Management for Nurses and Health Professionals
Theory into Practice

by
Alistair Hewison

Blackwell
Science

© 2004 by Blackwell Science Ltd, a Blackwell Publishing company

Editorial offices:
Blackwell Science Ltd, 9600 Garsington Road, Oxford OX4 2DQ, UK
    Tel: +44 (0) 1865 776868
Blackwell Publishing Inc., 350 Main Street, Malden, MA 02148-5020, USA
    Tel: +1 781 388 8250
Blackwell Science Asia Pty Ltd, 550 Swanston Street, Carlton, Victoria 3053, Australia
    Tel: +61 (0)3 8359 1011

The right of the Author to be identified as the Author of this Work has been asserted in accordance with the Copyright, Designs and Patents Act 1988.

First published 2004
3   2007

Library of Congress Cataloging-in-Publication Data

Hewison, Alistair.
    Management for nurses and health professionals : theory into practice / by Alistair Hewison.
        p. cm.
    Includes bibliographical references and index.
    ISBN 978-0-632-06433-5 (alk. paper)
    1. Nursing services—Administration. 2. Management. 3. Health services administration.
    4. Leadership. I. Title.

    RT89.3.H49 2004
    362.17′3′068—dc22

                                                                              2004041092

ISBN 978-0-632-06433-5

A catalogue record for this title is available from the British Library

Set in 10/12.5pt Palatino
by MHL Production Services, Coventry
Printed and bound in India
by Replika Press Pvt. Ltd

The publisher's policy is to use permanent paper from mills that operate a sustainable forestry policy, and which has been manufactured from pulp processed using acid-free and elementary chlorine-free practices. Furthermore, the publisher ensures that the text paper and cover board used have met acceptable environmental accreditation standards.

For further information on Blackwell Publishing, visit our website:
www.blackwellpublishing.com

Contents

Contents

Contents

Preface

The idea for this book has been with me for a long time. I have taught a number of different 'management modules' to students on a range of health related courses and one of the biggest challenges has always been demonstrating the relevance of management theory to the reality of practice. There are many excellent books which discuss and analyse management and organisational theory, indeed I have drawn on them in my teaching and in this book. There are also numerous 'How to do it' type management texts, yet the students on the modules often commented that they could not find anything that considered the theory in the context of practice. The experience of working with students on these modules and their comments about the utility of management theory suggested to me that there was a need to produce a book which brought elements of theory and practice together.

My aim is to demonstrate the relevance of management theory to practice, not only in terms of providing insights on what theory can tell us about being better managers, but also how it can be used to explain some of the problems experienced when trying to manage effectively. Management theory does not provide all the answers however it can help us develop a greater understanding of how the organisations we work in function. Ultimately the test of any book such as this is its usefulness for the reader, academically and practically. I hope you find it helps not only in completing your studies but also in approaching the management and organisation of health care with a different perspective.

Alistair Hewison
June 2003

Acknowledgements

I am grateful to Maggie Griffiths and Annie Young for their insights on NHS leadership programmes. Thanks are due to Claire Reece and John Couperthwaite for their help in drawing some of the figures. Comments on the manuscript provided by an anonymous reviewer were greatly appreciated. Finally the support and guidance of Beth Knight at Blackwell Publishing has been invaluable in the production of this book.

The following (authors and publishers) have kindly given permission for the use of copyright material:

Table 2.1 Doctrinal Components of the NPM. From Hood C. (1991) A public management for all seasons. *Public Administration* 69, 3–19.

Figure 3.5 The Components of Clinical Governance: Department of Health (1998) *A First Class Service Quality in the New NHS*. HMSO, London.

Figure 5.1 The Changing Nature of Change. This is a composite representing ideas from a range of presentations and ideas shared at a number of seminars/meetings. I am unclear as to the precise origin of this notion.

Figure 5.3 Receptive Contexts for Change: The Eight Factors. Reproduced by permission of Sage Publications Ltd from Pettigrew *et al.* (1992) *Shaping Strategic Change*.

Figure 5.4 Lewin's Forcefield Model. Iles V. & Sutherland K. (2001) *Organisational Change: A Review for Health Care Managers, Professionals and Researchers*. NCCSDO, London.

Chapter 6 Material Relating to the National Cancer Nursing Leadership Program. Management Research Group, 14 York Street, Suite #301, Portland, Maine.

Acknowledgements

Figure 6.2 What do Good Leaders do? Workforce and Development Leadership Working Group, London Region (2000).

Table 7.1 Ideal Type Contradictions between Managerialism and Professionalism. From Flynn R. (1999) Managerialism, Professionalism and quasi markets. In Exworth M. & Halford S. (eds), *Professionals and the New Managerialism in the Public Sector*, Open University Press, Buckingham, 18–36.

Table 10.1 Contrasting Attributes of Human Service Organisations and Business Industry. Kouzes J.M. & Mico P.R. Domain theory: an introduction to organizational behaviour in human service organizations. *Journal of Appled Behavioural Science*, 15(4), 169–174.

Figure 10.1 Domain Theory. Mark A. and Scott H. (1992) Management in the National Health Service. In Willcocks L. and Harrow J. (eds.), *Rediscovering Public Services Management*, McGraw-Hill Book Company, London, 197–234.

Introduction

Why study management?

Why do health professionals need to know about management? In what ways can management concepts and theories help health professionals understand more about the organisations in which they work? How can a knowledge of management help practitioners to deliver high standards of patient care? The purpose of this book is to provide some answers to these questions. The organisation and delivery of health care has been influenced by management ideas and theories throughout its history. However, in recent years this has become more evident. The intention here is to provide a context for this development and present a justification of the need for health professionals to study management. At the end of this introduction it should be clear why health professionals need to study management and how it can be of assistance to nurses and members of the allied health professions in the delivery of care to patients. However, it is not a 'how to do it' book, nor does it provide the definitive guide to managing. There are many texts which purport to provide 'the answer' to management (Collins 2000), yet as Trisolini has observed: 'Health care management textbooks and training programmes usually focus on only one or two models. The increasing pressures worldwide for efficiency and quality in health services means a wider perspective is needed' (Trisolini 2002, p. 296). The aim is that this book will encourage the development of this wider perspective by demonstrating how management and organisational theory impact on health care and the implications of this for health professionals.

What do we mean by management?

The word 'management' is derived from the Italian *maneggiare*, meaning to control or to train, particularly in relation to the management of horses; the Italian term was itself rooted in the Latin *manus*, meaning hand (Grint 1995). It is evident that management in some form has existed for as long as people have worked together collaboratively to achieve collective outcomes. The construction of Stonehenge, the Pyramids and the Great Wall of China could not have been completed without some form of planning, organisation, leadership and control, for example. Similarly if a more destructive activity is

1

considered, namely war, it can be appreciated that the capacity of people to organise the necessary logistics to execute a sustained campaign also needs to be managed, and the origins of key management terms such as 'strategy' and 'targets' become a little clearer. A further strand in the development of management can be traced to religious institutions, particularly the early Christian monastic orders (Grint 1995). Indeed, the longevity of the Roman Catholic Church is attributed to its success in organisational and management terms in remaining focused on its key purposes and having a clear structure (Handy 1997). Consequently the antecedents of management thought date back over many centuries, indicating not only that management has been a concern throughout history, but also that it is an area where opinions can diverge.

Different views of management

Whenever people work together with a common purpose there is the potential for a range of alternative and often competing explanations regarding how to organise this activity. As Shafritz & Ott observe:

> The basic elements of organizations have remained relatively constant through history. Organizations (or their important constituencies) have purposes (which may be explicit or implicit), attract participants, acquire and allocate resources to accomplish goals, use some form of structure to divide and co-ordinate activities, and rely on certain members to lead or manage others. Although the elements of organizations have remained relatively constant, their purposes, structures and ways of doing things, and methods of co-ordinating activities have always varied widely. (Shafritz & Ott 2001, p. 2)

To put it another way, we have to accept that any theory or perspective that we bring to the study of organisation and management, while capable of creating valuable insights, is also incomplete, biased and potentially misleading (Morgan 1997). There is no one best or universal way to manage in health care. Consequently managers need to understand a range of different models as this gives a broader array of methods to choose from when analysing problems, considering alternatives and implementing action plans (Trisolini 2002). Therefore it is important to examine a range of theoretical explanations of organisation and management in order to ensure their relevance for health professionals is clear. It is not a case of some theories being good or bad, or indeed one theory providing answers to all of the organisational problems people experience. Rather it is necessary to consider a range of views and theories and think about how they can inform us about health care organisation.

Surviving in organisations

Organisation and management have been around as long as people have worked together and yet management is a 'contested phenomenon' (Collins 2000). The way it is carried out varies from one organisation to another. Although there are general principles and approaches that can be applied in any organisation, there are inevitable variations. Mullins (2002) maintains that the common features of an organisation are people, structure and objectives. This may be so but the objectives of a hospital and restaurant are different. Similarly the two groups of people who work in a car factory and a community nursing team pursue different routes in terms of training and are motivated by different outcomes. There are certainly similarities between organisations, however the way management is carried out is different and this is shaped in part by the type of organisation and the activity in which it is engaged (Ranson & Stewart 1994).

Health care organisations have distinct features and are characterised by a particular set of values (New 1999). The way that the practice of management is carried out also varies depending on the person who has the responsibility to manage. This suggests that whatever can be done to understand more about the way organisations operate will be useful for health professionals. This can be at the level of recognising who is supposed to do what and why they are trying to do certain things, which can make managerial actions appear more understandable even if agreement as to the appropriateness of them is not so clear cut. This insight should enable those working within the organisation to at least find their way around, in management terms, and at best capitalise on this knowledge to enhance patient care. For example, knowing how patient referral mechanisms work, who is responsible for quality in the organisation, and how achievement of objectives is measured are all aspects of organisational performance that the health professional needs to be aware of in order to provide appropriate care. The chapters that follow all contain material that can be used in this way. However, there are other reasons why it is necessary for health professionals to be able to understand management and indeed adopt a critical approach to it.

Health professionals as managers

It has been suggested that if health professionals are to work effectively in the interests of their patients then an understanding of management would be helpful. In some ways this can be regarded as a minimum requirement. A recurrent theme in the organisation of health care is the recognition that if it is going to work then health professionals need to be involved in its management. In the National Health Service Bill (MOH 1946) it is stated that 'the minister is to assume direct responsibility, but he [sic] is to entrust the actual administration of the hospital and specialist services to new regional and local bodies ... they are to include people of practical experience and local knowledge and some with professional qualifications.' Although the term 'administration' is used it can be read as 'management' because at this stage of the development of the National Health Service (NHS) this was the term that was used in reference to the organisation and delivery of care and treatment, and here it indicates a belief that health professionals had a vital role in this. Similarly in 1972, before a later reorganisation of the NHS, Keith Joseph, the Conservative Secretary of State for Social Services at the time, explained the benefits that would follow: '... the organisational changes will ... bring positive gains to the professional worker. He – or she – will have the opportunity of organising his or her own work better and of playing a much greater part than hitherto in the management decisions that are taken in each area.' (DHSS 1972). Again there was an expectation that health professionals would play an active role in the management of the service. Similarly in 1983 the *Griffiths Report* (DHSS 1983) emphasised the importance of involving professionals in the management process. This report will be discussed in more detail in Chapter 2. However, it is referred to here because it provides more evidence of the drive at a policy level to integrate professionals into the active management of the service. Although the *Griffiths Report* is often regarded as having subordinated health professionals to management (Harrison *et al.* 1992), Griffiths himself expected the outcome to be somewhat different:

> I personally believed and intended it to be liberating in the sense that the doctors and nurses would have the opportunity of having a much greater say in the running of the Health Service and not be concerned solely with their professional work and responsibilities. It would also give them greater opportunities on a personal basis to take top management positions at all levels within the Health Service – on that basis they could become the best of all managers ... with an in-depth professionalism accompanied by the broadening of management experience. (Griffiths 1992, p. 65)

This recognition of the potential of nurses and health professionals as managers has been carried through into more recent pronouncements on health policy such as the *NHS Plan* (DOH 2000a). Here the introduction of 'Modern Matrons' was proposed as a means of improving the management and delivery of services. Guidance issued later (DOH 2001) reinforced the managerial nature and content of these new posts. The key terms used in the guidance were 'sufficient authority', 'leadership development', 'setting standards and controlling resources' and 'quality'. The role of the modern matron will be examined in more detail in chapter 10, however it is mentioned here to emphasise the continuing management role of nurses and health professionals and to provide a context for the chapters that follow. Finally there is evidence to confirm the presence of health professionals in management roles in health care. In a survey of managers in the NHS it was found that the most common primary professional qualification of the respondents was nursing (24 per cent with 9 per cent citing a qualification in one of the allied health professions (IHSM Consultants 1995a)). Also even if nurses and health professionals do not have the official title of 'manager', management still constitutes a significant part of their work. Organising the care for a group of patients, managing a case load and liaising with the multi-disciplinary team all require managerial capabilities. Having established that all health professionals manage in some form or another, what does the field of management theory have to offer?

The tools of management

The nature of management and managing is an area of continuing academic debate and dispute. In terms of its theoretical development it is still at a relatively early stage and there are differing views concerning what management is and what it should be (Hales 1986, 1993, Carrol & Gillen 1987, Whitley 1989, Willmott 1984, 1987). For example, the term can be used to refer to the activity of managing, the group of people who manage and the ideology that underpins the action of managing (Child 1981). This is complicated further because there is no consensus regarding the nature and content of management, and the speed at which new management 'truths' come and go implies a degree of instability about what management is (Reedy & Learmonth 2000). If this is the case what does management have to offer nurses and health professionals as they endeavour to manage care?

The response to this challenge is twofold. First, if nurses and health professionals understand the nature of management they will be in a better position to challenge inappropriate and underdeveloped approaches. Second, despite the lack of consensus there are principles and concepts from management that are useful and can be demonstrated to have positive benefits for care and service delivery, and in recognising this, nurses and health professionals can enhance their own practice. Nursing and the allied health professions, in common with many other professions, have a knowledge base that is derived from a number of areas of study (McKenna 1997). Management knowledge is one element in the amalgam of academic disciplines that constitute nursing and the allied health professions. One of the defining features of the work of health professionals is the way in which this package of knowledge is applied to the practice setting, and the aim of this book is to demonstrate how management concepts and theories can be used in this way.

Outline

This provides the basis for the approach to be taken in the chapters that follow. Each chapter examines either an element of management theory and its implications for health care, or explores the application of management principles to health care organisation and assesses the evidence for its success. Nurses and members of the allied health professions are increasingly expected to take a critical approach to their work and to embrace the principles of evidence-based practice as a central feature of professional activity (Harrison 1998, Wiles & Barnard 2001). This approach should also extend to the incorporation of management knowledge. It is a contested and often ideologically driven area of thought, and nurses and health professionals need to be aware of this if it is to inform their practice as clinicians and managers. In order to provide a framework to assist in this process the chapters examine specific aspects of management as they relate to nursing and health care. They have been written to be relatively self-contained and deal with each issue in detail. However, clear links are established between the chapters and the framework for the organisation of the material is established in chapter 2. This means that the most benefit will be derived from reading the chapters in sequence.

In chapter 1 the history of management in the NHS is discussed to demonstrate how management has always been a feature of health care and how this has been influenced by ideas from the field of general management. The transition from administration to management in health care is examined and reference made to developments that were occurring in the broader field of management theory. This places the chapters that follow in an historical context and serves as a point of contrast to indicate how health care management has developed in more recent years.

Chapter 2 locates the developments in the organisation and delivery of health care in the context of the New Public Management. This is a particular line of analysis that has developed in response to the changes that have occurred in health care and the public sector in the last twenty years. This further demonstrates the relationship between general management theory and health care, and the influence it can have on shaping the nature and structure of public sector organisations. The main purpose of this chapter is to illustrate how the current shape of health care management is a complex mix of a range of theories and concepts originating from a variety of sources. Later chapters will then analyse specific elements of this in more detail.

Chapter 3, for example, is the first in a series of four that examines particular aspects of management that have been introduced into health care as part of the general process of reform. It relates the work of the 'quality gurus' to health care and situates their contribution in the clinical governance framework. The need to improve the quality of health service delivery is a key concern of politicians, managers, professionals and patients. The contribution from management thought to developments in this area will be examined in this chapter.

This is followed by chapter 4 which presents an analysis of organisational culture and its usefulness to nurses and health professionals as a means of understanding organisations. Links will be drawn with the previous chapter where much writing on quality calls for a 'change in culture'. The key components of culture are identified and the central question posed: 'is culture something an organisation is or has?'. The intention in this chapter is to uncover some of the more problematic elements of this concept.

The pace of change within society generally and within the NHS in particular has created a situation whereby participation in and the effective management of change is required of health professionals. In chapter 5 theories related to change in organisations are examined. Particular emphasis is given to understanding the 'diffusion of innovations' as a means of bringing about change in the context of evidence-based practice (EBP). It is impossible to ignore the impact the concept of EBP has had on the discussion of health care issues. However, relatively little attention has been directed towards the difficulties in actually achieving the changes in practice necessary to make it a reality. A number of theoretical models relating to change are discussed to demonstrate the range of material available to health professionals which can be used to inform the management of change. The focus on 'getting research into practice' as part of the EBP agenda and the utility of the diffusion of innovations models in understanding the dynamics of this process, considered towards the end of the chapter, are intended to serve as a 'current' example of how this can occur.

Effective and 'strong' leadership are regarded as central to the achievement of both quality services and organisational change as part of the overall plan to 'modernise' the NHS (DOH 2000a). The commitment to developing 'clinical leaders', outlined in the *NHS Plan* (DOH 2000a), indicates that such roles are seen at government level to be crucial to the successful management of health care. Chapter 6 examines theories of leadership and their application in the contemporary NHS and offers some reflections on the progress and outcomes of the nurse leadership programme.

Chapter 7 will develop the theme identified towards the end of the previous chapter and examine the factors associated with health professionals being managers. The literature on 'hybrid management' indicates that there are particular issues that arise as part of this process and that hybrid management represents a new type of role in the NHS. The way this theory has informed the debate will be the central focus of this chapter.

An examination of middle management is included in chapter 8 because it is likely to be a career option available to many nurses and health professionals. Indeed many middle managers are hybrid managers and the combination of these two sets of circumstances renders the role in health care unique. The demise of the middle manager has been somewhat exaggerated in the general management literature and it remains a key role, particularly in health care, because it is a role many health professionals are likely to take on.

Current health policy stresses the need to develop interprofessional and multi-agency working in order to deliver an effective service (DOH 1999, 2000b, 2000c). However, this has been difficult to achieve in the past resulting in the fragmentation of care arising from a lack of cooperation and coordination amongst professionals and agencies. The purpose of chapter 9 is to locate this issue in its historical and theoretical context and demonstrate how ideas and theories derived from research in this area can be used to improve the delivery of interprofessional care. This is an element of service provision that confers further 'unique' features on management in health care and thus requires a distinctive approach which incorporates a combination of management principles/theories.

In chapter 10 a number of strands addressed in the previous chapters will be drawn together in the context of domain theory. Health care organisations are extremely complex, therefore contributions from a range of theories are necessary in order to build our understanding of the dynamics involved. A further example of this is explored in chapter 10. Domain theory is applied to health care in general and then to specific recent developments in order to assess its utility in developing understanding of the unique situation of health care organisations.

The drive for evidence-based practice (EBP), referred to in chapter 5, will be the focus of chapter 11 which examines the development of evidence-based management. This is a relatively recent phenomenon which has emerged as part of the EBP agenda. It is suggested that the application of the principles of EBP is possible, however it needs to take account of the nature of management theory and knowledge. In the conclusion the implications this examination of management has for nurses and health professionals will be outlined and the gaps in knowledge identified. Comment will also be offered on the opportunities that exist for professionals in terms of developing a management role and how examination of management and organisational theory will be of continuing relevance for all practitioners.

Terminology

It was noted earlier that there are difficulties in arriving at a precise definition of management and the same problem is encountered if attempts are made to define the term theory. Defining and explaining the precise nature of theory is a continuing enterprise in the literature (Denzin 1989, Hammersley 1985, 1990, 1992, 1995, Thompson 1995) and could constitute a study in itself. However, it is important to provide a definition of what theory is as a starting point for the consideration of its role in shaping management in health care. Gill & Johnson (1991, p. 26) contend that 'a theory is a network of hypotheses advanced so as to conceptualise and explain a particular social or natural phenomenon'. Similarly Hammersley (1995, p. 56) states 'The term theory refers to general principles that provide explanations for empirical phenomena'. Research, when viewed from a traditional or positivist standpoint, is then designed to examine the adequacy of the theory in terms of whether or not it continues to provide a logical and coherent explanation for phenomena.

These definitions provide a useful point of reference but are inevitably incomplete. For example, they do not explain the relationship of concepts to theories or the 'level' at which theories function. In sociology, for example, it is common to find references to 'grand theory', which is couched at an abstract conceptual level, and 'middle range' theories which function between the levels of minor working hypotheses and major conceptual schemes (Abercrombie *et al.* 1988). When concepts can operate at a number of levels in this way there is the potential for confusion. Also because of the nature of human or social activity it can be argued that, in this context, the role of theory is less precise than in the 'natural sciences'. Schön (1991, p. 273) suggests 'An overarching theory does not give a rule that can be applied to predict or control a particular event, but it supplies the language from which to construct particular interpretations'. Similarly Morgan (1997) argues that theory should be recognised as a metaphor and that no single theory will ever provide a perfect or complete explanation of phenomena. Therefore no one theory is likely to be a completely accurate representation of reality but some provide better insight to a particular phenomenon than others (Bond & Bond 1986). Consequently a range of theories and concepts drawn from management will be used in this way to provide the 'language' to examine the application of management in health care.

In relation to the term 'practice' a similar discussion could be presented. However, in the context of this book, 'practice' is taken to have a broad application to health care. It encompasses the practical working of health care organisations from the policy level to the ward/departmental level. Essentially it is wherever the theories and ideas from the study of organisations and management are applied to health care. This occurs at all levels and in a variety of ways. This approach is taken to direct attention to the influence and impact of management on health care. Whilst considering issues of terminology there is one further cautionary note that needs to be included here.

Language

Newman (1994a) has commented that 'management' is not a neutral term and she goes on to argue:

It is based on a body of knowledge that developed in the context of male controlled organizations (the military, factories, the civil service). It was written about and encoded into 'theories' principally by men, and the research which has established the norms of managerial practice has mainly been based on male subjects. Its concepts and images are predominantly drawn from the domains of order, hierarchy and rationality. Its goals are the control of the internal world of the organization and mastery of the external environment. (Newman 1994a, p. 185)

If it also considered that a 'glass ceiling' has existed in the NHS for many years which has prevented the progression of women up the managerial hierarchy (Dickson 1998, Brown & Goss 1993), many aspects of management may seem to be of limited relevance to nurses and the allied health professions. Seventy-nine per cent of the NHS workforce is made up of women (Langridge 1993) and nurses and the allied health professions are predominantly female and so a 'male' account of management and its application to health care may seem inappropriate. However, although the power of language to shape actions and influence our understanding of phenomena (Tannen 1995, Watson 1995a) is acknowledged, awareness of this can serve as a basis for revealing this element of management and thus make a more informed assessment of its utility to health professionals more likely. This is important because management is essentially a human social craft. It requires the ability to interpret the thoughts and wants of others – be they employees, patients, or colleagues – and the facility to shape meanings, values and human commitments (Watson 1994). Despite the potential difficulties involved, it is necessary for nurses and health professionals to study, appreciate and understand management in health care organisations. The intention is that in the chapters that follow this necessity will become clear and that the material included will provide some useful insights on management in health care.

1. The History of Management in the NHS

Introduction

Connelly (2000) has commented that the management of health care, as opposed to its administration, is a relatively recent development that has emerged only in the last 30 years. However, in order to understand the present it is necessary to look back and trace the origins of current events. Spurgeon (1995) has spoken of a 'cultural zeitgeist', where no learning occurs from changes that have happened and this results in the formation of poor policy as the mistakes of the past are repeated. This can also apply to the introduction of management ideas in that 'solutions' that have been tried in the past are repackaged and reintroduced, although not always successfully. An awareness of the history of NHS management provides a starting point for understanding how this occurs and the way events have unfolded in more recent years.

The purpose of this chapter then is to:

- examine the history of the NHS in order to identify the origins of current organisational structures and managerial approaches
- consider the nature of management theory
- relate changes in management and organisation in the NHS to general trends in management thinking.

The management problem in the NHS has been a persistent feature throughout its history. Indeed in 1988 Harrison maintained that for more than three decades the NHS has been obsessed with notions of 'better management'. The quest for improved management has spawned a succession of reforms and as the NHS moves into the twenty-first century the search for better management continues (DOH 2000a). In view of this a brief examination of the historical development of management in the NHS is necessary if an appreciation of health care management is to be placed in a chronological and theoretical context. The main points in this history are indicated on the 'timeline' (Figure 1.1) and explained in more detail in the sections that follow.

1948–1960
Manager as Diplomat
Service run on the basis of supporting professionals to deliver care and treatment. Management characterised by administration.

↓

1960s
Scientific Management and the *Salmon Report* (DOH 1966)
Introduction of more overtly management oriented approaches to service delivery and organisation.

↓

1970s
Classical Management and Systems Approaches and the 1974 Reorganisation
Moves to towards greater centralised management control of the service

↓

1980s
The Griffiths Report (DHSS 1983) and Managerialism
Introduction of 'private sector' management approaches and general management

↓

1990s
Working for Patients (DOH 1989) and the Internal Market
Service organised and managed on market principles

↓

2000–
The NHS Plan (DOH 2000a) and the 'Third Way'
Rediscovery of Public Service Management, combining a range of approaches?

Figure 1.1 Management theory in the NHS: a timeline.

This premise could be extended to include the 'pre-history' of organised health care before the formation of the NHS. However for our purposes the establishment of the NHS in 1948 will constitute the starting point for a discussion of the history of health care management. Examination of management in the NHS before 1983 provides the necessary background information and is included to present a picture of the past in order to provide a point of contrast with the radical programme of change that began to unfold later on. In the early years of the NHS the policy process resulted mainly in incremental changes to its management until *The Griffiths Report* (DHSS 1983) which signalled a profound change in thinking about health care in general and its management in particular. The intention here is to trace the effects of this process giving particular consideration to nurses and non-medical health care professionals as a group.

The impact of management theory on the NHS

The other aspect that is addressed in this first chapter is the impact of management theory on the development of management in the NHS. The NHS is the largest employer in Western Europe and absorbs expenditure at the rate of more than £1000 every second (DOH 1997). Consequently it is the subject of much attention in relation to its structure and organisation. One of the recurrent themes in the scrutiny that has been directed towards the organisation and delivery of the NHS is the application of the ideas and concepts of management as a means of improving health care. Therefore reference to key strands in general management theory will be made to indicate how it has influenced the design and organisation of health care. This will not be an exhaustive account as this is a major field of study in its own right, however key texts are listed at the end of the book so that further reading in this area can be undertaken. This is a worthwhile activity because the influence of management concepts and theories continue to be central to health policy (DOH 2000a) and so the more that health professionals know about this the more understanding they will have of the environment in which they work.

Theory

Barley & Kunda (1992) have traced the history of management theory and contend that the theoretical development of this field of study occurs in surges. Research is undertaken and recommendations made concerning appropriate management practice, which may not be enacted for some time. Often it can take up to 20 years for an idea to become part of accepted management wisdom (Bennis 1996). Also the nature of this process is not progressive, rather it is cyclical with what Barley & Kunda describe as surges of rational and normative ideologies holding sway at different points in history. Although focusing specifically on notions of management control, their categorisation usefully locates particular strands of management thought in their historical context. The ideologies they discuss are as much the product of their time as the outcome of formal study on the part of management researchers, which leads to their being publicised. Barley & Kunda (1992) argue that similar approaches are adapted and re-emerge. Table 1.1 outlines the main stages in the development of management theory and the key elements of each strand of theory. Yet it must be emphasised that the development and appearance of ideas is not a straightforward process. As will be seen ideas that have their origins in the early part of the twentieth century re-emerge and are applied in a modified way in the NHS at the end of that century. This occurs because the boundaries between ideology and theory are not clear cut. Ideology can be

Table 1.1 Trends in management theory.

Theory	Content	Period
1. Classical management (Scientific management, bureaucracy)	Rational, economic & scientific principles Specialisation and division of labour	1900–1923
2. Human relations	Motivation, group behaviour, leadership, social power	1923–1955
3. Systems rationalism	Inputs, processes, outputs, feedback loops, environment	1955–1980
4. Organisational culture	Basic assumptions, values, rites, rituals, symbols	1980–2000
5. Postmodernism and the information age	Information networks, globalisation, fragmentation	2000–

(Adapted from Barley and Kunda 1992).

defined as a complete and self-consistent set of attitudes, moral views, empirical beliefs and even rules of logical discourse and scientific testing (Robertson 1985). However, it can also be:

> [a] set of ideas which are located within a particular social group and which fulfils functions for that group. It helps defend, justify and further the interests of the group with which it is associated. (Watson 1995b, p. 378)

This is an important point to note because ideas and theories are not 'neutral', their development reflects particular concerns and interests on the part of their authors and the way the theories and concepts are used is not value free. They are often applied in particular ways to achieve certain outcomes. The other interesting feature of this process is that because it often takes some years for new theories to come to the attention of people working in organisations, by the time they reach some organisations ideas have already moved on and new prescriptions for management effectiveness have been developed. The irony of the NHS adopting management ideas that have subsequently been rejected by the 'private sector' has been noted (Willcocks & Harrow 1992). However the NHS is located in and influenced by its political, professional and managerial environment and the particular outcome of this, in management terms, will be examined. The intention is that the ideological element in this process will also be made clearer.

The establishment of the NHS

The establishment of the NHS has been characterised as the product of bargaining and negotiation in the health policy community and represented the achievement of what was possible at the time rather than what was desirable (Ham 1992, p. 15). The resulting structure, arising as it did from compromise and concession, contained many elements that were to lead to problems later.

Extensive and detailed histories of the development of the NHS have already been written (Webster 1988, 1998, Powell 1997, Allsop 1995, Klein 1995, Honigsbaum 1979) and it is not the intention to present another account of that history here. Rather it is to draw out some key milestones relating to the involvement of nurses and health professionals in management.

During the early stages of its history the main aim of management in the NHS was to administer the service so as to facilitate the practice of professionals (Harrison 1988). The assumption and belief was that the professionals, particularly medical staff, possessed the knowledge necessary to provide treatment and care and so the role of managers and administrators was to create the right circumstances for them to practise. As a result the professional groups developed their own internal hierarchies and organisational arrangements in order to deliver professionally determined care. Although slightly militaristic in style and characterised by a rigid hierarchy, the structures of the non-medical professions reflected a focus on professional care which did not take account of the broader organisational environment (Clarke 1995). Thus in terms of management the emphasis in the 1950s and throughout the early period of the NHS was on achieving its smooth running through care and maintenance rather than innovation and change (Klein 1995).

The role of the manager during this period has been characterised as that of the 'diplomat' (Harrison 1988). Although this analysis has been challenged and the title of 'technician' suggested as being more appropriate, because it more accurately reflects the technical expertise managers need to administer the service (Learmonth 1998), essentially the role of the manager/administrator was to ensure the service ran in the way the professionals felt it should operate. The resulting level of interest in management among the professional groups was limited as there was no real need for them to get involved. Throughout this period the size and complexity of the NHS workforce continued to increase. Allsop (1984) reports that one response to this development on the part of the government was to look to the principles of scientific management as a basis for organising the work of professionals. One of the early attempts to introduce the managerialist approach was the reorganisation of nursing services arising from the *Salmon Report* (MOH 1966).

Scientific management and the Salmon Report

Scientific management is the term used to describe an approach to the organisation of work which is based on the ideas of Frederick Winslow Taylor (1947). He advocated that managers use 'science' to measure all aspects of the production process, define tasks in great detail, and design the work process to maximise production specifying the precise content of every work task. He believed this would increase production and place control in the hands of managers. The separation of management and production were central tenets of his approach. This is reflected in the findings of the *Salmon Report*. The Committee of Enquiry recommended a division of labour between managers and practitioners through the abolition of matrons and their replacement with a hierarchy of nurse managers. The implementation of the recommendations of the *Salmon Report* (MOH 1966) relating to the nursing management structure resulted in a unidisciplinary approach to management. Based on an 'industrial' model it introduced several additional layers into the management hierarchy and required nurse managers to contribute to the overall management of the service through the medium of consensus management teams. As Carpenter (1977) observed: 'A different form of bureaucracy based on a fundamentally new kind of rationality was advocated by Salmon. This involved the creation of a managerial structure based on the industrial model of professionalised management, the application of techniques derived from aspects of capitalist rationality (Taylorism), and an emphasis on the managerial rather than the clinical content of nursing work' (Carpenter 1977). This point is also made by Manson (1977) who goes on to argue that the development of health care can only be understood by linking detailed analysis of the internal organisation of the service with wider social analysis (p. 210). The influence of management ideas in this process is clear in the antecedents to and effects of the *Salmon Report* and similar forces can be traced that contributed to the situation leading up to the 1974 reorganisation.

Classical management, systems approaches and the 1974 reorganisation

Another example of the NHS being shaped in line with managerial principles is the 1974 reorganisation. This followed a consultative document issued in 1971 and a White Paper (DHSS 1972), which outlined the legislation that would take effect in 1974 to coincide with a parallel restructuring of local government. Allsop (1984) regards this as 'the zenith of the managerialist phase'. There were five major objectives in this reorganisation:

1. To achieve greater integration of the service in order to provide more continuity and increase efficiency.
2. To introduce more central control vested in the Department of Health and Social Security to ensure policies were implemented and again to improve efficiency.
3. To create a clearer management structure and to improve accountability to the department and encourage delegation of tasks to health authorities.
4. To develop a more democratic decision-making mechanism.
5. To introduce a planning system in order to achieve goals and priorities.

The 'managerialist' content of these papers is probably best summarised as a combination of 'classical management' and 'systems' approaches. The classical school dominated organisational theory in the 1930s, but it remains influential to this day. As with most theories it has been expanded and refined over time, however its basic tenets include:

1. Organisations exist to accomplish production related goals.
2. There is one best way to organise for production, and that way can be found through systematic, scientific enquiry.
3. Production is maximised through the division of labour.
4. People and organisations act in accordance with rational economic principles (Shafritz & Ott 2001).

While this broad category includes the 'scientific management' discussed earlier in relation to the *Salmon Report*, it also incorporates work of other key management figures such as Fayol (1949), Gullick & Urwick (1937) and Weber (1948). The reflection of key elements of classical management theory can be discerned in the objectives of the 1974 reorganisation. The desire for central control and a structure which formalised clear lines of accountability and responsibility is evident, as is the focus on goals and priorities.

In contrast to classical theory, which views organisations as static structures, systems thinking regards organisations as complex ever changing processes of interaction among organisational and environmental elements (Shafritz & Ott 2001). Systems approaches have two major themes, the first being a view of organisations as akin to a living system, much like the human body, made up of a complex set of interrelated systems (e.g. the cardiovascular system, the digestive system and the nervous system) which are all part of the whole. In a similar way the personnel department, finance department and marketing department are all parts of a commercial enterprise that need to work effectively together if the organisation is to be successful. This is combined with the second theme of reliance on quantitative techniques to understand the complex relationships between the different elements of the systems.

Again in terms of the 1974 reorganisation the effect of this approach can be seen. The importance attached to integrating the different parts of the service reflect the influence of systems thinking as this integration was seen as a means of improving efficiency. Also the emphasis given to systematic, scientific enquiry can be attributed in part to the prominence of this approach in both 'scientific management' and systems theory.

Ranade (1997) maintains that health policy can only be understood within the context of the ideas and values which have shaped its development historically. The same can also be argued for health care management as the two are very closely interrelated. This brief sketch of the prevailing ideas and values at work during the early days of the NHS is intended to serve as a reference point for some of the more radical approaches that were to follow. This period of relative stability came to an end as a result of a number of factors.

The end of the post-war settlement

Until the late 1970s and early 1980s, the Welfare State had been described in terms of a social democratic consensus whereby there was a high level of agreement across political parties and political élites about the substance of public policy, especially the roles of the mixed economy and the welfare state (Farnham & Horton 1993).

The combination of the economic recession and the continuing increases in public expenditure on the public services provided the backdrop for the election campaign of 1979. The Conservative manifesto presented Britain as a failure, its values eroded, its economy disabled and its public services a burden on the taxpayer (Allsop 1995). Once in government a number of broad themes guided, and were reflected in, Conservative policy. These were:

1. Reduction in public expenditure.
2. Introduction of private sector management principles to the public sector, including the encouragement of market-based systems of operation.
3. Encouragement of self help and the transfer of the burden of care from the state to the family and the community (in the form of voluntary

sector service provision). (Ham 1992, Farnham & Horton 1993, Allsop 1995, Baggott 1998, Klein 1995)

Throughout the terms of the Thatcher governments, confidence within the Conservative administration grew and the 'New Right' ideas of economic liberalism, unregulated markets, free enterprise and a de-regulated economy were increasingly influential in the approach taken to the management of the public sector (Farnham & Horton 1993). The first major manifestation of this new approach in health care was the *Griffiths Report* of 1983. It marked the next, and most radical, stage in the introduction of managerialism into the NHS.

The Griffiths Report

The 'Griffiths prescription' is a significant point in the history of management in the NHS because it was the first report to advocate an explicitly 'private sector' model. It marked a turning point in the development of management in the NHS.

The *Griffiths Report* represents a break with tradition in terms of its approach and style (Klein 1995). Published in the form of a 25 page letter, the Griffiths recommendations were the outcome of an inquiry by four people who worked quickly and informally and completed their review in six months. This was in stark contrast to the Royal Commissions and Committees of Inquiry that characterised previous investigations into the workings of the NHS. Here was a reflection of the new government approach to policy making: brisk, decisive and often peremptory (Klein 1995).

The Griffiths diagnosis was that the NHS was institutionally stagnant; health authorities were swamped with directives without being given direction; consensus decision making delayed the management process and change was difficult to achieve. The recommendations made to remedy this situation were that a general management structure throughout the NHS was necessary. There should be a supervisory board chaired by the Secretary of State, below that a chief executive to carry through the objectives and decisions of the board, as well as provide leadership to the service as a whole. More significantly there were to be general managers at all levels of operation of the NHS and that they might well be recruited from outside the service to strengthen the management function. Although there was considerable opposition to the introduction of the Griffiths changes, most notably from the British Medical Association and the Royal College of Nursing, the recommendations were carried out almost to the letter (Klein 1995) and heralded a new approach to managing the NHS.

There are echoes here of the *Salmon Report* in that the provenance of methods that were felt to apply in the private or commercial sector were seen as superior in some way to public sector approaches to management and organisation. In the case of the *Salmon Report* the chairman had worked for the Lyons food company, and when the government was seeking someone to investigate the management of the NHS in 1983 it once again looked to the chairman of a large commercial organisation, the food retailer Sainsbury's. The precise origins of the package of management ideas that were at work here are not so clear cut and indeed it is probably more accurate to suggest that the enthusiasm for managerial solutions in this instance was driven equally by ideological factors as economic ones (Cox 1991). Cox (1991) goes on to identify the recurring themes of Griffiths' managerialism as action, effectiveness, thrust, urgency, vitality, management budgeting, sensitivity to consumer satisfaction and approaches to the management of personnel which rewarded good performance and sanctioned poor performance with dismissal. The *Griffiths Report* (DHSS 1983) is regarded as marking the end point of the transition from administration to management in the NHS (Barrett & McMahon 1990) and is made up of an amalgam of the management ideas summarised in Table 1.1. The need for clear authority is apparent (Fayol 1949) as is the notion of 'excellence', in relation to consumer satisfaction and vitality. However, the main way the Griffiths recommendations were articulated was in terms of concerns about 'who is in charge' and the need for strong mindedness and an ability to get things done, rather than professional expertise or training (Cox 1992). A concept of management was derived from the broad themes identified earlier that found expression in an action-oriented 'no nonsense' form. Management was about doing, and achieving results.

Researching the effects of Griffiths

In keeping with the prevailing Conservative government approach to policy implementation, no large, centrally organised systematic evaluation of the effects of the Griffiths proposals was conducted (Dixon 1998). Consequently, a range of research projects were undertaken which investigated various aspects of the changes.

The full impact of the changes introduced as a result of the Griffiths recommendations was beginning to be appreciated when the next package of reforms was introduced. The bulk of the empirical work evaluating the various effects of Griffiths was published in the late 1980s and early 1990s, just as the *Working for Patients* White Paper (DOH 1989) was being drafted and, to a degree, the Griffiths era can now be viewed as something of a transitional phase. It represents a period when general management was introduced into the 'old structure' before the whole configuration of health care was revised with the development of the internal market. However, it is a significant period in the history of the NHS and some of the effects of this report identified in the research are as follows.

- It caused widespread disruption and uncertainty particularly in the higher levels of the nursing hierarchy.
- Most unit structures were organised in such a way that separate lines of nursing management were eliminated.
- The number of middle managers was greatly reduced mainly to meet stringent financial goals.
- Nurses who were appointed to or continued in middle management roles spent much of their time involved in 'crisis' management and dealing with staffing issues.
- Many felt ill-prepared for such roles and complained of being overwhelmed by administrative tasks.

These findings were the outcome of an anthropological approach, a research strategy incorporating interviews, fieldwork and documentary analysis (Owens & Glennerster 1990, p. 164).

Harrison *et al.* (1992) employed an ethnographic approach, using interviews and extensive periods of observation of managers at work in their study and found that there was an increase in the speed of decision making in some areas but in many instances the rhetoric of a consumer-oriented organisation was not matched by the reality. Similarly although clearer lines of management accountability emerged there was a persistence of an unhelpful and constraining hierarchy. The lack of a clear set of objectives to be achieved was identified as a weakness as was the failure to eliminate political interference from the management process. The general managers' agenda was dominated by financial considerations particularly budget compliance and this limited the role of the manager. The overall conclusion reached by Harrison *et al.* was that:

> implementation of the Griffiths report has been handicapped by tensions and limitations which were inherent in the original report, by flawed understanding of the management problem in the NHS and by wider developments (the failure of the government to set clear priorities plus the deteriorating financial situation) which were beyond its remit. Despite this, its impact has been considerable, especially among managers and administrators themselves, and also with nurses. (Harrison *et al.* 1992, p. 72)

The consequences of the Griffiths Report

The implementation of the recommendations made in the *Griffiths Report* brought about a number of changes.

1. A trend towards greater centralisation of power within the NHS accompanied by increased bureaucracy.
2. An increase in confusion in accountability structures in the NHS.
3. Managers had different views of both their own leadership role and the part to be played by professionals, particularly medical staff, in the implementation of their agenda for change.
4. The status and power of the nursing profession declined within the new structures. Nurses were often given quality assurance roles which were seen as 'non-jobs' and the nursing influence on policy formation was reduced.
5. Because general management was introduced at a time when public expenditure was being tightly controlled, it became linked with the idea of financial cutbacks.
6. Improvements in quality largely took the form of improvements in 'hotel services' rather then in the quality of care. (Dopson & Waddington 1996)

Other work which sought to examine the impact of the *Griffiths Report* include a survey of 250 members of unit level staff and interviews with unit general managers conducted by Banyard. The findings from Banyard are summarised in Table 1.2.

Table 1.2   The effects of the *Griffiths Report* (Banyard 1988a,b,c,d).

1. Increased involvement of managers in setting and controlling budgets and greater clarity concerning budget arrangements.
2. Greater emphasis on cost awareness.
3. More devolving of responsibility to unit level.
4. Clearer and quicker decision-making processes introduced.
5. Authority and responsibility at unit level were more clearly defined.
6. Staff were better informed.
7. Individual character of the UGM was found to be a key determinant in the success of the unit.
8. Doubts were expressed over the utility of short-term contracts for UGMs.
9. Little real change was experienced at local level.
10. Little discernible improvement in staff morale.
11. Budgets were not related to workloads.

(UGM: unit general manager)

Whilst shedding light on the impact of the *Griffiths Report*, these studies also demonstrate how theory can be utilised in the conduct of research into health care management. Through the application of a particular theoretical perspective not only does each study examine different aspects of the reform process and thus contribute to our understanding of its complex nature and outcomes, they uncover the influence management theory has on the process of policy change. They also illustrate how the effects of such reforms are often very different to those anticipated at the outset (Dopson & Waddington 1996), which can be as a result of the inappropriate application of some of the management prescriptions. This further reinforces the importance of understanding management theory on the part of health professionals, if they are to understand the organisational environment they work in.

The internal market

However, as noted earlier, in many ways the general management structure ushered in by the *Griffiths Report* (DHSS 1983) served as a foundation for the more radical market-based reforms that were to follow. Although this was not a 'planned' progression it generated an impetus for change that was carried through following the publication of the White Paper *Working for Patients* (DOH 1989). The package of reforms that was implemented as a result of the 1989 White Paper is summarised in Table 1.3 and the management theory underpinning them examined in chapter 2. The reforms centred around three main principles: large publicly-owned hospitals could opt to become self-managed trusts which, while still publicly-owned, were given greater freedom to control their own affairs. The main aim was to remain financially viable and use resources more efficiently. They could also pay staff on rates negotiated at a local level which were different from nationally agreed pay deals. Health Authorities became buyers or purchasers (later commissioners) of services and could purchase care and treatment for their populations from private as well as NHS providers. The role and function of the District Health Authorities thus changed from a managerial/supervisory role, to that of a 'buyer' in a health care market. The purchasing and providing of care and treatment was organised through the agreement of contracts between the purchaser (Health Authority or GP Fundholding Practice) and the provider (the NHS Trusts or private providers). Also large General Practices could become 'fundholders' and be both purchasers and providers of care. They could provide primary care services for their patients and were also able to choose which hospital to send their patients to for secondary care.

This is a very brief summary, and extensive research has been conducted to investigate the impact of *Working for Patients* (DOH 1989) (see for example,

Table 1.3 Key features of *Working for Patients* (DOH 1989, Teasdale 1992, Maynard 1994).

Working for Patients (DOH 1989)

Seven key changes

1. The introduction of greater flexibility and the more effective matching of patient needs and care. More local decision making at organisational level.
2. The establishment of self-managed trusts which could provide a better service for patients. This was to be facilitated by the trusts borrowing capital, within annual financing limits, and setting local rates of pay.
3. Money was to 'follow the patients' through the system of purchasing and providing of care.
4. Waiting times were to be reduced and 100 new consultant posts were created.
5. GP practices could become GP fundholders with their own budgets and be able to purchase services from hospitals.
6. Health Authorities and Trusts to be organised on 'business' lines with executive and non-executive directors.
7. To improve services rigorous systems of audit were introduced.

Baggott 1997, Dawson *et al.* 1995, Flynn *et al.* 1996, Glennerster *et al.* 1994, Hughes & Griffiths 1999, Malek *et al.* 1993) and some of the main findings are summarised in Table 1.4. The changes that were made in the 1990s had a profound effect on the NHS and were part of a wider programme of reform which is examined in more detail in chapter 2.

Conclusion

It has been demonstrated that throughout the recent history of the NHS the influence of management ideas has had a significant impact on the organisation and delivery of health care. Wide ranging changes have been introduced in an attempt to ensure the NHS is 'managed' more efficiently and effectively. This process has continued with the introduction of the *NHS Plan* (DOH 2000a). These measures can be seen as part of a wider programme of change throughout the public sector and the term used to describe the outcome of this process is the New Public Management (NPM). In chapter 2 the broad theoretical context of the managerial changes in health care that are encompassed within this term will be examined.

Table 1.4 Summary of the main research findings relating to *Working for Patients* (based on Dixon 1998, Appleby 1994, Ham 1994, Mohan 1996).

The Effects of *Working for Patients* (DOH 1989)

1. There appears to be value in separating purchaser and provider roles, particularly in the opportunity to enable purchasers to focus on the population's health needs.
2. Purchasers must be supported if they are to carry out their responsibilities effectively. Purchasers are more than payers and need to call on a range of skills to enable them to negotiate on equal terms with providers.
3. As purchasers have gained experience and confidence, they have demonstrated their ability to hold providers to account and to improve standards of service delivery.
4. A purchaser/provider system is more expensive to administer than an integrated system and the transaction costs involved in a managed market are considerable.
5. Markets can act as a powerful stimulus to change and improved performance but they need to be used in conjunction with planning and regulation.
6. Giving budgets to groups of GPs has empowered them to bring about improvements in services for patients but has increased transaction costs and raised concerns about equity.
7. Budgetary incentives remain underdeveloped and money is not yet following patients. Patients are 'following the money'. Information systems need to be improved and purchasers need to take more risks in contract negotiations.
8. The contracts used as a basis for organising service delivery do not have the status of a contract in law.
9. There is a lack of reliable evidence on which to base definitive conclusions regarding the 'success' of the reforms.
10. Evaluating the success or otherwise of the reforms is dependent on the criteria used to make such a judgment.

2. *The New Public Management*

Introduction

It is widely accepted that the term the 'New Public Management' (NPM) consists of a 'bundle' or a 'shopping basket' of measures intended to bring about reform in the public sector (Pollitt & Summa 1997). It is often presented as a 'neutral or transferable technology to improve the public sector without offending traditional values (Gray & Jenkins 1995). However, its precise nature varies depending on the country into which it is introduced; the aspects of the NPM that are applied; and the measures used to judge its success (Pollitt 2000). Contemporary health care management is a complex blend of theories and concepts arising from a range of sources and, although the term NPM is imprecise, it does give a sense of how this complex blend came to have a profound effect on the organisation of health care. The intention is that in examining the NPM, the reasons for the introduction of particular management methods into health care will be revealed and that the value of theory in uncovering this process will become evident.

The purpose of this chapter then is to:

- discuss the origins of the term the 'New Public Management'
- examine its utility in explaining recent changes in the management and organisation of health care
- identify the components of the NPM and thereby establish a rationale for the selection of content in the remaining chapters.

The NPM

When reflecting on the widespread effects of the public sector reforms enacted by the post-1979 Conservative government, Clarke *et al.* comment:

> It is not possible to avoid discussing the economic, political and ideological conditions in which the micro-processes of organizational change have occurred. (Clarke *et al.* 1994, p. 226)

The purpose of this chapter is to locate the transformation from consensus management to a more active 'managerialism' in the context of theoretical accounts of this New Public Management. The literature which attempts to provide a coherent analysis of these developments and their effects on management in the public services demonstrates how a number of political, economic and ideological forces coalesced to produce an impetus for change. In essence the new managerialism incorporates the application of private sector management systems and techniques to the public services (Farnham & Horton 1993). However, there is a danger in simplifying the situation in this way. There is no single or unified model of the NPM, rather it is a short-hand term for a range of principles which have been applied in a variety of ways and have had different effects (Wilson & Doig 1996). Ferlie *et al.* (1996) confirm that no consensus exists on the precise nature of the NPM:

> There is no clear or agreed definition of what the new public management actually is and not only is there controversy about what is, or what is in the process of becoming, but also what it ought to be. (Ferlie *et al.* 1996, p. 10)

However, some detailed explanations of this trend in public sector management have been produced. Hood (1991) contends that there are seven doctrinal precepts which appear in most discussions of the NPM (Table 2.1). He regards the NPM as a 'marriage of opposites', of two different streams of ideas. One is the new institutional economics of public choice, transactions cost theory, and principal-agent theory, which generated a set of administrative reform doctrines built around the ideas of contestability, user choice, transparency and the use of incentive structures. The other element in this combination is the business type 'managerialism' drawing on notions of scientific management and incorporating a set of doctrines based on professional management, freedom to manage and high discretionary power for the manager (Hood 1991). The rise of the NPM was inextricably linked with the prevailing political situation in the UK in the 1980s and early 1990s.

Debate concerning the NPM

The work of Hood (1991) signalled a new departure in the study of management in public sector organisations such as the NHS. Before this the study of public administration, as it was called, was based on the belief that there is a major difference between private and public administration and management (Chandler 1991). Indeed some commentators have argued strongly that this distinction should remain because the unique purposes, values and conditions of the public domain cannot be resolved by models of

Table 2.1 Doctrinal components of the NPM. Reproduced by permission of Blackwell Publishing from Hood, C. (1991) A public management for all seasons. *Public Administration* 69, 3–19.

No.	Doctrine	Meaning	Typical justification
1.	'Hands-on professional management' in the public sector	Active, visible, discretionary control of organisations from named persons at the top, 'free to manage'	Accountability requires clear assignment of responsibility for action, not diffusion of power
2.	Explicit standards and measures of performance	Definition of goals, targets, indicators of success, preferably expressed in quantitative terms, especially for professional services	Accountability requires clear statement of goals; efficiency requires 'hard look' at objectives
3.	Greater emphasis on output controls	Resource allocation and rewards linked to measured performance; break-up of centralised bureaucracy-wide personnel management	Need to stress results rather than procedures
4.	Shift to disaggregation of units in the public sector	Break up of formerly 'monolithic' units, unbundling of U-form management systems into corporatised units around products operating on decentralised 'one-line' budgets and dealing with one another on an 'arm's length' basis	Need to create 'manageable' units, separate provision and production interests, gain efficiency advantages of use of contract or franchise arrangements inside as well as outside the public sector
5.	Shift to greater competition in the public sector	Move to term contracts and public tendering procedures	Rivalry as the key to lower costs and better standards
6.	Stress on private sector styles of management practice	Move away from military-style 'public service ethic', greater flexibility in hiring and rewards; greater use of PR techniques	Need to use 'proven' private sector management tools in the public sector
7.	Stress on greater discipline and parsimony in resource use	Cutting direct costs, raising labour discipline, resisting union demands, limiting 'compliance costs' to business	Need to check resource demands of public sector and 'do more with less'

organisation and management built for the private sector (Ranson & Stewart 1989, 1994). Similarly Ackroyd *et al.* (1989) concluded that because public sector managers have to manage the highly discretionary and evaluative activity of those who deliver services, they have to reconcile diametrically opposed demands of external 'controllers' (policy makers) and internal carers (professionals). They suggest it is this task of balancing client need with the political direction of the service that renders public sector management unique. Barrett & McMahon (1990) have also argued that the adoption of orthodox prescriptions from the private sector have limited relevance in the health care setting because of the small number of individuals in such organisations who work autonomously and are able to influence outcomes. Flynn (1993), Metcalfe & Richards (1990) and Pollitt (1993a) also contend that the uniqueness of the public sector means that the 'private sector prescriptions' aimed at improving the management of a range of public services are fundamentally flawed.

On the other hand some believe that this distinction is unhelpful and that a 'generic' approach to management is possible (Chandler 1991, Gunn 1989). Others contend that the NPM is the result of a fusion between the best of both traditions (Osborne & Gaebler 1992) incorporating clear notions of public service with the recommendations made by management 'gurus' such as Deal & Kennedy (1982) and Peters & Waterman (1982). The influence of Peters & Waterman (1982) for example, was considerable. Their book *In Search of Excellence* is the world's bestselling business book (Kennedy 1998). In it they identify eight attributes of excellence which are present in successful organisations. These are:

- A bias for action: this means getting on with things.
- Close to customer: this means learning from and meeting the needs of the customer as a central concern of the organisation.
- Autonomy and entrepreneurship: this means giving people the freedom to be inventive and take responsibility for improving the way the organisation operates.
- Productivity through people: this means treating people well, fostering teamwork and recognising that people deliver quality.
- Hands on value driven: this means that managers are visible and involved. Also there is a sense of shared values in the organisation which results in a unity of purpose. People all have a clear idea of what the organisation is trying to do.
- Stick to the knitting: this means concentrating on the business that the organisation is good at.
- Simple form lean staff: this means having a clear simple structure that everyone understands and the minimum number of staff necessary to do the work.

- Simultaneous loose-tight properties: this means that if everyone agrees on the aims and purpose of the organisation there is less need for rules and regulations. Consequently if shared values are present there is 'tight' control over performance whilst at the same time there are 'loose' structures which enable people to innovate and feel autonomous.

However, five years after the book was published two-thirds of the organisations included in the original study, which was the basis for the book, were experiencing problems and only 14 of the 43 'top' companies could be classified as 'excellent', judged against the original criteria (Kennedy 1998). Also the methodology used by Peters & Waterman (1982) has been criticised on the basis of the sampling procedures and representativeness of the sample (Guest 1992). One of the authors even changed his position, later stating 'there are no excellent companies' (Peters 1988).

This illustrates how influential ideas can be, even when events have moved on, and it has been demonstrated that the recommendations made have limitations. It is also clear that despite the lack of precision concerning the exact nature of the NPM it has undoubtedly had an effect on the NHS.

NPM *ideal types*

Ferlie *et al.* (1996) respond to this lack of precision in the terminology by proposing a typology of new public management 'ideal types'. This leads them to suggest that there are at least four models of NPM and while each of them represents a move away from traditional public administration models, they also contain important differences and distinctive features (Ferlie *et al.* 1996). The notion of 'ideal types' derives from the work of Weber (Gerth & Mills 1948) who employed them as a means of comparing social phenomena. An ideal type is not a moral judgment, in the sense of what is best morally, nor is it an ideal in the sense that it is the best or average example. It is an abstract tool which focuses attention on a particular set of factors that are regarded as important. It represents the essential or 'pure' elements of the phenomenon as a basis for comparison and analysis (Watson 1995b, Bond & Bond 1986). They are 'pure' ideas, never to be found in their purity in the real world (Albrow 1997). Ideal types are examples of heuristic devices, in that they provide a point of comparison involving the use of an artificial construct which can serve as a basis for study and research to increase our understanding of the nature of certain phenomena (Marshall 1994). We now go on to discuss each of these four models.

NPM 1: The efficiency drive

Ferlie *et al.* (1996) contend this is the earliest model to emerge and that it was dominant throughout the early 1980s. It represents an attempt to make the public sector more business-like and is dominated by crude notions of efficiency. The driver for this model was the new Thatcherite political economy in which the public sector was seen as wasteful, bureaucratic and underperforming and a series of institutional reforms were introduced from the top of the political system to correct this situation. It incorporated command and control approaches and has been characterised as 'neo-Taylorist' (that is a new application of the principles developed by Taylor discussed in chapter 1) (Pollitt 1993a).

Examples
The introduction of the various targets to improve the management of waiting lists is an example of the efficiency drive. In an attempt to increase efficiency, targets are expressed numerically and success is judged in terms of how many people are taken off the waiting list, or the extent of the reduction in waiting times. Generally these are 'crude' targets that are easy to measure. They may not reflect issues relating to clinical priority. For example, if the target is to reduce the number of people on the waiting list one way of doing this is to treat a large number of 'routine' minor cases, so five hernia operations could be performed in the time it takes to do one complex procedure to treat an abdominal carcinoma. On one level efficiency has been increased because more people have had an operation, however those five people could wait longer without a major risk to their health, whereas the patient with the abdominal carcinoma cannot wait. Efficiency may have increased, in terms of meeting the target set, however the service to individual patients may deteriorate.

Focusing solely on efficiency as part of the NPM had other limitations. In attempting to measure performance and output more rigorously a range of indicators can be used. One that led to some difficulties was finished consultant episodes (FCEs). Again the basis of this way of monitoring performance is counting the number of FCEs as a reflection of activity. The logic behind this is that the more episodes that are recorded, the more patients are being seen and treated. However, a patient may be admitted to hospital under the care of one consultant and not actually see that consultant at any point because staff were unaware that the 'take' had changed, and so the patient is reassigned to the care of another consultant. Consequently an FCE is recorded although no activity has occurred.

Other extreme examples include anecdotes of patients in Accident and Emergency departments, awaiting transfer to the ward, being asked to get off their trolleys and sit in chairs for short periods, before being helped back onto

31

the trolley, to avoid the department exceeding the maximum 'trolley wait' target. Because the patient sat on a chair for a few minutes and then got back on the trolley the waiting time starts again from that point, for monitoring purposes. These examples illustrate some of the unintended consequences of the efficiency drive. It did have an effect on performance and there was an increase in efficiency, when measured on this basis. However, there were also some questionable outcomes.

NPM 2: Downsizing and decentralisation

This is seen as reflecting wider trends in the restructuring of organisations across the public and private sector. It is reflected in the movement away from large vertically integrated organisations to more decentralised and flexible units, which involved the contracting out of services and large-scale 'unbundling' to improve responsiveness and reduce costs. This model of organisation is increasingly referred to as 'postfordist' (Walby *et al.* 1994) and is regarded as a general trend in the development of organisations. Fordism is a pattern of industrial organisation and employment policy which combines mass production, deskilling of jobs, and a recognition of employees as consumers (Watson 1995b) and is a development of Taylorism. The term derives from the car production plants established by the industrialist Henry Ford, where the principles and practice of mass production within a tight system of managerial authority were the basis of the organisation. 'Postfordism' is a term now used to contrast the newer 'flatter' organisations, that is those with fewer levels in the management hierarchy, and those which ostensibly afford employees greater freedom and autonomy, with the old 'fordist' organisations which had rigid structures and exerted tight control over the workforce. This incorporated the internal market, the separation of purchasers and providers and the contracting out of services. Ferlie *et al.* (1996) argue that this model was not as dominant as NPM 1 in the 1980s but is now of increasing importance.

Examples
This model was reflected in the creation of clinical directorates within NHS trusts. This involved the grouping together of collections of usually similar services as business units. Based on an organisational model developed at the Johns Hopkins University Hospital in the USA, groups of wards and departments were designated as directorates, e.g. the Medical Directorate, the Surgical Directorate, Critical Care Directorate, Speciality Services Directorate, and so on. This decentralisation within trusts mirrored the new structures that had been introduced nationally with trusts being identified as independent organisations with greater freedom from Health Authority control. The idea behind this decentralisation was that the

individual units (be they trusts or the directorates within them) could focus on the 'business' they were engaged in. The intention was that these smaller units would have more control over their own affairs and that the people working in them would feel more involved and committed to them, be innovative, and respond to the needs of the patients more directly.

However, the unintended consequences were that in many trusts, directorates were placed in direct competition for staff and other resources. The approach taken to managing scarce resources in many instances was that if one directorate wanted to develop a new service, e.g. an out-of-hours clinic, it would first have to produce a 'business case' justifying the need for such a service and indicating how much it would cost to run. This 'bid' would then be considered along with similar bids and requests for staff submitted by the other directorates. In this way the budget allocated to the trust as a whole could be divided up. Although this is a way of managing scarce resources, it runs counter to notions of cooperation and collaboration between departments and directorates as they are all competing for scarce resources.

NPM 3: 'In search of excellence'

This model is associated with the 'excellence literature' of the 1980s (Deal & Kennedy 1982; Peters & Waterman 1982). It highlights the role of values, culture, rites and symbols in shaping how people behave at work. It also incorporates notions of the 'learning organisation' and human relations approaches to management. There is an emphasis on charismatic and transformational leadership often associated with the imperative to change the organisation.

Examples
This is reflected in the emphasis placed on the management of culture in organisations (see also chapter 4). The creation of new letter heads, corporate logos and job titles are all intended to change the way people think and feel about the organisation they work in or are treated by. Ward sisters become ward managers, the general manager becomes the chief executive and a director of communications is appointed to ensure the trust presents a positive image when dealing with the media. Such changes in title and new appointments signal a more 'corporate' and business-like approach to the delivery of health care. They are intended to raise the level of performance of the organisation by instilling a culture of excellence. The addition of 'quality marks' such as 'Investors in People' and 'Charter Mark' to all organisational literature is a public statement of excellence expressed by the organisation. However, difficulties can arise when staff and client expectations generated by such expressions are not met. For example, if a member of staff applies for a course of study and is informed she can only attend if she meets the costs of

the course, this will run counter to the impression of the organisation as an investor in people. Similarly if a patient receives confusing communication giving conflicting dates for an appointment the credibility of the charter mark status is called into question and affects the patient's confidence. Consequently the impression of excellence needs to be constantly reinforced in the actions of the organisation.

NPM 4: Public service orientation

This model is the least well developed and is still to reveal its full potential. It represents a fusion of private and public sector management ideas. It confers legitimacy on a new style public sector which has moved on from its 'bureaucratic' past but retains a sense of distinct identity and purpose. It places emphasis on quality services, public service values and the need for a more user centred approach.

Examples
As Ferlie *et al.* (1996) suggest this variation of the NPM is still being developed. It reflects a concern that in introducing management methods to the NHS and the public sector there is a danger that the fundamental purpose of the organisations it is applied to will be overlooked. An early development of this brand of the NPM is evident in a report compiled by the Office for Public Management in collaboration with the NHS Women's unit in 1994, which concluded that a new framework for public management was required. Central to this was the notion of 'managing for social result'. This involved managers balancing the demands for efficiency, effectiveness and value for money whilst maintaining 'social result' as the guiding public management principle (OPM/NHSWU 1994). This reflects the public service orientation of NPM 4.

A more recent manifestation of this is in the New NHS Modern Dependable (DOH 1997) and its reference to a 'third way'. It states there will be a 'third way' of running the NHS, which combines the best from the past with new approaches. 'It will neither be a model from the 1970s nor the model from the early 1990s. It will be new model for a new century.' It is founded on six principles which reflect elements of the NPM:

- commitment to a national service
- combined with local responsibility and standards
- partnership working throughout the NHS
- efficiency, through the elimination of bureaucracy and improving performance
- excellence, arising from improved quality systems
- rebuilding public confidence in the NHS, rediscovering the public service ethos.

This is further underpinned by a statement of ten core principles at the start of the *NHS Plan* (DOH 2000a) which are intended to ensure that the overall aims of the NHS are retained as it is modernised over the next ten years. As Ferlie *et al.* (1996) observed, the final form of this variation of the NPM is yet to be realised.

This typology provides a model which draws the disparate elements of the NPM together. It is a useful and detailed continuum which demonstrates the different elements of the NPM. The NPM is a term that is used to summarise the broad thrust of management reform that has affected the public sector over the last decade, however it is important to recognise the different dimensions within it to appreciate the organisational and management context of health care.

The number of managers

Given the emphasis on the importance of management in the NPM, it would be logical to assume that there was a concomitant rise in the number of managers working in health care as a consequence of its impact. However, the evidence to support such a view is not clear cut. Allsop (1995) maintains that since the health reforms there have been large increases in the numbers of administrative, clerical and managerial staff in the NHS. Ham (1997), for example, reports that the number of managers rose from 6,091 in 1989/90 to 20,478 in 1992/93, and that over the same period the number of administrative and clerical staff increased from 144,582 to 166,363. This is demonstrated in the costs to trusts. Management and administrative costs of NHS trusts in England and Wales represent, on average, 10.5 per cent of their revenue (Audit Commission 1995). This reflects a general increase in managers and administrators since between 1989 and 1994 the number of managers increased fourfold and the number of other administrative staff rose by just over 10 per cent (DOH 1995a). Although there appears to be a clear increase in the number of managers, the consideration of administrative and clerical staff, and different levels of management together makes it difficult to obtain an accurate representation of the actual increase in 'management' that has occurred.

It is evident that some growth in the 'general and senior manager' category has occurred, because staff have transferred from what were predominantly management jobs in other categories (e.g., nursing, the allied health professions, and medicine), yet the unreliability of the data makes it impossible to draw firm conclusions about the extent or pace of any real growth (Audit Commission 1995). Indeed in view of the lack of reliable data in this area the Audit Commission (1995) called for a wider debate to define management and produce a clearer idea of management objectives in the

NHS, because in the absence of a consensual definition of management it is extremely difficult to measure the rate of increase of management. However, what is beyond dispute is that as a result of the changes inherent in the NPM greater emphasis was placed on management as a means of delivering health services. Some of the research that has been conducted to examine the effects of this is now discussed.

Researching the NPM

Much of the interest in the NPM has taken the form of commentaries and 'overviews' of the changes that have occurred in the public sector (Ackroyd *et al.* 1989, Hood 1991, Dunleavy & Hood 1994, Wilson & Doig 1996), with comparatively few projects investigating the development of the NPM within organisations. Two exceptions are Broussine (1990), and Dopson & Stewart (1990a), and their studies will now be examined to illustrate some contrasting views on the NPM.

Broussine (1990) found that local authority chief officers and their private sector counterparts identify more differences between them than actually exist. Drawing on the results of a postal survey of 110 executives and directors in the public and private sector; three seminars involving 44 local authority chief officers, 21 private sector managers and 10 senior managers from the NHS, which explored perceptions the groups had of each other through group work and the completion of a personality profile questionnaire and a job characteristics questionnaire, Broussine (1990) concludes that the two groups are remarkably similar in terms of their reported skills and personality types. He ascribes the perceived differences to negative stereotypes which, once challenged, become less of a barrier and that this act of confronting distorted views can help to narrow the gap which exists between the private and public sector.

Dopson & Stewart (1990a), on the other hand, found that some public sector managers saw commercially oriented working practices as inimical to public services because they undermined traditional values and the distinct sense of professional identity and ethos. They found themselves in a paradoxical position where the government was demanding more of them but offering no support. They were given the responsibility but not the necessary power to achieve specified targets. Using data obtained from case study research into middle managers' attitudes to change, Dopson & Stewart (1990a) contend that the fundamental areas of difference centred around achievements and resources. Achievements go unrecognised in public sector organisations, so managers operate defensively and try to avoid making mistakes rather than being innovative and embracing change. Also managers in the private sector have a greater feeling of control over their work because of their control of resources. Public sector managers, however, do not have this control and so are less able to achieve their objectives. Dopson & Stewart (1990a) see leadership as crucial in bringing this about.

NPM *and health care*

These two studies present some interesting material concerning the relationship between public and private sector approaches and establish the broad context of the NPM. They also indicate how different public and private sector approaches vary depending on the setting. However, if a more complete understanding of the NPM and its effects on health care is to be achieved it is necessary to examine in more detail the component parts of the NPM and how they relate to the work of health professionals. The framework that will be used to highlight these component parts is derived from two of the latest major policy pronouncements from the Labour administration elected in 1997 and re-elected in 2001. *The New NHS Modern Dependable* (DOH 1997) and the *NHS Plan* (DOH 2000a) can be located in NPM 4 (Ferlie *et al.* 1996) as they both represent attempts to combine elements of 'old' and 'new' managerial thinking and elements of all four NPM models can be discerned in their content. The NHS Plan is the blueprint for the organisation and delivery of health services for the next ten years. Therefore it is appropriate to use the main elements of the plan as a guideline for the content of the remaining chapters. In order to do this the components of the plan are summarised in Table 2.2, along with the implications they have for nurses and health professionals. However, this can only be a brief summary as the document itself is extremely comprehensive running to some 144 pages. Rather, the purpose here is to indicate how the material addressed in the remainder of the book is relevant to and necessary for nurses and health professionals.

Conclusion

The NPM is a useful theoretical device for drawing together the diverse strands in management thinking that have shaped health care in the 1980s and 1990s. The *NHS Plan* (DOH 2000a) represents the next phase in the development of health management and it has a number of implications for nurses and other health professionals. In the final part of this chapter the main areas that need to be considered have been identified (Table 2.2) and will be examined in more detail in subsequent chapters. It is important to understand the broad context in which nurses and health professionals work because it is a crucial factor in determining how they deliver care. It is part of the policy domain (Kouzes & Mico 1979) (see chapter 10) which is influential in creating the environment in which all health care personnel work. A specific dimension of the NPM is its emphasis on quality.

Table 2.2 The *NHS Plan* and its implications

The *NHS Plan* (DOH 2000) A Summary of Key Changes

Plan	Details	Management implications
Facilities		
7,000 extra beds in hospitals and intermediate care	7,000 extra beds by 2004	Change
Over 100 new hospitals by 2010	19 new hospitals open by 2004	(Chapters 4 and 5)
500 new one-stop primary care centres	Inner city practices to be targeted	
Over 3,000 GP premises modernised	Refurbished or replaced by 2004	
250 new scanners	£300 million to be invested in equipment to achieve target by 2004	
Modern IT in every hospital and GP surgery	Bedside televisions, telephones, IT infrastructure	
Clean wards better food		
Staff		
7,500 more consultants and 2,000 more GPs	By 2004	IWL Standards
20,000 extra nurses and 6,500 therapists	45,000 nurses and midwives, 13,000 therapists qualifying by 2004	(Chapter 3)
1,000 more medical school places	New pay system	
Extra pay in shortage areas to attract staff	By 2004 (£30 million allocated to this)	
100 on-site nurseries	Improving Working Lives Scheme	
Improvements in the working environment		

Table 2.2 Continued

The *NHS Plan* (DOH 2000) A Summary of Key Changes

Plan	Details	Management implications
Systems		
Devolved responsibility	Primary care trusts earned autonomy	Standards
Core national standards and targets	National service frameworks	Change
Modernisation agency	Teams to bring about change	Management
Publication of performance information	Annual reports on performance	(Chapters 3, 4 and 8)
Inspection to assure quality	Commission for health improvement	
£500 million performance fund	£5 million for trusts achieving targets from performance fund	
Intervention in failing trusts		
New ways of running the NHS		
Changes for health and social services		
One-stop health and social care services	Partnership working	Interprofessional working
£900 million investment in intermediate care services	New joint teams	Standards/Inspection
Joint best value inspections of health and social care	Commission for Health Improvement,	Quality
New health and social care trusts	Audit Commission and Social Services Inspectorate	(Chapters 3 and 9)
Changes for nurses, midwives, therapists and other NHS staff		
New skills and roles for nurses	Removal of barriers between professions	Interprofessional working
£140 million to develop staff skills	Continuing professional development	Clinical leadership
Individual learning accounts for all staff	£150 annual learning account for all staff	Hybrid management
Modernised education with a core curriculum	Interprofessional training	(Chapters 6, 7 and 9)
Modern matrons	Nurse leaders	
1000 nurse consultants. Consultant therapists	By 2004	
NHS leadership centre		

3. Clinical Governance and Quality Management

Introduction

Clinical governance is defined as:

> a framework through which NHS organisations are accountable for continuously improving the quality of their services and safeguarding high standards of care by creating an environment in which excellence in clinical care will flourish. (DOH 1998, p. 33)

Clinical governance provides the current policy framework for the management of quality in the NHS and the ideas that inform it have their roots in management thought. The purpose of this chapter is to examine some of the main trends in management thinking that have contributed to the development of quality management systems in health care. This is necessary because a focus on quality is a central feature of current government approaches to the management of health care. It is stated in the *NHS Plan* that:

> Patients should have fair access and high standards of care wherever they live. So at national level the Department of Health will, with the help of leading clinicians, managers and staff, set national standards in priority areas. (DOH 2000a, p. 58)

The relationship of this approach to general quality management principles is examined and the problems that occur when attempts are made to apply 'general' management methods in health care explored. This serves as a starting point for consideration of what will be required if clinical governance is to be implemented successfully in health care. To summarise then this chapter seeks to:

- examine the difficulties and challenges involved in defining quality in health care
- establish the importance of quality as a central concern, through reference to significant failures in the NHS

- discuss the work of the 'quality gurus' and their influence on heath care quality
- assess the success of managing quality in health care.

Defining quality

There are particular difficulties associated with defining the term quality in the context of health care. For example, if the definition of clinical governance is considered what is meant by 'excellence'? Will notions of what is excellent vary from person to person? Similarly what are high standards? There are a number of dimensions that affect the construction of any definitions that are used. Maxwell (1984, 1992) has usefully summarised a number of the issues involved and demonstrates that the development of statements which are intended to define quality, or aspects of it, is by no means a straightforward process (see Figure 3.1). Each of the dimensions highlights a particular aspect of quality and can help increase awareness of the complex nature of health care quality. They can also point the way to the need for a range of quality indicators if the quality of a service as a whole is to be comprehensively assessed.

The surgeon may be technically skilled and carry out a surgical procedure based on the best available evidence. However, if the patient has to wait two years for this surgery, suffering discomfort and the operation is postponed on two occasions, what would be the overall judgment of the quality of service received in this case? Similarly if a patient needs a course of treatment which can only be accessed within the next year if the patient is prepared to travel 70 miles to a hospital that has some spare capacity and which has mixed wards, is this a quality service? The answer to such questions is always conditional, it depends. Judgments about the service provided are made against notions of what is expected. If a rapid, responsive service is expected and is not forthcoming then the perception will be that the quality is poor. However, if an acute life threatening illness is being experienced and the patient's life is saved as a result of treatment this will be regarded as a positive outcome and good quality. The key point is that perceptions of quality are varied and contingent upon expectations and past experience as well as the service provided. Recognition of this situation is important as it helps to explain divergent opinions on quality which are informed by fundamental beliefs about what the NHS is there to do.

The poles of the debate in this area can be summarised by a simple analogy. Is the NHS there to provide a Rolls Royce or a Ford Escort service? Is it there to provide the best possible care that could be delivered, or is its role to provide a minimum, basic or acceptable service as cheaply as possible? In many ways the theoretical accounts and management

---

Questions that help to define and expand the label 'quality'

Effectiveness
Is the treatment given the best available in a technical sense, according to those best equipped to judge? What is their evidence? What is the overall result of the treatment?

Acceptability
How humanely and considerately is this treatment/service delivered? What does the patient think of it? What would/does an observant third party think of it ('How would I feel if it were my nearest and dearest?') What is the setting like? Are privacy and confidentiality safeguarded?

Efficiency
Is the output maximised for a given input or (conversely) is the input minimised for a given level of output? How does the unit cost compare with the unit cost elsewhere for the same treatment/service?

Access
Can people get this treatment/service when they need it? Are there any identifiable barriers to service – for example, distance, inability to pay, waiting lists, and waiting times – or straightforward breakdowns in supply?

Equity
Is this patient or group of patients being fairly treated relative to others? Are there any identifiable failings in equity – for example, are some people being dealt with less favourably or less appropriately in their own eyes than others?

Relevance
Is the overall pattern and balance of services the best that could be achieved, taking account of the needs and wants of the population as a whole?

Figure 3.1 Six dimensions of quality (Maxwell 1984, 1992).

prescriptions that have been presented in the area of quality can be viewed as systems and approaches designed to deal with such issues. They generally incorporate a particular definition of quality on which they are based and then set out how quality, as defined, can be achieved. However, before examining some of these in more detail it is necessary to explore the difficulties in defining health care quality a little further.

Øvretveit (1992) maintains that a quality health service is one that satisfies a number of sometimes conflicting requirements and interest groups. He

---

The three dimensions of health service quality

Client quality
What clients and carers want from the service (individuals and populations).

Professional quality
Whether the service meets the needs as defined by professional providers and referrers, and whether it correctly carries out techniques and procedures which are believed to be necessary to meet client needs.

Management quality
The most efficient and productive use of resources, within limits and directives set by higher authorities/purchasers.

Figure 3.2 The three dimensions of health service quality (Øvretveit 1992).

summarises this as consisting of three dimensions (see Figure 3.2) which correspond to the major interest groups that must be integrated to specify the quality of health services. This is similar to the analysis of Pollitt (1993b) in which he identifies what he terms three 'species' of quality in the NHS. These are:

- **Medical quality**: a professional, highly technical exercise conducted exclusively by doctors.
- **Service quality**: the aspects of quality that remain once the 'doctors' business' has been artificially extracted.
- **Experienced quality**: dimensions of the patient experience which the patient thinks important.

What these 'dimensions' and 'species' of quality indicate is that definitions of quality used by people working in or accessing health care are not the same. This can result in confusion and disagreement concerning how quality should be measured and managed.

Example
An elderly patient is admitted to hospital with abdominal pain. During assessment in the Accident and Emergency (A&E) department she is classified as 'non-urgent' as the pain has been present for a few days and on examination it does not appear to be an 'acute abdomen'. Consequently immediate treatment is not required. As a result of this classification she waits for four hours in the department until a bed becomes available on a

ward. Once on the ward she is seen quickly and a diagnosis of chronic constipation is made. The next day, following administration of an enema, the constipation is relieved and the patient feels better. A decision is made that the patient can go home as no further medical or nursing care is required. However, some supervision and support at home is necessary to prevent a recurrence of the constipation. Organising the necessary support at home takes a few days. Whilst waiting for the arrangements to be put in place the patient is moved several times to other wards to make beds available for emergency admissions. As a result of this she loses several items of clothing during transfers.

Is this a quality service?

- **Medical perspective**: The patient received appropriate treatment and the condition was resolved. A good service was provided.
- **Nursing/professional perspective**: The frequent transfers compromised continuity of care. There was a lack of opportunity to support the patient in her preparation for discharge.
- **Service/management perspective**: Treatment was delivered on the basis of need. As long as the wait in A & E did not exceed the waiting time directive, that aspect of care was satisfactory. The loss of clothing is a concern as a complaint may follow.
- **Client perspective**: Initially concerned at having to wait; later satisfied as the problem was resolved; probably followed by dissatisfaction with the delay in discharge and the loss of personal items.

When considered in this way it becomes clearer why quality is a difficult aspect of care to manage. People approach it with different expectations. These perceptions and expectations can also be influenced by the nature of the problem. For example, when first admitted to hospital the relief of pain may be the first concern. When this has been dealt with the next requirement is an accurate diagnosis and explanation of the treatment required. Then skilled and efficient administration/performance of the necessary treatment/intervention is expected. Finally information and aftercare to support discharge arrangements or continuing care is needed. At various points along this continuum patients may start to focus on other aspects of care as quality issues. Once the pain has been relieved the patient may be more aware and more concerned about the way she is spoken to. Similarly when the initial treatment is underway or has been performed successfully then the quality of the surroundings or the food may be become more of a concern. So not only do perspectives on quality vary depending on the person/group concerned, perceptions and concerns can change over time. This indicates why there are challenges in managing quality in health care. In many instances the response to this challenge is to use fairly 'basic' measures. Essentially everyone can recognise a chronological or numerical target and these are often used as a means of managing quality. For example, the time patients have to wait before receiving an appointment, before being seen, or before having surgery can be quality targets. Reducing the number of patient complaints could be a target. These can all be useful and play a part in an overall quality system. However, difficulties emerge when other aspects of quality need to be assessed such as the patient's level of satisfaction with the service as a whole; the quality of the environment; and the treatment outcome, because of the different starting points for evaluation outlined above.

Quality failures

If it is then considered that managers and professionals are not homogeneous groups and that there will be divergent opinion as to the best route to quality among the people within these groups, the picture is complicated further. Also, it is not particularly helpful to approach client or patient quality as a single entity because the range of experience and expectation is hugely variable. This situation has been compounded by the very public failings of the NHS which have been so comprehensive that they span all of these dimensions and have contributed to a situation whereby demands to improve quality can no longer be ignored.

The Inquiry into the Management of Care of Children receiving complex Heart Surgery at the Bristol Royal Infirmary 1984–1995 (2001) discovered that quality failings resulted in the deaths of babies. The report is 'an account of a time when there was no agreed means of assessing the quality of care. There were no standards for evaluating performance and there was confusion throughout the NHS as to who was responsible for monitoring the quality of care'. In the period 1991–1995 between 30 and 35 more children under one year of age died after open heart surgery in the Bristol unit than would be expected in other similar units. The report goes on to make 198 recommendations aimed at ensuring safe care and the improvement of quality. Reflecting on the report Coulter (2002) concludes: 'If we want to centre quality improvement efforts on the needs and wishes of patients we must first understand how things look through their eyes' (p. 650). This will involve empowering patients to become more involved in decisions about their care which will in turn need leadership from within the clinical professions, more training and a willingness to change (Coulter 2002). All key aspects of any quality system.

Similarly a review of cardiac services in Oxford found that the combination of a lack of leadership, surgeons working autonomously, difficulties in recruiting and retaining nursing staff and a culture of complacency and secrecy all contributed to a decline in the quality of services (Dobson 2000). The main recommendation of the review was that the surgeons should work as a team and devise a system for managing operating theatre lists (Dobson 2000), both basic components of quality management.

When reflecting on the death of a young patient as a result of an erroneous intrathecal injection of the cytotoxic drug vincristine, intended for intravenous use, Berwick (2001) concluded the remedy was to change systems of work. People are fallible but they can create safer systems based on quality principles. The example he cites is the change to the connecting fittings of nitrous oxide and oxygen supply lines in operating theatres. The connections have been made incompatible so that it is impossible to inadvertently connect the nitrous oxide line to the oxygen supply, and vice versa, during anaesthesia. This has almost eliminated the small number of deaths that used to occur each year as a result of incorrect connection of lines.

Other failings such as 'unprofessional, counter-therapeutic and degrading' treatment of elderly people, and the death of a patient following the removal of a healthy kidney instead of the diseased one (Kmietowicz 2000) indicate that there are many quality problems in health care. Such events, along with more 'routine' lapses in quality including drug administration errors, poor standards of hospital cleanliness and unpalatable meals, are evidence that quality is an issue that needs to be managed. The current approach to this is through the system of clinical governance. This is reflective of a series of quality principles that have been propounded by key management theorists. These include W. Edwards Deming, Joseph Juran, Philip Crosby and John Oakland. Their work is considered in terms of how it relates to clinical governance to demonstrate how management theory and ideas drawn from management are of enduring and contemporary relevance to nurses and members of the health professions.

The work of the quality gurus

The main principles identified by individuals who have come to be referred to as 'quality gurus', will be presented as a means of summarising the broad sweep of ideas that were very influential in the 'private sector' and which later came to influence management in health care and are a feature of the NPM discussed in chapter 2. The term guru is generally applied to a spiritual leader or a wise man. When used in a management context it is used to denote an elite, yet diverse grouping, who simultaneously comment on management while acting to change its practice (Huczynski 1993). Huczynski goes on to argue that there are three types of management guru:

- the academic guru
- the consultant guru
- the hero manager.

The background and work of the quality gurus considered below display elements of all three types in that they have studied quality and written extensively on it (academic guru); they have acted as advisors and experts to help companies and indeed countries, in the case of Deming and Juran, develop quality management systems (consultant guru); and have themselves managed organisations in line with the principles of quality (hero manager).

These individuals developed different aspects of a management approach to quality which over time developed into a system which came to be known as total quality management (TQM). The different contributions that they made are summarised and evaluated below and then the way their ideas relate to current approaches in health care is examined. This also involves an assessment of the success of TQM initiatives in health care. Finally current guidance on clinical governance and quality in health care is explored.

TQM

TQM has been defined as

> an approach to improving competitiveness, effectiveness and flexibility in a whole organization. It is essentially a way of planning, organizing and understanding each activity and depends on each individual at each level. For an organization to be truly effective, each part of it must work properly together towards the same goals, recognizing that each person and each activity affects and in turn is affected by others. (Oakland 1993, p. 22)

Oakland goes on to state that TQM needs to gain ground rapidly and become a way of life in many organisations. There are many definitions of TQM (Mullins 2002); however, its essential features can be regarded as a combination of the work of Deming, Juran, Crosby and Oakland.

Deming and TQM

W. Edwards Deming is famous as the man who taught the Japanese about quality. Deming obtained a doctorate in mathematical physics in 1928 (academic guru). He worked for the US government in the National Bureau of Census and brought about a sixfold increase in productivity (hero manager). After the Second World War Deming was sent to Japan to help in the reconstruction of the infrastructure and industry (the consultant guru) (DTI 1995). Deming's (1988) fourteen points for quality management are as follows:

1. Create constancy of purpose toward improvement of product and service. If organisations are to survive, they must allocate resources for long-term planning research and education, and for the constant improvement of the design of their products and services.
2. Adopt the new philosophy. Government regulations that represent obstacles to competitiveness must be revised. Transformation of companies is needed.
3. Cease dependence on mass inspection. Quality needs to be designed and built into the processes, preventing defects rather than attempting to detect them after they have occurred.
4. End the practice of awarding business on the basis of price tag alone. Lowest bids lead to low quality. Organisations should establish long-term relationships with single suppliers.
5. Improve constantly and forever the system of production and service. Management and employees must search continuously for ways to improve quality and productivity.
6. Institute training. Training at all organisational levels is a necessity, not an option.
7. Adopt and institute leadership. Management's job is to lead, not to supervise. Leaders should eliminate barriers that prevent people from doing the job well and from learning new methods.
8. Drive out fear. Unless employees feel secure enough to express ideas and ask questions, they will do things the wrong way or not do them at all.
9. Break down barriers between staff areas. Working in teams will solve problems and thus improve quality and productivity.
10. Eliminate slogans, exhortations, and targets for the workforce. Problems with quality and productivity are caused by the system, not by individuals. Posters and slogans generate frustration and resentment.
11. Eliminate numerical quotas for the workforce and numerical goals for people in management. In order to meet quotas, people produce defective products. Instead, management must take decisive steps to replace standards, rates, and piecework with intelligent leadership.
12. Remove barriers that rob people of pride of workmanship. Deming views individual performance appraisals as one of the greatest barriers to pride of achievement.
13. Encourage education and self improvement for everyone. Education should never end, for people at all levels of the organisation.

14. Take action to accomplish the transformation. Commitment on the part of both top management and employees is required.

Juran and TQM

Joseph Juran began his professional life as an engineer and as a result of this published a quality control handbook (1992) which led him to international eminence (hero manager). Like Deming he was invited to Japan to work on the postwar reconstruction programme (consultant guru) and he went on to publish twelve books which have been translated into thirteen languages (academic guru) (DTI 1995). He outlined ten steps to quality improvement:

1. Build awareness of the need and opportunity for improvement.
2. Set goals for improvement.
3. Organise to reach the goals (establish a quality council, identify problems, select projects, appoint teams, designate facilitators).
4. Provide training.
5. Carry out projects to solve problems.
6. Report progress.
7. Give recognition.
8. Communicate results.
9. Keep score.
10. Maintain momentum by making annual improvement part of the regular systems and processes of the company (Juran 1992).

Kennedy (1998) has noted that Juran and Deming are so closely linked by age, experience and their part in the Japanese economic miracle that it is sometimes difficult to differentiate between their contributions. Although there are differences in approach among the gurus considered here, there are some overall themes in their work which can be regarded as broadly accepted quality principles and these are identified below. First, though, the work of Philip Crosby and John Oakland is outlined.

Crosby and TQM

Philip Crosby is a graduate of Western Reserve University and started work in the US Navy. He later worked for ITT and for fourteen years was Corporate Vice President and Director of Quality (hero manager). In 1979 he left ITT and established Philip Crosby Associates (consultant guru) and the Quality College (academic guru) to provide training for organisations on how to management quality (DTI 1995). Like Deming, he also offers fourteen steps to quality improvement however he prefaces these with four 'absolutes' of quality. These are:

- Definition – conformance to requirements.
- System – prevention.
- Performance standard – zero defects.
- Measurement – price of non-conformance.

which underpin his fourteen points:

1. Make it clear that management is committed to quality.
2. Form quality improvement teams with representatives from each department.
3. Determine where current and potential quality problems lie.
4. Evaluate the cost of quality and explain its use as a management tool.
5. Raise the quality awareness and personal concern of all employees.
6. Take actions to correct problems identified through previous steps.
7. Establish a team for the zero defects programme.
8. Train supervisors to actively carry out their part of the quality improvement programme.
9. Hold a 'zero defects' day to help all employees realise that there has been a change.
10. Encourage individuals to establish improvement goals for themselves and their groups.
11. Encourage employees to communicate to management the obstacles they face in attaining the improvement goals.
12. Recognise and appreciate those who participate.
13. Establish quality councils to communicate on a regular basis.
14. Do it all over again to emphasise that the quality improvement programme never ends. (Crosby 1979, 1985)

Oakland and TQM

In terms of total quality management, John Oakland (1993) has also been a key figure, particularly in the UK. He has been Professor of Total Quality Management and Head of the European Centre for TQM at the University of Bradford (academic guru), following a career in industry (hero manager). He established O & F Quality Management Consultants (consultant guru), a company which has advised many organisations on quality matters. Again he identifies a series of steps to TQM, coincidentally there are fourteen:

1. Understanding quality.
2. Commitment and leadership.
3. Design for quality.
4. Planning for quality.
5. Systems for quality.
6. Measurement.

7. Costs of quality.
8. Tools and techniques for improvement.
9. Capability and control.
10. Organisation for quality.
11. Communications for quality.
12. Teamwork for culture change.
13. Training for quality.
14. Implementation of TQM (Oakland 1993).

Clearly summarising the work of others as a series of 'key principles' or steps runs the risk of oversimplifying their contribution and failing to convey its comprehensive nature. However, the emphasis here is not so much on a detailed examination of the work of these gurus as this can be undertaken by accessing the original work, listed in the references. Rather it is on tracing the influence of this work on current approaches to quality in health care. So what are the broad areas of agreement among the gurus which constitute broad organisational quality principles? They are:

- Quality is the responsibility of management.
- Teamwork is essential to the achievement of quality.
- The quest for quality is a continuous process.
- Both systems management and people management approaches are required.

Limitations of TQM

Although there is a level of agreement concerning the overarching principles of quality management systems, this is not to suggest that their application is straightforward. There are conceptual and practical difficulties. For example, based on a review of the introduction of TQM in the USA in the 1980s, Cole (1998) concludes that Deming's work lacks a unified coherent theory and detailed guidelines on how to implement quality improvement. However, because US manufacturing firms were 'in crisis' at this time and were seeking radical solutions, TQM was enthusiastically seized upon, if not always introduced as its authors intended. Hackman & Wageman (1995) suggest that rhetoric is winning out over substance and that what many organisations are implementing is a pale or highly distorted version of TQM. Also little research has been undertaken to demonstrate the effectiveness and value of TQM. It seems that the almost evangelistic tone of the proponents of TQM was successful in gaining acceptance for the ideas before they had been subjected to scrutiny and testing (Pollitt 1993b, Collins 2000).

The reality of the situation is much more complex and it is more helpful to approach the challenge of delivering quality based on an acceptance that there are different types of quality for different purposes and that different systems will be required to achieve this (Bouckhaert 1995) rather than seeking recourse to a single solution such as TQM. Indeed when an attempt was made to introduce TQM into the NHS it met with limited success (Joss & Kogan 1995). This was partly as a result of the programme not being adequately resourced; however, there were also difficulties in terms of the nature of TQM not coinciding with the structures within the trusts; poor integration of the existing range of quality systems such as audit; low take up rate (1–5 per cent) of doctors undergoing training in TQM; and a lack of information systems necessary to monitor quality. One of the main barriers to its effective introduction to the NHS was its origins in the commercial sector.

Failing to acknowledge the differences between the two sectors (public and private) made it inevitable that some staff would find it difficult to accept both the principles and the implementation schedules. The lack of participation of medical staff was also a serious blow to the credibility of the approach (Joss & Kogan 1995). These findings were borne out by the work of Hearnshaw *et al.* (1998) who found that the introduction of quality methods developed for use in private sector organisations into the NHS is not without its problems. They report on a project designed to foster quality improvement in general practices based on the principles of TQM. Of the 147 practices invited to participate only six practice teams commenced the programme, and of these only five completed a quality improvement project. Three years later only three practices reported that the changes made were still in place. This illustrates that there are many barriers to improving quality in health care. Øvretveit (1994a) identifies four reasons why TQM failed in the NHS:

1. The political nature of the NHS means that there are frequent changes of policy and directives which demand immediate management action and thus make it difficult to pursue the long-term strategy necessary to achieve TQM.
2. NHS organisations have difficulty obtaining the financial investment necessary to support genuine TQM strategies because the link between service improvement and increased income is not as clear as in private sector organisations.
3. Meeting customer requirements is much more than giving customers what they want. Patients often do not know what they need or whether they have received what they need.
4. The NHS customer is a complex mix of patients, carers, commissioners of services, referrers and other interest groups. This renders the simple concept of 'fully meeting customer requirements' inherently problematic.

Audit

Similarly, more modest attempts at introducing quality mechanisms have met with difficulties. Clinical audit is a way of demonstrating the effectiveness of health care interventions through meeting defined standards and it is also a way of developing the quality of service that clinicians provide (Exworthy 1996) (Figure 3.3). Medical audit, nursing and therapy audit were introduced in 1991 following the publication of *Working for Patients* (DOH 1989). These audit streams subsequently became known as clinical audit to reflect the increasing participation of all clinical groups in multi-professional audit (Exworthy 1996).

Yet the basic process of audit, in its various forms, has been difficult to establish in health care for a number of reasons. This has resulted from a series of related issues. Lord & Littlejohns (1994) found that clinicians believed the results from audit would be used to penalise them or to justify management decisions on cost rather than on quality. Conversely managers distrusted what they saw as professional secrecy and protection of professional interests against those of the patient. This professional-managerial tension was an impediment to the progress of audit.

In the same year Thomson & Barton (1994) feared that audit was losing its impetus and direction because of uncertainties in the following areas:

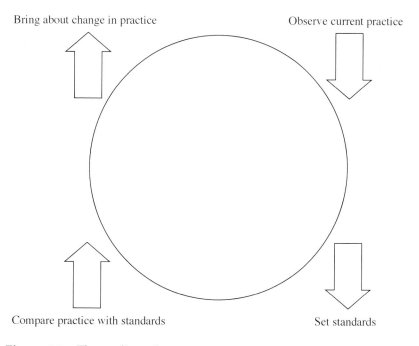

Bring about change in practice   Observe current practice

Compare practice with standards   Set standards

Figure 3.3 The audit cycle.

- Hierarchical doctor-nurse relations
- Poor teamworking
- Practical difficulties in arranging multidisciplinary group meetings
- Interprofessional differences in approaches to audit
- Nursing audit perceived as less credible than medical audit
- Lack of commitment from senior doctors or managers in supporting multidisciplinary audit
- Lack of or insufficient influence of purchasers
- Nurses with little professional autonomy
- Audit in early stages of development in the team or organisation
- Widely differing levels of audit knowledge and experience within the team
- Lack of limited support for teams (facilitation by audit staff)

Figure 3.4 Reported obstacles to multidisciplinary audit (Cheater & Keane 1998).

negative attitudes towards audit on the part of medical staff and a lack of organisation in its management; audit being conducted outside other information management strategies; lack of education on the part of those carrying out audit; the lack of coordination with other initiatives; the lack of research into the effectiveness of audit; and the lack of prioritising that was going on resulting in misplaced effort. Earlier Packwood (1991) had found that in the initial stages of medical audit it was too episodic and inconsistent to be beneficial in educational or management terms. Time pressures were also identified as problematic in that hard pressed clinicians were expected to carry out audit in addition to already heavy workloads. Consequently the level of professional leadership and the educational or managerial benefits that could realistically be expected from the process were limited. A later study found that many barriers remained to the successful introduction of multidisciplinary audit (Cheater & Keane 1998) (see Figure 3.4). This indicates that although many nurses were enthusiastic supporters of audit, several structural, organisational, interprofessional, and intraprofessional factors hampered its progress (Cheater & Keane 1998). An awareness of this is important because audit will need to become part of everyday practice if the requirements of clinical governance are to be met.

Barriers to implementing audit

In a comprehensive review of 93 publications which investigated various aspects of audit in health care, Johnston *et al.* (2000) identified five main barriers that impede the introduction of audit. This usefully summarises much of the material discussed earlier. These barriers are: lack of resources; lack of expertise in project design and management; lack of an overall plan for audit; relationship problems; and organisational impediments. Whilst recognising that these can be overcome and that audit can contribute to the delivery of quality in health care, Johnston *et al.* (2000) sound a note of caution in relation to future developments. They suggest that if it is to be effective the introduction of clinical governance must be informed by the lessons learned from the history of audit in health care. In a similar vein Leatherman & Sutherland (1998) argue that advancing quality in the United Kingdom means building on the legacy of the past, capitalising on existing knowledge, experience, and technologies, and integrating these with a vision for the future of quality in the NHS. It seems the government has attempted to do this with its proposals for quality in health care (DOH 1998, 2000a). The remainder of the chapter will consider this initiative in the light of the general quality principles discussed earlier and attention will be given to the actions necessary for clinical governance to be successful.

Clinical governance

The definition of clinical governance was presented at the start of this chapter to provide a basis for the discussion of the development of quality management in health care. This new approach to quality management is comprehensive in its scope and is summarised in Figure 3.5.

Essentially clinical governance involves the delivery of standards at local level within trusts. The National Institute for Clinical Excellence (NICE) conducts and coordinates studies of the effectiveness of new and existing treatments. This work is used to inform the development of evidence-based National Service Frameworks which set out what patients can expect to receive from the NHS in relation to care, e.g., mental health, cardiac care, elderly care, diabetes care. NHS Trusts ensure that these standards are met through implementing a system of clinical governance whereby all organisational efforts are directed to achieving the standards. This involves managing systems of audit; systems of risk management; and continuing professional development. The effectiveness of these systems is then monitored by the Commission for Health Improvement (CHI) through a system of inspection and through comparison of progress with milestones set out in the National Performance Framework (NHSE 1999). The detail of how this works in practice can be found in *A First Class Service Quality in the New NHS* (DOH 1998); however, the key principles of quality management are clear. Standards are set, the organisation is structured to achieve the standards and achievement of the standards is monitored through

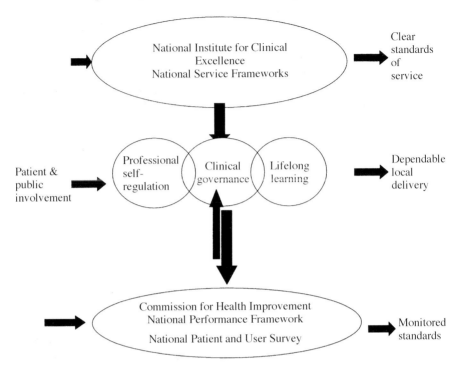

Figure 3.5 The components of clinical governance. Reproduced with permission from DOH (1998) *A First Class Service Quality in the New NHS*, HMSO, London.

Notes: National Service Frameworks will set out common standards across the country for the treatment of particular conditions. The National Institute for Clinical Excellence will act as a nationwide appraisal body for new and existing treatments, and disseminate consistent advice on what does and does not work.

inspection. Management theory in this area provides a framework for management of quality.

This is an ambitious plan for reform of quality management and although, as has been demonstrated earlier in this chapter, quality management should involve everyone in the organisation and all the activities within the organisation should be directed towards quality, the situation in health care is somewhat different. Clinical governance is just part of a very crowded agenda that health care managers and professionals are having to deal with. The framework of clinical governance (Figure 3.5) should provide a means of integrating these diverse demands on health care. However, the reality often dictates that it becomes one more 'target' among many. For example, evidence-based practice (see chapter 5), interprofessional working (see chapter 9), NHS staff shortages (Bradshaw 1999, Finlayson *et al.* 2002), and the delivery of health improvement programmes (DOH 2000a) are all major challenges in their own right. The policy process results in decisions concerning priorities and the delegation of tasks which inevitably means that progress in some areas will be more rapid than others, and that some 'priorities' become sidelined in response to a range of pressures (Green & Thorogood 1998, Allsop 1995, Walt 1994). The need to deliver on short-term targets such as waiting times can mean that other longer-term targets such as quality can be neglected. The limited amount of evidence that is available on the implementation of clinical governance suggests that progress may be modest, owing to some familiar 'barriers' noted earlier in the chapter.

Progress with clinical governance

In a survey of clinical governance 'leads' in primary care, Roland *et al.* (2001) received an 81 per cent response rate. This in itself is a notable finding as it indicates that key people have been designated as responsible for clinical governance in primary care organisations. However these people reported that there were barriers to the successful implementation of clinical governance and these included: a lack of time and resources; too much change leading to 'initiative fatigue'; the attempt to combine quality assurance and quality improvement approaches in a single strategy; and the lack of clarity surrounding what should be determined locally and nationally in terms of guidance on clinical governance. Roland *et al.* (2001) argue that these barriers may impede the implementation of clinical governance and go on to recommend some measures that need to be adopted if this is to be overcome. These were:

- provide time for quality improvement
- reward teamworking
- involve professionals
- support the development of professional leaders at all levels
- support lifelong learning.

These observations confirm much of the work considered earlier in the chapter related to previous attempts to manage quality in health care. Teamwork is crucial and it is important that the teams involve all professionals. This in turn requires skilled leadership at all levels of the organisation based on a philosophy of continuing education and lifelong learning. However, if this is to be achieved it will take time. It seems that some of the problems evident in past attempts persist and may impair the introduction of clinical governance. Roland *et al.* (2001) argue that it is too early to conclude if the changes made have improved quality but some of their concerns are echoed in other work.

Franks (2001) analysed twenty-one annual clinical governance reports from acute NHS trusts in the Northern and Yorkshire Region. He found that responsibility for the introduction of clinical governance had been devolved and that it was difficult to determine from the reports how it was being monitored. The involvement of doctors in clinical governance was patchy, and risk assessment and clinical audit were managed separately. Finally, it is interesting to note that there was a lack of consistency in the presentation of the reports. Some were as brief as ten pages whilst others ran to fifty pages plus appendices. Given that the bedrock of quality systems is standardisation it is surprising to discover that such variability in format is acceptable. If comment on progress and standards is not presented in a uniform way, how can meaningful comparisons about progress be made? The other notable observations made by Franks (2001) relate to the separation of different elements of quality processes. If risk and audit are dealt with separately within trusts it is unlikely that they will be brought together in a coherent quality management system. Similarly, if doctors are not involved in clinical audit how valuable is the process to the overall management of quality in the trusts?

This need for full integration of quality processes into the 'normal' operation of the organisation is identified in other accounts reflecting on the introduction of clinical governance. For example Holt (1999) contends that based on experience in his trust, quality management is integral to 'business as usual' not something to be grafted onto routine operation. Similarly Harrison (1999) and Haslock (2000) argue that clinical governance needs to be bedded into day-to-day management and that it should not be regarded as an 'add on'.

The need for such change is clear at the level of national policy as a *First Class Service* (DOH 1998) recognises that meaningful and sustainable quality improvements in the NHS require a fundamental shift in culture. The importance of changing the culture in order to bring about new ways of managing and delivering the service is a feature of much current policy (DOH 1997, 1998, 2000a). However, when it comes to achieving such change there are many challenges to be faced. In chapter 4 the nature and significance of organisational culture, in managerial terms, is considered.

Conclusion

Ellis & Whittington (1993) trace the development of quality in health care through three distinct phases: embryonic, emergent and mandatory.

Embryonic is when measures for quality are in place yet tend to be implicit and not specifically referred to in quality terms. This is followed by an *emergent* stage when the term 'quality assurance' gains currency and explicit quality management mechanisms are introduced to assure quality. Finally health care systems arrive at a *mandatory* stage whereby the government imposes a centrally determined regulatory framework to ensure the management and improvement of quality. This point has now been reached in the NHS. There are five new national agencies which have been established to regulate the different elements of quality (Walshe 2002):

- National Institute for Clinical Excellence
- Commission for Health Improvement
- Modernisation Agency
- National Patient Safety Agency
- National Clinical Assessment Authority.

This indicates that quality is likely to remain a prominent issue for both managers and professionals. An understanding of the underpinning principles on which these initiatives are based may help people working in health care to overcome some of the barriers to implementation noted earlier. Quality systems are basically simple; however, they need to be applied to the 'business' of health care carefully.

4. *Organisational Culture*

Introduction

Shafritz & Ott (2001) locate total quality management (TQM) in the category of a 'cultural reform movement'. They suggest it is one of a number that was intended to increase productivity, flexibility, responsiveness and customer service by reshaping the culture of organisations. However, it was demonstrated in the previous chapter that the application of 'quality methods' to health care in the UK is not without its problems. This is partly because the attempts at 'cultural reform' referred to by Shafritz & Ott (2001) were often based on a partial understanding of the nature of organisational culture. The purpose of this chapter is to demonstrate the complexity of this concept and consider the ways it can be useful to health professionals in the management of health services.

The chapter has three main aims. The first is to demonstrate that culture is a multi-layered and complex concept derived originally from the discipline of anthropology and more lately organisational studies. This will illustrate how the origins of the term affect its application and how the current widespread use of the term can be problematic, because the meaning attributed to it varies depending on the particular perspective employed, and this is not always made explicit. Second, three categories for the study of culture will be presented to demonstrate that it is not a unitary concept and to emphasise the importance of clarity in the use of the term. This contention is then explored through an examination of the utility of the concept in its application to health care in the UK. If organisational culture is clearly defined and used appropriately it can be a useful analytical concept in increasing our understanding of the organisation of health care. This understanding can also serve as a basis for more effective management of the service as managers will have a keener appreciation of the environment they are operating in and the forces at work in that environment.

Therefore the chapter will:

- examine the origins and definition of culture
- present three categories of the concept of culture in order to convey its complexity

- discuss these categories in relation to health care in order to demonstrate how the concept of culture can contribute to our understanding of health care organisations
- identify the problems that can occur when the term is used in an inappropriate way.

Why is culture important?

The word culture has a variety of meanings. It can be used to refer to the cultivation of the soil and plants; the customs, civilisation and achievements associated with a particular period of history or people; the arts and other manifestations of human intellectual activity and refinement; and a society's system of knowledge, ideology, values, laws and day-to-day ritual. Recently, however, it has increasingly come to be used with reference to organisations. Indeed as Shafritz & Ott (2001) observe, almost all the literature about organisational culture has been published in the last fifteen years. The use of the term culture has also become commonplace in a wide range of literature concerned with health care organisations, particularly in the context of managing change (Newman & Clarke 1994, Pollitt 1993a, Harrison *et al.* 1992, Thomson 1992). This reflects the enormous influence the work of Peters & Waterman (1982) and the 'quality gurus' had in attributing managerial success to the effective management of organisational culture. This theme was taken forward by others and the central premise of culture management is that by 'strengthening' the corporate culture, organisational performance is improved as a result of the greater flexibility and commitment secured from employees (Deal & Kennedy 1982, Ouchi 1981, Pascale & Athos 1986). Willmott (1993) suggests that this approach to managing has been endorsed by sufficient numbers of gurus, corporate executives and state mandarins to ensure that it has had more than a passing influence on management theory and practice. So what is meant by the term organisational culture? This is an important question because there is often a lack of clarity and precision in the way the term is used. For example, problems of an obdurate workforce have been attributed to a closed professional culture (Roberts *et al.* 1995), also the need for a particular type of culture is identified by many commentators on health care. For example, this can range from a 'proactive health and safety culture' (Chamings & Keady 1995) to a 'positive culture for public involvement' (Lupton & Taylor 1995) through to a 'culture of consensus' (Macara 1995). Another consequence arising from the widespread and often superficial application of the term to organisations is that the potential it has for uncovering areas of interest and concern is not always realised.

The complexity of culture

Culture is a very yielding word which can be used to refer to almost any situation (Spurgeon & Barwell 1991). Indeed within one short article in the *Health Service Journal*, the term is used in three different ways: to refer to a culture of secrecy; express the need for cultural change; and to recommend the introduction of a marketing culture (Spiers 1995). Similarly Young (1994) highlighted the culture of contemporary health care, in a list of pressures facing nurse managers. The inclusion of the term culture by these authors is reflective of a general trend in the literature whereby it is used as a form of shorthand to signify the general climate or feeling in an organisation. It is also used to characterise the way organisations as a whole approach things. For example, using the labels, a quality culture or a culture of fear is a way of communicating how the organisation operates. In many ways it has become a general term which is called upon to describe a complex set of circumstances which contribute to the distinctive 'atmosphere' or 'feel' of an organisation. However there is potential for confusion because the precise meaning people are trying to convey is often unclear and evidence for the assertions being made is often lacking.

Alvesson (1993) maintains that culture is a word for the lazy because it can be conveniently employed to refer to all of the 'soft' organisational features such as attitudes, values and feelings that defy more exact definition. It may be that the work of writers such as Handy (1993), Deal & Kennedy (1982), Peters & Waterman (1982) and Ouchi (1981) have raised the profile of organisational culture to the extent that people assume there is a level of agreement concerning its meaning, but this assumption is open to question. Alvesson (1993) cautions against oversimplification, feeling it can be very misleading. Also Spurgeon & Barwell (1991) recognise that the construct of culture has become so malleable that there is a danger it can become devoid of any practical meaning. There is a need to look beyond the shorthand use of the term and explore it more thoroughly. The first step in this process is to recognise the diverse applications and meanings inherent in the concept.

Defining culture

The concept of culture has been central to the discipline of anthropology throughout its history. Indeed as far back as 1952, Kroeber & Kluckhohn produced a landmark study in this field identifying 164 definitions of culture drawn from the anthropological literature. Not only does this underline the complexity of the concept; it also goes some way towards explaining the increasingly liberal use of the concept to refer to a wide range of situations and issues. The fact that there are so many available definitions makes it impossible to comprehend the concept in total, therefore a convenient definition is selected to serve a specific purpose (Allaire & Firsirotu 1984). Although it is important to appreciate this complexity in order to understand the way the concept has come to be used, it in no way justifies the lack of rigour that often accompanies the indiscriminate and sometimes limited application of the concept because adopting a particular definition of culture is a commitment to specific conceptual assumptions and ways of studying it (Allaire & Firsirotu 1984).

However, these conventions may be ignored and the concept applied in an inappropriate way. Another related issue is raised by Bourne & Ezzamel (1986) who recognise that to single out any one approach as the only way of analysing organisations is misleading because any one perspective only offers a partial view of organisations and the methods of analysis used under any one precept have limitations. This demonstrates that to make a contribution to the understanding of health care organisations the nature and scope of the term culture, as it is to be used, must be made clear. Once this is achieved the information from a variety of perspectives can be pieced together to build a more comprehensive picture of how health care organisations function.

The original purpose of using the notion of culture in the field of organisation studies was to increase understanding and interpretation and there is nothing fundamentally wrong with borrowing concepts from another discipline as this has resulted in important theoretical innovations, the danger is that in the process of transfer the concepts can become stereotyped or distorted (Meek 1988). To some extent this has been a feature of the way the culture has been used in its application to health care organisations.

Refining the definition

Through the addition of the prefix organisational to the term culture, some boundaries are immediately imposed on the discussion. However, even a consideration of the concept in the context of organisations reveals a variety of applications. Wright (1994) contends that in organisation studies it is generally used in four ways:

1. To refer to the problems of managing companies with production processes or service outlets in a number of countries each with a different national culture.
2. When management is trying to integrate people with different ethnicities into a workforce in one place.
3. The identity, informal concepts, attitudes and values of a workforce.
4. To refer to the formal organisational values and practices imposed by management as a 'glue' to hold the workforce together and to make it responsive to change.

Applications 3 and 4 are the ones most commonly used in the context of health care. The need to change the culture, to respond to events or indeed to shape them is a common theme as is the notion that a 'strong culture' will contribute to organisational success. The way the term has been used in organisation studies in general and in health care specifically has been somewhat limited. Indeed Wright (1994) uses the categories she identifies to demonstrate how the term has been transformed in the process of its appropriation from anthropology. Culture has changed from being something an organisation *is* into something an organisation *has*, and from being a process embedded in context to an objectified tool of management control (Wright 1994). In an effort to address this issue Anthony (1994) draws a distinction between the espoused version of culture and the reality. To aid clarity he suggests that the espoused version be referred to as corporate culture and the reality as organisational culture. Yet even within this refinement there is the possibility that other dimensions of the concept may be overlooked.

The increasing demands being made of professionals and managers working in health care organisations, arising from policy changes, government targets and professional initiatives, would seem to suggest that any means of making these processes and their effects more understandable would be welcome. For example:

> The point has been made repeatedly to us that achieving meaningful and sustainable quality improvements in the NHS requires a fundamental shift in *culture*, to focus effort where it is needed and to enable and empower those who work in the NHS to improve quality locally. (DOH 1998, p. 71)

Yet what does this mean? Is a fundamental shift in culture something that can be managed? There is a need to demonstrate how different facets of the concept of organisational culture can be beneficial in increasing understanding of contemporary health care organisations. A more informed use of the concept of organisational culture has the potential to inform this endeavour.

Three categories of culture

One way of dealing with the complexity of the term is to categorise the uses of the concept. The underlying contention of this section is that if a degree of clarity and specificity is made explicit in the application of the concept it can be valuable in helping to uncover some of the dynamics at work in health care organisations. It needs to be dissected into manageable proportions so that it can be used in the interpretation of organisations (Meek 1988). The three categories adopted to render the concept more manageable are instrumental, cognitive and interpretive.

In some ways the classification offered here would be regarded by many to be a gross oversimplification in itself. However the intention is not to produce the definitive account of organisational culture because much more detailed and erudite taxonomies are available (see, for example, Alvesson 1993, Allaire & Firsirotu 1984, Gregory 1983, Smircich 1983). Nor is it to suggest that organisational culture will take on a neat and ordered appearance as a discrete series of categories. Rather it is an attempt to find a relatively straightforward way through the complexity in order to demonstrate how the concept can be used whilst urging caution against its indiscriminate application to all 'soft' organisational issues.

Instrumental

The first category is instrumental. This is perhaps one of the most common understandings of organisational culture and it is a relatively recent conceptualisation. It derives largely from the corporate culture literature which argues that a 'strong culture' is desirable and can be managed (Denison 1984). The work of people such as Kilmann *et al.* (1985), Peters & Waterman (1982), Deal & Kennedy (1982) and Ouchi (1981) have been very influential in popularising this particular version of organisational culture. The apparent evidence that successful organisations have strong cultures led to an upsurge in interest in how this might be achieved. Anthony (1994) maintains that the reality behind this drive to manage culture resides in the possibility of using the evident strength of culture as a means of control, the idea being that if control can be exerted at a broad level over organisational values and beliefs, legends and myths, stories, rites, rituals and ceremonies, then the culture can be harnessed as a force to achieve the organisation's objectives. Indeed several books have been produced with the express intention of helping managers to do this (Williams *et al.* 1993, Spurgeon & Barwell 1991, Kilmann *et al.* 1985, for example).

A common theme in much of this work is that if all the members of an organisation share common values and beliefs there is less need for complex organisational structures to exert managerial control as people will direct their energies and enthusiasm toward the corporate enterprise willingly. It is in this sense that the term is still commonly used.

Recommendations concerning the need to change the culture are, in effect, advocating a re-focusing of values and encouraging people to think differently about what they do. The identification of a dynamic culture or a culture of excellence, for example, is used to signify the values people are expected to aspire to. Such wide ranging requests for a change in the culture still appear frequently in the literature, but are seldom accompanied by a clear idea of how this is to be brought about. Aside from the deficits associated with the application of the concept in this way, there are other difficulties. Meek (1988) contends that the assumption that a corporate culture can be created runs counter to everyone's experience of organisational life.

Sub-cultures

This would certainly seem to be the case in the NHS which cannot realistically be regarded as an homogenous organisation because it is made up of a complex mix of many different occupational groups, some with their primary allegiance outside the organisation (Williams *et al.* 1993). For example, nurses and the allied health professions may feel their overriding concern and loyalty should be to the patient, rather than the organisation they work in. This approach also ignores that fact that cultures can be divisive and that there can be a range of competing sub-cultures (Bourne & Ezzamel 1986, Gregory 1983, Morgan 1997). It has been suggested that it may be more fruitful to think of organisations as collections of sub-cultures rather than attempting to manage a single culture, that in reality can never really exist (Morgan 1986).

Programmes of organisational change are often based on a presumption of changing the culture. However, this rests on the premise that organisations consist of a single unified culture. In organisations generally, and in the NHS in particular, culture is a good deal more complex than this. Bourne & Ezzamel (1986) found that the existing values of the NHS were in conflict with those being imposed as a direct consequence of the recommendations arising from the *Griffiths Report* (DHSS 1983) and predicted the increase of financial control systems that later materialised. These were introduced to overcome the resistance of medical and nursing staff to different elements of the proposals. Similarly, Newman (1994b) and Henry (1994) pointed to the clash of values arising from the market oriented reforms and the public service and professional ethos of groups of staff in the NHS.

This particular problem can be exacerbated if culture is regarded by managers as simply another way of exerting control. Willmott (1993) maintains that culture is management control in a new guise. It is used as a tool to systematise and legitimise a mode of control that shapes and regulates the practical consciousness and unconscious strivings of employees. He goes on to state:

> Though masquerading as a 'therapy of freedom' that expands the practical autonomy of employees, corporate culture identifies cultural values as a powerful under utilised media of dominance. (Willmott 1993, p. 523)

In extreme forms, then, the concept of culture can be manipulated to capture the 'hearts and minds' of employees in a manner synonymous with Lukes' (1974) third dimension of power, where power is exerted over people but in such a subtle and pervasive way that they remain unaware of it. This ensures employees are compliant and acquiescent to the demands of the organisation. This rather bleak conclusion illustrates the immoderate way the concept can be applied and how it can be used to mask other objectives. However it can also provide a means of identifying that such a process is underway and reveal that although the term culture is being applied what is actually going on is an attempt to impose control.

An appreciation of what can realistically be achieved through attempts to manage culture is necessary if managers are to be able to function effectively in a changing environment. Attempts to change the culture of an organisation demand a great deal of time and effort. Real and lasting change will not occur quickly. Rapid change can be brought about but this can be superficial or, as Willmott (1993) suggests, a veiled form of control. If managers are to manage the corporate culture effectively and prevent it taking on sinister overtones and, as a consequence failing, a deeper understanding of what organisational culture can mean would be a useful resource. This can be achieved if other dimensions of the concept are considered.

Cognitive

The cognitive perspective on culture arises from the assumption that culture is not something that can be imposed on a social setting, rather it develops out of social interaction (Morgan 1986). Culture is not something that can be 'managed' rather it is part of the way an organisation is. Culture is not a power, something to which social events, behaviours, institutions, or processes can be causally attributed; it is a context, something within which they can be intelligibly – that is, 'thickly' – described (Geertz 1973). Organisations as cognitive enterprises are, in effect, organised patterns of thought and categories of shared understanding among people, and this is the reality of what the organisation 'is'. Schein, a very influential figure in the literature concerning organisational culture, defines it in the following way:

> Organizational culture is the pattern of basic assumptions that a given group has invented, discovered, or developed in learning to cope with its problems of external adaptation and internal integration, and that have worked well enough to be considered valid, and, therefore, to be taught to new members as the correct way to perceive, think and feel in relation to those problems. (Schein 1984, p. 3)

Organisational culture then can be thought of as a system of knowledge and learned standards for perceiving, believing, evaluating and acting (Allaire & Firsirotu 1984). This approach is particularly useful in highlighting the 'climate' or 'feel' of an organisation. Pettigrew *et al.* (1992) suggest that the perceived failure of recurrent structural reorganisation in the NHS directed attention to the deeper issues of organisational culture as a shaper of belief systems. This interest was motivated by a desire to understand the culture in order to change it, however it has also led to an appreciation of the complexity of health care organisations. Morgan (1986) contends that in all organisations there are many different and competing value systems, rather than a single unified culture. This is particularly relevant to health care organisations and the work of Strong & Robinson (1990) confirms this view. They found that general managers trying to introduce standard management practices, in the wake of the *Griffiths Report*, identified 'tribalism' among health care professionals as being a major source of frustration.

The unique value systems and shared cognitions which characterise the different occupational groups in health care organisations are a result of history, specific bodies of knowledge and beliefs about the nature of organised health care. People working in health care organisations are all multiple members of, and participate in, other social institutions and forms, many of which can be expected to exert a more powerful influence on values, beliefs, behaviour and performance than the stated organisational credo (Linstead & Grafton-Small 1992). All occupations have an informal culture of attitude and practice (Turner 1987) and this can be viewed as a barrier to change or it can be viewed as revealing important information about how such organisations function.

Nursing culture
This is significant for managers, whatever their background, wishing to discover more about the dynamics of their organisations. For example, Turner (1987) discusses the culture of nursing in some detail. He maintains there is a significant split in the occupational discourse of compliance and complaint. The official ideology specifies how tasks should be accomplished whereas the 'vocabularies of complaint', shared by nurses, focus on the lack of autonomy they experience. Turner goes on to identify five main functions of these vocabularies of complaint:

1. To underline the independent contribution and importance of nursing in the therapeutic process.
2. To de-legitimise the system of authority and hierarchy in their place of work.
3. To deflate the unwarranted idealism of new nurses by describing the real and mundane nature of nursing.
4. To create a sense of solidarity of nurses against intrusion and dominance from other groups.
5. To act as a safety valve which releases emotion and frustration – thus allowing the nurses to continue in their role.

In this way not only do the vocabularies of complaint outline methods of survival, they strengthen the distinct identity of nurses as a group within the organisation. An awareness of the specific forces and concerns involved in the development of this particular occupational culture could help managers to understand it. The recognition and acceptance that people create and enact their reality is a powerful way of thinking about culture (Morgan 1986). The development of shared meanings in culture is both a natural process of their evolution and a feature central to their identity, without them cultures do not exist and cannot survive (Anthony 1994). Morgan (1986) goes on to suggest that it must be understood as an active, living phenomenon through which people create and recreate the worlds in which they live. This can be applied at the everyday level of working in a collaborative manner with particular groups, rather than against them. If managers appreciate the origins and specialist skills of different professional and occupational groups in health care, they will be more able to encourage interprofessional cooperation.

For example, the holistic approach advocated by both nurses and occupational therapists can be used as a common starting point for dissolving unhelpful professional barriers. Such knowledge can also serve as a basis for designing new, and more responsive, organisational structures as a means of ensuring changing patterns of service delivery are accommodated.

In viewing culture as a monolith (Meyerson & Martin 1987) managers restrict their conception of it to its superficial manifestations, such as the values espoused by top management. Basing managerial action on a partial understanding of the concept of culture is likely to lead to difficulties when attempts are made to change the culture of an organisation.

Interpretive

The interpretive approach, in organisational culture, has – at its simplest – sought to determine the meanings of particular relationships and symbols in organisations (Linstead & Grafton-Small 1992). Linstead & Grafton-Small (1992) advocate that culture in organisations should be read as a text to gain an understanding of its meaning. The interpretive approach involves analysis of the networks of meanings conveyed by symbols, forms and the organisational context. One of the foremost exponents of this approach is Clifford Geertz. Building on the work of the German sociologist Max Weber he states:

> Man is an animal suspended in webs of significance he himself has spun, I take culture to be those webs, and the analysis of it not an experimental science in search of law but an interpretive one in search of meaning. (Geertz 1973, p. 5)

Wright (1994) suggests this has led to greater attention being directed towards issues of language and power and how they are manipulated in organisations. Organisations can be examined in terms of what the common language, symbols displayed and rituals performed actually mean. For example what is the purpose of the consultant ward round? Is it the most logistically efficient way of ensuring patients are seen by the appropriate personnel? Or is it, as Fox (1992) contends, an elaborate ritual designed to reinforce the power of the consultant through potent symbolism and control of the discourse surrounding surgical care. Alternative explanations of everyday organisational events such as this illustrate one of the main benefits an interpretive approach can bring.

In a similar vein Walsh & Ford (1989) used some elements of this approach in their comparison of the 'real world' of clinical nursing with research findings concerning clinical practice. They concluded that mythology in the realm of care and nursing procedures abounds with many practices being ritualistic and of no demonstrable benefit, if not potentially harmful to patients. They employ the notions of myths and rituals throughout the book to build a case for a more research-based approach to practice. Although employed specifically as a device to demonstrate how widespread out-moded and potentially dangerous procedures are in nursing, employing the terms myths and rituals emphasises the benefits of applying this perspective of culture. Through examining familiar activities and procedures and interpreting or reinterpreting them, new insights and improvements in practice can occur.

The linking of culture to organisations legitimates attention to the subjective, interpretative aspects of organisational life which in the past have been regarded as sources of error and variance in research rather than as valid subjects of enquiry (Jelinek *et al.* 1983). Pettigrew *et al.* (1992) discuss the symbolism of language, in this case in the early days of the NHS reforms arising from the 1989 White Paper *Working for Patients*. They chart the moderation of the language from 'boards of directors' to 'new NHS Authorities' and 'opting out' becoming the establishment of 'self-governing trusts'. As they conclude, who could object to a trust? Attention to these areas and the interpretation of the meaning of the symbols and language, results in an alternative explanation of what is really going on. The language was used in this situation to convey a particular image about how things should be, but had to be refined in light of the reality of experience.

This brings the argument full circle to the instrumental approach, because as well as being read and interpreted, symbols and language can be consciously manipulated to change the culture.

Components of culture

These categories of culture can be used to inform the management of or the study of culture. The culture of an organisation develops over time and in response to a complex set of factors. However it is possible to identify a number of key influences that are likely to have an important role in its development. These are:

- history
- primary function and technology
- goals and objectives
- size
- location
- management and staffing
- environment (Handy 1993, Mullins 2002).

So in the case of the NHS these influences would be:

- **History**
  The NHS developed in the postwar society based on notions of collective provision of welfare services. It was professionally driven and founded on an ethos of public service.

- **Primary function and technology**
  Its primary function was the treatment and prevention of disease and illness, although it came to be associated mainly with acute hospital care. Technology was developed to support this function.

- **Goals and objectives**
  The provision of health care free at the point of delivery on the basis of need is the overriding objective of the NHS. Numerous targets and supplementary goals have been added over the years.

- **Size**
  The NHS is one of the largest organisations in the world and this has an influence on the culture. The size of individual units within the NHS also has an effect on how cohesive they are.

- **Location**
  Similarly whether or not the organisation is situated in a rural or city centre area partly determines what it is 'like'. Its proximity to other providers (competition) can also be a defining feature in how the organisation functions.

- **Management and staffing**
  The NHS has a highly specialised and 'tribal' workforce. Pettigrew *et al.* (1992) use the term a 'scientific community' to convey the particular

background of the health professions. They have different training, views about patient care and quality and this in part characterises the culture of NHS organisations.

- **Environment**
  The wider environment of which the organisation is a part also has a powerful influence. The respective environments created by the Conservative and Labour administrations affect the culture of NHS organisations.

This information relating to the culture of the NHS can be approached or used in different ways depending on how the concept is viewed. They can be managed (instrumental), understood (cognitive), and read (interpretive). So, for example, the history of the NHS can be seen as a key element in the development of the NHS and any new measures put in place need to be sensitive to this. This is reflected in the introduction of the modern matron, which can be regarded as an attempt to introduce a new form of management which is connected with the history of NHS (cognitive), aimed at changing the way the organisation works (instrumental), in a visible way illustrated in the requirement that the post holders have a distinctive uniform (interpretive).

Similarly the management and staffing of NHS organisations can be regarded as 'tribal' (cognitive), illustrated in the rites and rituals of the way the different professions work such as consultant 'firms', nursing hierarchy, and grading structures (interpretive). Managers may decide that these are arcane and not consistent with 'modern' approaches to management and they need to be dismantled and changed, for example through the introduction of clinical directorates (instrumental).

Levels of culture

These components also need to be considered in terms of the level at which they exert this influence. There are different layers which contribute to the overall culture (Figure 4.1). Schein (1985) identifies three:

- **Level 1: Artefacts**
  This is the visible level and includes the symbols of a culture, for example space, type of building, language, overt behaviour, uniforms, corporate image material such as logos and letter heads.

- **Level 2: Values**
  This is the level at which the values of the organisation shape it and these are 'deeper' than the more superficial symbols and signs.

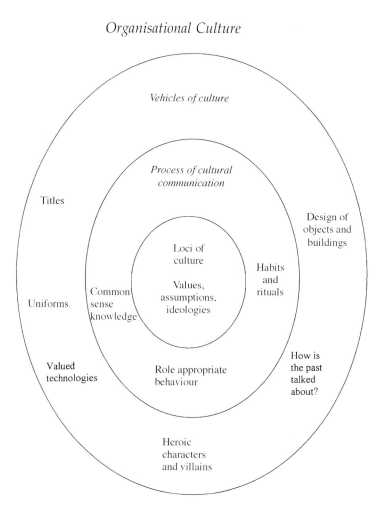

Figure 4.1 The levels of organisational culture.

- **Level 3: Basic underlying assumptions**
  Finally there are the deeply held assumptions amongst people which shape the values, which in turn determine the 'feel' or culture of the organisation.

An example of how this operates in organisation is presented in Figure 4.1. This can be used to analyse organisations and build a clearer picture of their culture. It can help to clarify why the organisation functions in the way that it does.

In terms of managing culture, the deeper the level, the stronger the influence. Consequently it may be possible to change the artefacts and the appearance of the organisation, however it is more difficult and takes longer to change the basic underlying assumptions.

Is the concept of culture useful?

The concept of organisational culture has the potential to be useful to health professionals as a way of stimulating new ways of thinking about the organisations they have to manage. It can be used to indicate ways of managing the culture if this is desired, or perhaps more usefully it can increase understandings of the complex dynamics that need to be handled with sensitivity and skill. In health care, attempts have been made to survey the culture (MacKenzie 1995) and improve it (Jackson & Hinchliffe 1999). Principles derived from the culture literature have been used to inform the management of mergers and acquisitions (Cavanagh 1996). However it is difficult to draw definitive conclusions from such work. One clear conclusion reached by Sackman indicates how this process will need to develop in the future:

> If culture is to survive its fashionable wave and turn into a useful and meaningful concept both for organization researchers and for prac- titioners, it is necessary to spend more effort on empirical research rather than debating options. (Sackman 1991, p. 3)

This is confirmed by Schein (1996) who maintains that there is a need to test some of the ideas contained within this literature more thoroughly in practice before they are used to inform wide ranging programmes of change. Concepts for understanding culture in organisations have value only when they derive from observations of real behaviour in organisations, when they make sense of organisational data, and when they are definable enough to generate further study (Schein 1996). There is still a long way to go before this level of certainty and clarity in the concepts is achieved.

Davies *et al.* conclude:

> For all the interest in defining and assessing organisational cultures, the crucial generic question of whether and how organisational culture impacts on organisational success or performance remains empirically poorly explored. A simple causal relationship between cultural characteristics and success has not yet been demonstrated. (Davies *et al.* 2000)

Conclusion

Organisational culture can be defined as the commonly held and relatively stable beliefs, attitudes and values that exist within an organisation (Williams *et al.* 1993), however it has been demonstrated that proceeding from such 'basic' definitions can lead managers into difficulties. For example in many 'culture management' projects new values, assumptions and ways of working are imposed on the employees. This seems to arise from a basic misunderstanding surrounding the nature of organisational culture arising from approaching culture as something an organisation *has* rather than something an organisation *is*.

Hope & Hendry (1995) contend that such 'prescriptive' approaches were pursued throughout the 1980s and that processes of cultural change often work in the opposite direction to the values being inculcated. This leads to staff feeling they are being manipulated, leading to anger, lack of cooperation and cynicism. These failed attempts can result in the managers being isolated through their advocacy of organisational values that are not shared by the rest of the workforce (Anthony 1994) thus making their job more difficult. The management of culture can become a process which is intended to produce secure but secret influence on the behaviour of organisational members (Anthony 1994). This outcome is also identified by Willmott (1993), which was noted earlier. However, despite these perceived sinister overtones, many efforts at culture management may be inappropriate at a more fundamental level. The values and norms which comprise 'corporate culture' have very limited direct impact on organisational effectiveness in terms of work behaviour and willingness to work (Alvesson 1993), so at best the efforts of management may be misplaced and at worst be counter productive.

The concept of organisational culture and its management is an extremely complex area and has been subject to a great deal of analysis (see, for example, Gagliardi 1986, Linstead & Grafton-Small 1992, Meek 1988, Smircich 1983). However, it has been applied in health care management in a limited way. The potentially negative effect this can have demands that managers gain a greater understanding of the concept before it is used as a basis for wholesale culture change. The intention is that this chapter has provided some useful information to assist in this process. Also by introducing other dimensions of the concept that new ways of analysing the organisation have been introduced.

5. Change in Health Care Organisations

Introduction

'Who hasn't heard the mantra: change or perish? It's a corporate cliché by now. And like many clichés it happens to be true' (Abrahamson 2000, p. 75). The need for organisations to constantly adapt and change in order to achieve commercial success has, as Abrahamson suggests, now become part of orthodox management thinking. The policy changes and reforms affecting health care have contributed to a situation where organisational change is a permanent feature of life in the NHS as well. This drive for change is unlikely to diminish as the *NHS Plan* (DOH 2000a) contains many references to the continuing change that will need to occur. For example:

> The NHS has been too slow to change its ways of working to meet modern patient expectations for fast, convenient, 24 hour personalised care. (p. 26)

Similarly:

> Managers and clinicians across the NHS must make change happen. (p. 82)

and a Modernisation Agency has been established to ensure this occurs because:

> Rapid, effective service improvement requires targeted expert support to spread best practice and stimulate change locally. It mirrors the change management approach taken in much of the private sector. (p. 60)

However these exhortations appear to be based on an assumption that change is a straightforward process that is amenable to being 'managed'. The purpose of this chapter is to demonstrate that in reality the situation is a good deal more complex than that conveyed in policy documents and much of the management literature. It was noted in chapter 1 that contrasting explanations concerning the nature of organisations and management arise, in part, from the particular ideological and theoretical orientation of their originators. This means that consideration of a range of approaches needs to be undertaken if more than a superficial understanding of the issue at hand is to be achieved. Collins has commented:

> there can be no single theory of change since there is no single body of thought that would be accepted by all organizational members, theorists and commentators as a valid account and explanation of organization. (Collins 1998, p. 138)

Similarly, following a comprehensive assessment of the accumulated evidence on the nature of change management and its applications in health care, Iles & Sutherland concluded:

> No single method, strategy or tool will fit all problems or situations that arise. Managers in the NHS need to be adept at diagnosing organisational situations and skilled at choosing those tools that are best suited to the particular circumstances that confront them. (Iles & Sutherland 2001, p. 19)

Consequently in this chapter it is necessary to:

- address the nature of change;
- examine the range of theoretical explanations that have been developed to increase our understanding of the change process;
- evaluate the models that have been advocated as tools for the management of change;
- consider the utility of change management approaches in the context of evidence-based practice.

The importance of this area is reflected by the fact that the Government, in the form of the NHS Service Delivery and Organisation National Research and Development Programme, has commissioned a series of large-scale research projects to investigate the nature of change in health care. This is based on a recognition that change is necessary, as stated in the *NHS Plan* (DOH 2000a), yet the way in which lasting change can be brought about is still far from clear. This chapter will focus on some of the fundamental issues that it is important to appreciate, if this complex area of practice is to be understood.

The nature of change

Abrahamson (2000) has commented that 'change has been with us forever, and it always will be, but the idea of change itself is changing' (p. 79). We are living in very confused times, because many of the things that gave structure to our lives are disappearing. Institutions on which we relied, particularly the work organisation, are no longer so sure or certain (Handy 1997).

These commentators suggest that the environment we live in is in a state of flux. The nature and pace of change is such that its impact is felt by everyone. A number of factors have combined to create a situation where change and change at a very fast pace is inevitable and this has particular implications for the management of health care organisations.

> Change is a necessary condition of survival, be we individuals or organisations, and such differences are a necessary ingredient in that change, that never ending search for improvement. The challenge for the manager is to harness the energy and thrust of the differences so that the organisation does not disintegrate but develops. (Handy 1993, p. 291)

This is one view of change: it is about progress and adaptation. Dawson (1994) outlines some of the forces for change that drive this development.

- Technological obsolescence and the need to introduce new technology. Organisations which specialise in high technology products are particularly prone to this form of pressure.
- Major political and social events.
- An increase in the size and complexity of an organisation. This may result in the growth of specialist areas and a need to develop appropriate coordinating mechanisms.
- The internationalisation of business.
- Competition.
- Economic climate.

However, what is significant about organisational change in its current form is its pace. Figure 5.1 illustrates how the pace of change has changed. Before the Industrial Revolution, change occurred in a relatively gradual way and people were able to adapt and learn about new technologies and ways of doing things. Now major technological advances render past knowledge and skills obsolete at an increasingly rapid rate (Pascale *et al.* 1997). In Figure 5.1 the loops represent how in the past it took at least three generations for a major technological change to take full effect and so people were able to adjust gradually to its effects and impact. Now three major technological changes occur within one generation thus making adaptation to the change more challenging.

For example, consider the advances in mobile telephone technology, computers and health care technology. Mobile telephones have evolved rapidly from large unwieldy items in the 1980s to compact units which can access the internet, send images, and communicate across continents. This 'revolution' in communications has occurred in less than a generation. Similarly computer technology has developed at such a rate that access to

Pre-Industrial Revolution

One major technological change

Three generations to adapt to the change

Present day

Three major technological changes

Within one generation

Figure 5.1   The changing nature of change.

information and complex programs is almost unlimited in ways that were almost unimaginable just ten years ago. In the case of health care, improvements in treatments and practices render established approaches obsolete with increasing frequency. For example 'key hole' endoscopic techniques have revolutionised surgery; CT scanning has changed diagnostic procedures; and new approaches to mental health care have resulted in the closure of large institutions and a move to care based in the community.

Organisational change theory

Practitioners and academics have considered the management of change in organisations ever since management emerged as a discipline and so there is a large body of literature about change (Iles & Sutherland 2001). Yet it is by no means a coherent and systematic body of knowledge. Collins (1998) has commented that in attempting to uncover and apply practical insights the field concerned with change and its management has been notable, not so much for the rigour and coherence of its approach, but for its eclectic plundering of a range of subject areas and disciplines (p. 129). Spurgeon & Barwell (1991) refer to *descriptive* and *prescriptive* perspectives on organisational change. Descriptive perspectives are concerned, as the name suggests, with describing the change and trying to explain it to increase the level of understanding of the process, whereas prescriptive models are intended to guide the management of the change process. This broad assessment is a useful starting point for categorising the literature, however the problem is more complex than this distinction would suggest. Iles &

Sutherland (2001) identify six reasons why the literature about change management is difficult to access:

1. It contains contributions from several different academic disciplines including psychology, sociology, business policy, social policy and others.
2. Its boundaries can be set differently, according to the definition of change management employed.
3. Valuable contributions to the literature have been made in all of the last five decades, with the later not necessarily superseding the earlier.
4. It contains evidence, examples and illustrations generated in a wide variety of organisations and from a diverse range of methodologies with varying degrees of rigour.
5. Some material is not readily accessible to non-specialists and does not readily lend itself to cumulative review.
6. The concepts included within it range in scale from whole academic schools, through methodologies to single tools.

This underlines the point made earlier that there are many ways of conceptualising change and particular theoretical accounts or prescriptive models will affect the way change is managed. Some of the main theoretical models and prescriptive approaches are summarised below. It is beyond the scope of this book to examine all of the approaches in the appropriate level of detail and useful reviews are already available (see, for example, Iles & Sutherland 2001, Collins 1998, Dawson 1994). The intention is to illustrate the range of theoretical resources available to professionals and managers by examining four in each category (see Figure 5.2) and then to focus on one

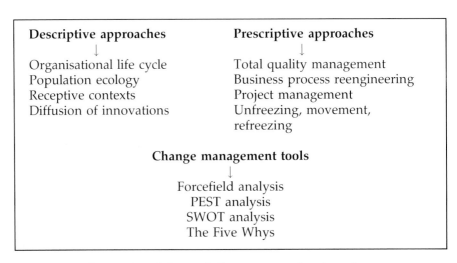

Figure 5.2   Categories of theoretical resources related to change.

particular approach which centres around the key concern of evidence-based practice. This is intended to demonstrate the ways in which specific approaches can be useful in understanding and bringing about a particular type of change.

Summary of approaches

Theoretical perspectives

Organisational life cycle (e.g. Kimberly & Miles 1980)
In some ways the development of this approach is representative of a field at an early stage in its theoretical development, in that there is a tendency to look elsewhere and use metaphors and analogies from other fields. Essentially this approach uses the metaphor of a biological organism to understand changes in organisations. It emerged as an attempt to explain the dynamic situation in terms of the development and demise of organisations.

New businesses and organisations are continually being created both in the public and private sectors, yet businesses fail with great frequency and are particularly vulnerable in the early stages of their 'life'. Similarly, agencies shut down or restructuring occurs, which is how organisations fail in the public sector, for example the various manifestations of Health Authorities over the years. In theoretical terms this can be viewed as birth, life and death. All organisations have a birth point, a life and ultimately a demise. As Kimberly & Miles suggest:

> biological metaphors, imperfect though they most certainly are, can serve a very useful purpose in the study of organizations. By forcing theorists to think through carefully where the metaphors are appropriate and inappropriate, their use can lead to the raising of important new questions and perhaps to the recasting of old ones. (Kimberly & Miles 1980)

This work has been developed further and now focuses on a biographical approach to the study of organisations. This perspective views organisations as evolving through time in response to, or in anticipation of, both external and internal forces (Kimberly & Rottman 1987). It can then be used as a framework for researching change in organisations and ultimately predicting those which are likely to be able to respond effectively to change.

Population ecology (e.g. Singh *et al.* 1986, Hurley & Kaluzny 1987)
Extending the metaphor of organisations as biological organisms all competing for survival in a hostile environment the population ecology approach suggests that notions of 'survival of the fittest' can be applied in

organisational studies. It is seen to be especially appropriate where there is a volatile environment, for example where a large number of small firms are in fierce competition with each other for customers and resources. It has been applied in the study of restaurants and also to health care organisations in the United States. Research conducted by population ecologists seeks to understand how social conditions affect the rates at which organisations change forms and the rate at which forms die out.

An ecology of organisations also emphasises the dynamics that take place within organisational populations. Population ecologists are concerned with large numbers or sets of organisations which share a common organisational niche and the resources it contains. Over the long term those forms or structures which survive within a population do so because their niche has selected them out as being most successful in the endemic struggle to secure and retain those resources that guarantee organisational survival. A theoretical approach such as this must take account of wider institutional contexts such as industrial sector and the class structure. A key underlying assumption is that environmental pressures make competition for scarce resources the central mobilising force in organisational change. The model itself sets out to explain how organisational forms or structures are established, survive and become diffused throughout a population or, conversely, fail to become established and die out. Drawing on work conducted in the USA, Hurley & Kaluzny (1987) observe that this perspective recognises that much of the ongoing change within health services is a function of chance and necessity rather than purpose and does not necessarily represent progress but simply better fit with the environment. This statement is likely to have some resonance with most people working in health care in that much change is often perceived as being externally imposed and politically driven.

Receptive contexts (e.g. Pettigrew *et al.* 1992)
The complexity of change as a process is illustrated by the variety of theoretical explanations that have been put forward to account for change. Pettigrew and his colleagues developed this model because of their dissatisfaction with existing explanations of change in organisations. It emerged from extensive research conducted into health care organisations involving interviews (400 in total), observation of meetings, archival work and observation. They concluded that there were differences in the receptivity to change dependent on the context. This affected the rate and nature of change in the eight health districts they studied.

Following a literature review, conducted as part of the study Pettigrew *et al.* (1992) identified deficits in the research base on change in the NHS. They argued that research into change in the NHS is insufficiently:

- processual (that is, involving an emphasis on action as well as structure)
- comparative (there is a need for comparative case studies as well as single cases)
- pluralist (there is a need for description and analysis of the often competing versions of reality seen by actors in the change process)
- contextual (the research does not operate at a variety of different levels and does not specify the linkages between those levels)
- historical (there is a need to take into account the historical evolution of ideas and stimuli for change as well as the constraints within which decision makers operate).

In response to this they advocate studying change over time in a contextualist mode. In other words studying the change where it takes place whilst taking account of the wider forces impinging on it. This extends to locating the change in a timescale. The change has a past, present and future which it is important to appreciate. There is also a need to consider if and how the context is a product of action and vice versa. Their central assumption, and the basic premise underpinning their work, is that the causation of change is neither linear nor singular. The search for a simple and singular grand theory of change is unlikely to bear fruit. Rather the task is to identify the variety and mixture of causes of change and to explore them through time in some of the conditions and contexts in which these mixtures occur. As they conclude:

> For the analyst interested in the theory and practice of changing, the task is to identify the variety and mixture of causes of change and to explore through time some of the conditions and contexts under which these mixtures occur. (Pettigrew *et al.* 1992)

This is best illustrated in the diagrammatic representation of this model (Figure 5.3). In order to understand the nature of the change process in health care organisations, attention needs to be directed to these eight factors and the way they interact. This will uncover new insights on the content, process and context of change.

Diffusion of innovations (e.g. Rogers 1983, 1995)
This perspective emerged in the 1960s and developed into a substantial body of work in later years. Its key concern was to determine the characteristics of adopters of innovations and distinguish them from non-adopters. This is intended to help explain the different rates of diffusion in different groups or markets. The original focus of the research was on farmers before it moved on to doctors and health care. Originally the approach was somewhat limited as it focused exclusively on the decision-making processes surrounding the adoption or non-adoption of the

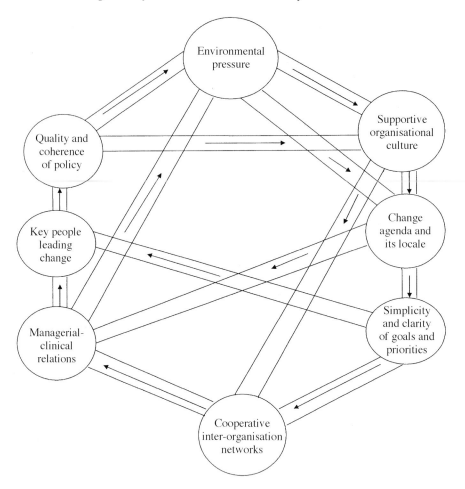

Figure 5.3 Receptive contexts for change: the eight factors. Reproduced by permission of Sage Publications Ltd from Pettigrew *et al.* (1992), *Shaping Strategic Change*.

innovation. There is now much greater attention to how historical factors can influence decisions and the differences between individual and organisational adoption.

In health care particularly, the studies revealed the importance of interpersonal networks at work through which subjective evaluations of an innovation are transmitted, and suggested that the role that 'opinion formers' could play in encouraging adoption of new technologies could be expanded. The adoption of innovations by hospitals is associated with large size, existence of teaching and research facilities, hospital ownership of the technology and urban location. Although Rogers (1983, 1995) and his colleagues have brought together over 4,000 studies on the diffusion of innovations identifying the key characteristics of the people and the processes involved, interest in diffusion approaches fell away in the 1980s with the emphasis shifting to top down restructuring as a key factor in organisational change. However, it is now experiencing a resurgence of interest in the context of evidence-based practice and is explored further later.

Prescriptive approaches

The prescriptive approaches share some similarities in that they are what Collins (1998) refers to as *n*-step guides to change. They incorporate a 'rational' analysis of change; a sequential approach to the planning and management of change; a generally upbeat and prescriptive tone (Collins 1998). They all imply that if the steps or actions advocated are followed then change will occur.

Total quality management
This approach to managing quality, which was examined in chapter 3, can also be regarded as a means of managing organisational change. It includes fourteen steps which have to be taken to achieve TQM (Oakland 1993, p. 425). There is a considerable amount of detail included to explain what these steps are, however, essentially TQM is a step-by-step guide to changing the organisation to achieve quality.

Business process reengineering
The 'official' definition of reengineering is: the fundamental rethinking and *radical redesign* of business *processes* to bring about *dramatic* improvements in performance (Hammer & Stanton 1995). The basic idea behind re-engineering is that organisations need to identify their key processes and make them as lean and efficient as possible (Crainer 1998). Although it places emphasis on discontinuous thinking and the development of radical solutions to organisational problems, it does this by recommending the completion of a series of steps:

- Prepare the organisation. (Look at what it does and how it does it now.)
- Rethink the way the organisation operates. (Examine how things can be done differently.)
- Restructure the organisation to operate in a new way based on this rethinking.
- Implement new systems to reinforce the changes made.

Reengineering became synonymous with redundancies in many organis-ations (Crainer 1998), however it has been widely employed in the commercial sector and in some health care organisations to bring about change (Packwood *et al.* 1998).

Project management
This is a very common and familiar approach to managing change. For a change to be amenable to being 'project managed' it must have a discernible beginning and end (Iles & Sutherland 2001). Once again this is an *n*-step model (Collins 1998) as outlined by Iles & Sutherland (2001). It has five stages.

1. Defining the project's goals – ensuring that these are measurable and attainable.
2. Planning the work programme in order to achieve the objective or objectives set.
3. Leading the project implementation.
4. Monitoring the progress of the project.
5. Completing the project and ensuring it is integrated into the mainstream activity of the organisation.

For complex change a series of projects can be managed together to address different dimensions of the change. This approach is similar to the other prescriptive models as it rests on an assumption that rational management solutions are appropriate to bring about change.

Unfreezing, movement, refreezing
First proposed by Lewin (1951), this model has since gained considerable currency in management thinking and is still widely used today as a basis for managing planned organisational change. It represents an intentional attempt to improve the operational effectiveness of the organisation involving three phases.

Unfreezing
↓
Movement
↓
Refreezing

Unfreezing involves reducing those forces which maintain the past behaviour and establishing the need for change. It sometimes involves the deliberate disruption of the organisation in order to achieve the beginnings of change. The unfreezing phase consists of three major elements:

- Disconfirmation or lack of confirmation (recognition of the need for change).

- Creation of guilt or anxiety.
- Provision of psychological safety (in order to cope with uncertainty).

Movement refers to development of new attitudes, behaviour and the implementation of the change. This occurs when the readiness for change is present. It may follow a long period of unfreezing. Four elements are identified as being part of the 'movement phase'.

- Acceptance of reality (of the change).
- Testing (seeing how the new order works).
- Search for meaning (understanding what has occurred).
- Internalisation (final acceptance of the change).

Refreezing entails stabilising the change at the new level and reinforcement through supporting mechanisms, for example the development of new policies, structures to formalise it.

In the application of the prescriptive models of change a number of tools can be used to help inform decisions concerning planned change. There are many that have been developed (see Iles & Sutherland 2001, for example). However, only four will be considered here to demonstrate how they relate to the overall process of change. Their purpose is to inform the assessment of the situation or organisation that is to undergo change, by providing a mechanism for systematically collecting important information. Each one has a slightly different focus and purpose.

Change management tools

Forcefield analysis

This tool is mainly used as a way of identifying where energy needs to be directed to bring about change. Developed by Lewin (1951), in conjunction with his change model, it is a means of identifying the driving forces and the restraining forces for change in a given situation (see Figure 5.4). A forcefield analysis can help managers assess the progress of a programme of change diagrammatically. If the restraining forces are stronger than the driving forces change will not occur. It recognises that group norms are an important element in shaping and resisting organisational change. Accessing this information enables the manager to take action to work to reduce the restraining forces. This is a more fruitful approach than trying to increase the driving forces as this also increases the restraining forces (Iles & Sutherland 2001).

This is perhaps the most common of these sorts of tools and it serves as a template for a series of others that have been developed subsequently, for example, 'sources and potency of forces' (Beckhard & Harris 1987),

Lewin's Force Field Model

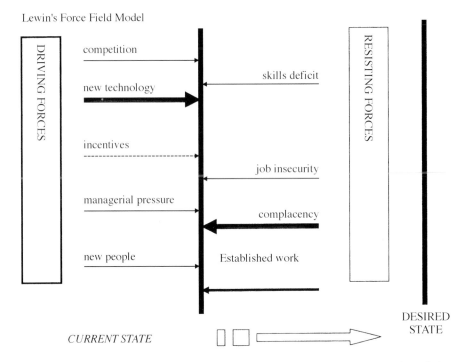

Figure 5.4 Force field analysis, based on Lewin (1951). Reproduced by permission of NCCSDO, from Iles & Sutherland (2001) *Organisational Change: A review for health care managers, professionals and researchers*, NCCSDO, London.

'Commitment, enrolment and compliance' (Senge 1992). At a more basic level there are tools which simply stimulate thought about change.

PEST analysis

Iles (1997) contends that using a PEST is a good way of scrutinising the external environment in terms of its effect on change in an organisation. The acronym stands for political, economic, sociological and technological factors and it can be used to increase understanding of the context of the change that is taking place.

- **Political** – focuses attention on national political factors such as legislation and policy, as well as local and internal politics.
- **Economic** – the nature of the competition faced by the organisation, its financial position and the priorities and perspectives of those who control resources.
- **Sociological** – local demographic issues, changing attitudes to service provision.

- **Technological** – technological factors/advances that will result in or affect change.

In some respects this is again similar to Lewin's (1951) Forcefield Analysis, as the PEST analysis is intended to direct attention to the factors in the environment that are helpful in supporting change and those that are likely to impede progress. It extends the principle employed by Lewin to focus on the environment external to the organisation.

SWOT

Strengths, weaknesses, opportunities and threats is an acronym that grew out of Ansoff's (1987) work on strategic change. This is another widely used tool in the management of change (Iles & Sutherland 2001) and is designed to inform data collection around these issues.

- **Strengths** are the positive aspects of the organisation which it can build upon, for example good facilities, good staff, effective systems.
- **Weaknesses** are those deficiencies in the present skills and resources of the organisation which need to be corrected or their effect minimised before change can occur. Examples are staff shortages, poor estate.
- **Opportunities** usually arise from changes in the external environment, for example the *NHS Plan* (DOH 2000a) and the opportunity to achieve foundation trust status.
- **Threats** are external developments which are likely to endanger the operation of the organisation, for example the possibility of losing an A & E facility to a regional trauma centre.

The Five Whys

Finally the Five Whys is a simple tool which addresses single problem events rather than generic organisational issues (Iles & Sutherland 2001). It explores the interrelationships which underlie an unfavourable event that has occurred in an organisation in order to find out more about it and to assist managers in focusing on causes of problems rather than symptoms. It involves asking why did a problem happen? And then asking why a further four times in an attempt to ensure the problem is fully investigated.

Summary

The reason for examining theories, models and tools in this way is to indicate the range of conceptual and practical resources that are available in understanding and managing change. Similarly it is to emphasise that there is no single solution to the challenge of managing change, rather different tools and approaches will be required depending on the context and the nature of the change. No one approach or model is better than another, rather they have been developed in different ways to address different issues. The challenge for managers is to use this material so that it informs their practice. In the final part of this chapter recent research on the diffusion of innovations, as a means of promoting evidence-based practice in health care, will be discussed as an example of this process in action.

Evidence-based practice and the diffusion of innovations

During the last decade, evidence-based health care has become a priority in the NHS with increasing emphasis on changing practice in the light of quality evidence, rather than continuing to base interventions on traditional ways of working (McInnes *et al.* 2001). It has been defined as: 'The conscientious, explicit and judicious use of current best evidence in making decisions about the care of individual patients' (Sackett *et al.* 1996).

Harrison (1998) argues that it is the doctrine that professional clinical practice ought to be based upon sound biomedical research evidence about the effectiveness of each diagnostic or therapeutic procedure. It is very much a common-sense aspiration for the NHS, because as he enquires: who wants to be the object of ineffective interventions? The acceptance of evidence-based practice has also reached the level of government which has stated its aspiration that public policy be based on evidence (Macintyre *et al.* 2001).

However, despite the fact that evidence-based practice is 'an idea whose time has come' (Harrison 1998), this does not necessarily mean that changes in practice based on the most up-to-date evidence will be made. As Davies *et al.* (1999) conclude: 'Even in health care, for all the richness of the research base, it remains unclear how best to bring about changes in professionals' behaviour that are congruent with the evidence' (p. 4). The naive assumption that when research information is made available it is accessed by practitioners, appraised and then applied in practice is now largely discredited (EHCB 1999). If this particular type of change is to be better understood and managed particular contributions from the field need to be examined and used as a basis for action. One area of work that is useful in this respect is the diffusion of innovations. Detailed assessments of specific strategies that can be employed to implement evidence-based practice already exist (see, for example, Hallady & Bero 2000, EHCB 1999, Bero *et al.* 1998) and are summarised below. The purpose of this section is to demonstrate how a broad theoretical approach can be useful in informing understanding of the process as a whole. The combination of specific interventions is likely to be more successful in bringing about change than relying on isolated single actions. Such interventions are listed below.

Specific interventions

- Disseminating research findings in simple and accessible formats.
- Using training regimes to put key messages across.
- Issuing evidence-based guidelines to practitioners.
- Identifying opinion leaders, advocates and 'product champions'.
- Establishing inspection or audit regimes to monitor the implementation of evidence-based guidelines.
- Creating the demand for evidence by introducing tailor-made performance targets.
- Identifying existing best practice, coupled with incentives for these successful programmes to share their strategies with others (Nutley *et al.* 2000).

These can be incorporated in a broader approach to change.

The diffusion of innovations

Diffusion is the process by which an innovation is communicated and adopted (or rejected) by members of a social system (Nutley & Davies 2000). The importance of social and communication networks is a central theme in the theory (Ashford *et al.* 1999) and the role of opinion formers and experts was noted earlier. The classical diffusion model is a relatively centralised one where decisions about what needs to change are made at government level and then diffusion flows from the top down (Nutley & Davies 2000). However, it is now generally recognised that the process of diffusion can also be decentralised in its origins and nature (Rogers 1995).

Researching the diffusion of innovations in health care

Fitzgerald *et al.* (1999) note that little prior research has taken place in the UK to explore why professionals adopt innovations, which sources and modes of compunction of evidence influence them, and what makes the evidence credible. In order to address this deficit they undertook a series of comparative case studies to investigate the career of four 'critical change issues' in the acute hospital sector and to establish their relative impact Ferlie *et al.* (2000). The change issues studied were:

- devolution of an anticoagulation clinic from secondary care to primary care
- the use of low molecular weight heparin as a prophylactic measure in orthopaedic surgery
- change in maternity provision in the light of *Changing Childbirth* (DOH 1993)
- minimal access surgery repair for inguinal hernia repair.

They found that the 'strength' of evidence for the benefits of the particular change was not reflected in the extent of the diffusion of the innovation. Indeed the very nature of the evidence itself is contested. They concluded that their data demonstrated that scientific evidence is not clear, accepted and bounded. Rather there are competing bodies of evidence and the relative 'weight' attributed to the evidence has more to do with the professional group involved than the nature of the evidence itself. Thus the same evidence does not produce the same response in every profession (Fitzgerald *et al.* 1999). Similarly the diffusion and the degree of adoption of the change varied depending on the group involved (Ferlie *et al.* 2000). The evidence itself is a socially constructed reality, rather than a fixed point, and diffusing evidence into practice is a construct of debate and agreement among practitioners (Fitzgerald *et al.* 1999).

In a more recent study examining the diffusion of innovations in primary care (Fitzgerald 2001) some of these findings were confirmed, for example few clinical professionals found it possible to identify the point at which they decided the evidence on an intervention was sound. It was also found that opportunities for the sharing and debate of evidence between the professions did not exist, although interprofessional collaboration will be necessary if the innovations are to be taken forward. The role of 'opinion leaders' as a positive force for innovation was also confirmed. The importance of these particular social networks in health care in bringing about change in this area is a factor that has been revealed through the application of diffusion theory.

Based on their work West *et al.* (1999) recommend that if effective dissemination of evidence-based practice is to occur it needs to be founded on a knowledge of the characteristics of the audience and its social context. The changes that can occur when an active 'network' of professionals is established (Thomas *et al.* 2001) further illustrates the benefits that can accrue if this aspect of diffusion theory is capitalised upon. Active networks of practitioners in primary care have been found to facilitate change and the dissemination of research evidence, yet they operate in a variety of ways (Thomas *et al.* 2001). Theory concerning the diffusion of innovations will not provide all the 'answers', however it has the potential to inform the management of change in that specific issues relating to evidence-based practice and its implementation can be considered before a plan for change is developed.

Conclusion

Garside (1998) suggests that the term 'change management' has become devalued across sectors and industries because it has negative connotations and has often been used inappropriately. The purpose of this chapter has been to demonstrate that the complexity of change has resulted in the production of a large number of theories and recommendations intended to explain the process of change and present prescriptions of how to manage it.

As with many aspects of management there are no simple solutions or correct answers. The range of theoretical and prescriptive literature is probably best regarded as a collection of resources that contains a range of useful information which will be applicable at different times and in different settings dependent on the nature and the context of the change. This makes things very challenging for those wishing to understand and indeed manage change. There is a need to employ what Collins (2000) has termed a 'critical-practical perspective', that is an approach to ideas which locates them in their context and facilitates their critique, when considering change theory. This will help inform the assessment of the utility of theory which will in turn help determine its applicability to practice. This is also the conclusion reached by Ashford *et al.* (1999) based on an evaluation of a range of change strategies. They found that awareness of the approaches available and their respective strengths and weaknesses is essential if an appropriate strategy is to be selected. This needs to be combined with a thorough knowledge of the context of the change, including the barriers to change, the characteristics of the groups involved and the facilitators (or opinion formers). This combined with the relevant knowledge from the literature can then be combined to develop an appropriate strategy to bring about change (Ashford *et al.* 1999).

The theories and approaches addressed in this chapter will be effective in some situations but not in others. An example of this in action was the focus of the final part of the chapter in which the theory of the diffusion of innovations was examined in the context of evidence-based practice. This theoretical approach is useful for generating insights and guidance concerning the implementation of this innovation because of the central role played by professional groups in the assessment and assimilation of evidence. This particular strand of theoretical knowledge, together with an understanding of setting, contributes to a more informed basis for managing this particular innovation or change. In other settings and with different changes a different combination of theoretical resources would be needed.

Change is a complex and dynamic process and is not amenable to a 'one size fits all approach'. Its effective management is the outcome of an appropriate melding of theory and experience. The other crucial element in bringing about change is leadership and this is the focus of the next chapter.

6. *Leadership in Health Care*

Introduction

During the 1980s and the early 1990s the emphasis in the UK health service was on improving management. Managerialism played a central role in the reorganisation of health care because as an ideology it legitimated change and on a practical level management was presented as a business-like approach to getting things done (Poole 2000, Clarke & Newman 1997). More recently the focus has shifted from management of the health service to the development of leadership of the people within it, as a means of delivering high-quality care and treatment. This is reflected in the *NHS Plan* (DOH 2000a) which states: 'Delivering the plan's radical change programme will require first class leaders at all levels of the NHS' (p. 86) and, 'we need clinical and managerial leaders throughout the service' (p. 87). In order to produce these 'first class leaders at all levels', a number of leadership development programmes have been introduced. The National Cancer Nursing Leadership Programme and the Leading Empowered Organisations (LEO) project are examples of this approach and are examined later in the chapter.

The purpose of this chapter is to examine the broad categories of leadership theory, and to consider some specific examples from each, in order to provide a context for discussing the types of approaches to developing leadership capacity that have emerged within the NHS. The purpose of this chapter then is to:

- discuss the definitions of leadership that have been developed
- summarise the main theoretical approaches to the study of leadership
- examine current approaches to leadership development in the NHS
- seek to provide fresh insights on the nature of management.

Defining leadership

Bennis & Nanus (1997) discovered more than 850 definitions of leadership when undertaking their work on 'leaders'. Consequently it is difficult to generalise about leadership, but essentially it is a relationship through which one person influences the behaviour of other people (Mullins 2002). However, the way that influence is exerted and the elements involved in it are extremely complex. This is reflected in the range of theoretical explanations that have been developed to expand our understanding of leadership in organisations. Mullins (2002) identifies six main categories of theories which have informed the study of leadership, and these are:

- qualities or traits approach
- the functional or group approach
- leadership as a behavioural category
- styles of leadership
- the situational approach and contingency models
- transformational leadership.

Handy (1993) also concludes that examination of a range of approaches is necessary as he concludes:

> the search for the definitive solution to the leadership problem has proved to be another endless quest for the Holy Grail in organization theory. There is no secret trick. (Handy 1993, p. 97)

Consequently examples to illustrate the main points behind each of the broad approaches identified will be considered before moving on to examine current attempts to improve leadership in health care.

The qualities or traits approach

The qualities or traits approach rests on the assumption that leaders are born and not made. Leadership arises from a set of characteristics or personality traits possessed by the individual. This explains why only some people become great leaders, because those in possession of the right combination of traits are a rarity. Based on this view research was undertaken to try and identify the traits necessary for effective leadership (Handy 1993). However, although this type of work identified lists of traits they tended to be overlapping, contradictory and have little correlation for most features (Mullins 2002). As Handy (1993) reports, by 1950 there had been over 100 studies of this kind. Unfortunately when considered together only five per cent of traits were found to be common to all of the studies. To some extent this lack of convergence probably reflects the different starting points of the researchers concerned and the range of research approaches adopted. Ironically the resulting extensive list of traits undermines the approach. The leaders studied had such a wide range of traits that it became clear that there was no 'typical' package that could be associated with good leadership. However the common areas identified were:

- **Intelligence**: above average but not genius level, good at solving complex and abstract problems.
- **Initiative**: independence, initiative, the ability to perceive the need for action and a desire to take it.
- **Self-assurance**: self-confident with high aspirations.
- **Helicopter factor**: the ability to rise above the particulars of a situation and perceive it in its overall context.

In addition most leaders appear to have good health, be above average height or well below it, come from the higher socio-economic groups in society. Other traits identified in the studies include: enthusiasm, sociability, integrity, courage, imagination, decisiveness, determination, energy and faith (Handy 1993).

The functional or group approach

This approach focuses on the functions of leadership, rather than the personality of the leader. The functional approach views leadership in terms of how the leader's behaviour affects, and is affected by, the group of followers (Mullins 2002). Perhaps the best known and most widely used example of this approach is action centred leadership (Adair 1988). Leadership requires that three areas of need within the work group are met. These are task needs, team maintenance needs and individual needs. If all of these needs are met Adair (1988) argues that effective leadership will be achieved. This model of leadership is represented in Figure 6.1. Task functions include agreeing objectives with the group, defining tasks, planning and monitoring the work of the group. Team functions include getting the group to work as a team by maintaining morale, ensuring that good communication occurs, and providing training when needed. Individual functions centre around meeting the needs of the individuals within the group by giving praise, handling conflict and understanding individual needs. Kennedy (1998) observes that Adair includes theory which is 'borrowed and re-evaluated' from Maslow (1970) and Fayol (1949) as part of his model.

This is another illustration of the interdependence of theory in the area of management generally. Adair (1988) also includes chapters on planning, controlling, evaluating and organising, which indicates that leadership needs to be underpinned by a firm foundation of management skills, if it is to be effective.

Leadership as a behavioural category

In this approach the focus is on the behaviours exhibited by people who are leaders. The assumption is that if the right combination of behaviours can be

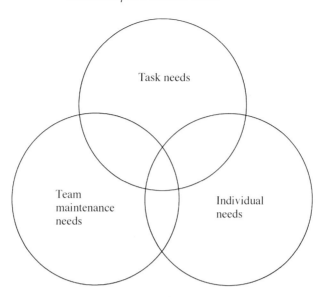

Figure 6.1 The three circles model of action centred leadership (adapted from Adair 1988).

identified then leaders simply need to adopt them to achieve success. One of the most well known is the work of McGregor (1960) on theory X and theory Y. Theory X and theory Y represent two extremes of leadership behaviour arising from contrasting assumptions about the nature of people and motivation. In general the emphasis is on managers developing leadership behaviours consistent with theory Y. These assumptions are outlined below.

Theory X assumes that:

- People are lazy and dislike work.
- Employees need to be controlled, directed and threatened with punishment if the work is to be done.
- People avoid responsibility, lack ambition and prefer to be directed.

Consequently the leadership behaviours required centre on direction and control built around a system of authority and punishment.

Theory Y assumes that:

- People want to work.
- Employees will work hard if they are committed to what the organisation is doing.
- In the right conditions employees will seek and accept responsibility.
- Employees have the potential to be creative and solve organisational problems.
- Employees' intellectual potential is only partly utilised in organisations.

In this case the leadership behaviours required are those which create the circumstances in which individuals feel motivated and are able to achieve goals. These include trust, delegation, good communication, and a participative approach to problem solving. McGregor (1960) maintained that leadership based on theory Y is the best way to do this.

Leadership styles

Closely associated with the actual behaviours leaders display is the way in which they do this. This constitutes another area of study in leadership. Generally the way in which the function of leadership is carried out can be classified within a broad threefold heading (Mullins 2002).

- **The authoritarian or autocratic leader:** This is where the leader holds all the power and controls the flow of communication; takes decisions and determines policy; allocates work and controls rewards and punishment.
- **The democratic or participative leader:** Shares the leadership function with the team; encourages discussion and interaction; decisions arise from discussion and debate; team members are encouraged to be involved in the leadership function.
- **The laissez-faire leader:** Often regarded as the leader abdicating responsibility and allowing the team to get on with things without support or direction. Mullins (2002) however emphasises that a 'genuine' laissez-faire style arises from a conscious decision to pass the focus of power to the group members. The team is encouraged to take on the tasks and responsibility and the leader is available to support this.

Other work in this tradition includes the 'tells, sells, consults and joins' model of Tannenbaum & Schmidt (1973) in which four main styles of leadership are needed for the different tasks facing the work team. The degree of management/leadership authority maintained is adapted in response to the nature of the task to be completed.

The situational approach and contingency theories

The situational approach focuses on the importance of the situation in terms of leadership. The basic premise is that different situations require different types of leader and the person who is best suited to lead in a given situation will come to the fore. However, the material considered earlier indicates that leaders tend to be people who display particular behaviours in particular ways and so whilst the situation is an important factor it is less significant than some of the others.

Contingency theories of leadership build on the situational approach by providing a means of explaining the interaction between the situation and leadership behaviour (Mullins 2002). Contingency theories suggest that there is no single model of leadership that is applicable to all situations. Depending on the specific circumstances and variables involved a different model will be required. The types of variables studied include: leadership attitudes (Fiedler 1967); quality of leadership decisions (Vroom & Yetton 1973); employee expectations (House 1971); readiness of team members (Hersey & Blanchard 1993). This further demonstrates the complexity of leadership as an area of study. Added to this new approaches and refinements of existing ones are being developed all the time. An example of this is transformational leadership.

Transformational leadership

Current trends in thinking about leadership focus on its capacity to revitalise and transform organisations (Mullins 2002). The nature of trans-formational leadership is often described by contrasting it with transactional leadership.

Transactional leadership is the type of leadership that traditionally existed in large organisations. It has echoes of the theory X approach in that it is based on the setting of goals and objectives by the leader and appeals to the self interest of the team members. It is transactional in the sense that the relationship between leader and team members is based on a relationship in which rewards are exchanged for compliance, and punishment for deviation.

Transformational leadership, on the other hand, echoes theory Y in that it is about creating high levels of motivation and commitment among the team. This arises from a clear vision and is based on notions of trust and loyalty. It is transformational in that this approach changes the way people work and thus changes the fortunes of the organisation. As Bennis & Nannus conclude:

> It is collective, there is a symbiotic relationship between leaders and followers, and what makes it collective is the subtle interplay between the followers' needs and wants and the leader's capacity to understand, one way or another, these collective aspirations. Leadership is 'causative', meaning that leadership can invent and create institutions that can empower employees to satisfy their needs. Leadership is morally purposeful and elevating, which means, if nothing else, that leaders can, through deploying their talents, choose purposes and visions that are based on key values of the workforce and create the social architecture that supports them. (Bennis & Nanus 1997, p. 202)

This belief that leadership can bring about transformation and deliver new ways of working is a central feature of current approaches to leadership in the NHS.

Leadership in the NHS

The need for leadership in the NHS has never been more clearly recognised at national, regional and local levels (Edmonstone & Western 2002, DOH 2000a). Edmonstone & Western (2002) summarise the range of leadership development programmes that have been devised to meet this need:

- *National programmes (centrally funded).* Examples include the Chief Executive Development Programme, the NHS Management Training Scheme, Nursing and Advanced Health Practitioner programmes.
- *National programmes (self-financing).* Examples include programmes offered by the King's Fund, and the Office for Public Management. These are prestigious national programmes run on the basis of income generation.
- *Regional programmes.* These are leadership programmes developed for and delivered in specific NHS regions.
- *Local programmes.* As the name suggests these are organised at a more local level in a variety of ways.
- *Employer programmes.* This is where NHS trusts organise 'in-house' leadership development programmes for its employees.
- *Individual initiative.* Many NHS staff fund their own development through attendance at a range of undergraduate and postgraduate taught courses.

Examples of the types of activities undertaken as part of the different levels of programme are discussed below to demonstrate how the principles derived from theories of leadership are being applied in practice.

The National Cancer Nursing Leadership Programme

Elements drawn from this extensive body of work can be found in the overall approach taken in the NHS Leadership Programme. This is usefully summarised in the statement concerning the philosophical approach of the programme:

> There is an ongoing debate about whether management effectiveness is best defined by a set of competencies or in terms of the pursuit of an organisational ethos and culture which frees people's creative abilities. The approach to leadership development adopted in this programme strikes a balance between developing knowledge, skills and competencies on the one hand and working with participants to develop their self-awareness, helping them identify their inner strengths and build courage and self confidence, on the other. (NHSE/King's Fund 2000, p. 4)

The programme aims to help its participants increase their self knowledge and personal direction; create a greater breadth of vision and ability to think and act strategically; improve their leadership ability and confidence to the extent that they are able to originate and lead change within their working environment; develop an understanding of diverse environments, situations and personalities; and to improve their ability to operate constructively and positively within diverse environments (NHSE/King's Fund 2000).

This involves a range of learning experiences including classroom and small group activities, learning sets, personal reflection and one-to-one mentoring. Opportunities are provided to learn about theories of leadership, strategy and change and to develop self-awareness and skills in sharing experiences and networking. The balanced approach referred to is an acknowledgement of the complexity of the area and illustrates how a range of theoretical material needs to be used if leadership is to be understood. This is reflected in one of the tools used in the National Cancer Nursing Leadership Programme (Centre for the Development of Nursing Policy & Practice/Royal Marsden 2000). Leadership Effective Analysis^{TM} (LEA) (Management Research Group 1998) is central to this programme. LEA is a method of developing individuals and increasing their effectiveness. It defines the leadership role in terms of 22 behavioural characteristics (or sets). It provides an individualised feedback profile of the approach individuals take to the leadership role. It identifies areas which need the most development. It provides a framework for the creation of action plans to address specific needs. This approach arises from a belief that competence and effectiveness in leadership result from the management of relationships with superiors, peers and subordinates within the organisation. The way this is done is by using the information provided in the Leadership 360$^{®}$ Report (Management Research Group 1998). This tool is designed to present self and observer feedback and scores on the 22 sets that constitute effective management practice.

Observer feedback is provided by superiors, peers and subordinates, this information is then collated and presented to the participant in a personal feedback report. This feedback is then combined with input on management and personal action plans and mentorship to develop the individual's leadership capability. The 22 sets are organised under five broad headings which reflect the dimensions of leadership that are expected in modern organisations, some of which were discussed earlier. The sets are shown below.

Creating a vision
A vital ingredient of leadership is vision. The five sets that are involved in creating a vision are:

- **Traditional:** Studying problems in the light of past practices to ensure predictability, reinforce the status quo and minimise risk.

- **Innovative:** Feeling comfortable in fast-changing environments; being willing to take risks and to consider new and untested approaches.
- **Technical:** Acquiring and maintaining in-depth knowledge in your field or area of focus; using your expertise and specialised knowledge to study issues in depth and draw conclusions.
- **Self:** Emphasising the importance of making decisions independently; looking to yourself as the prime vehicle for decision making.
- **Strategic:** Taking a long range, broad approach to problem solving and decision making through objective analysis, thinking ahead and planning.

Developing followers

In order to make their best contribution, leaders must get others to respond positively to their ideas and efforts. The ability to influence others is to do with the strength of the logic of people's approach, insight, imagination, and communication skills, rather than position in the organisational hierarchy. The four sets involved in developing followers are:

- **Persuasive:** Building commitment by convincing others and winning them over to your point of view.
- **Outgoing:** Acting in an extroverted, friendly and informal manner; showing capacity to quickly establish free and easy interpersonal relationships.
- **Excitement:** Operating with a good deal of energy, intensity and emotional expression; having a capacity for keeping others enthusiastic and involved.
- **Restraint:** Maintaining a low-key, understated and quiet interpersonal demeanour by working to control your emotional expression.

Implementing the vision

This is about setting things in motion and developing systems and procedures to support the total effort. It requires communication, training, and the setting of standards for judging as a basis for judging success. The four sets involved in implementing the vision are:

- **Structuring:** Adopting a systematic and organised approach; preferring to work in a precise, methodical manner; developing and utilising guidelines and procedures.
- **Tactical:** Emphasising the production of immediate results by focusing on short-range, hands on, practical strategies.
- **Communication:** Stating clearly what you want and expect from others; clearly expressing your thoughts and ideas; maintaining a precise and constant flow of information.

- **Delegation:** Enlisting the talents of others to help meet objectives by giving them important activities and sufficient autonomy to exercise their own judgement.

Achieving results
This reflects the pressure in organisations to deliver higher levels of performance in a situation where there are limited resources. Leaders need to remain focused on results and set challenging goals in order to achieve. There is a need to make sure everyone makes their maximum contribution, barriers are broken down, expectations are exceeded. The three sets involved in achieving results are:

- **Management focus:** Seeking to exert influence by being in positions of authority, taking charge and leading and directing the efforts of others.
- **Dominant:** Pushing vigorously to achieve results through an approach which is forceful, assertive and competitive.
- **Production:** Adopting a strong orientation toward achievement; holding high expectations of yourself and others; pushing yourself and others to achieve at high levels.

Team playing
This category arises from the recognition that leaders can achieve little without the support of others. Part of this involves acting as a follower as well as a leader. Developing and using abilities as a follower can contribute to the success of the organisation, and this is also a good way to gain the cooperation of others. The individual who is able to build positive and trusting relationships throughout the organisation is likely to achieve more. The four sets involved in team playing are:

- **Cooperation:** Accommodating the needs and interests of others by being willing to defer performance on your own objectives in order to assist colleagues with theirs.
- **Consensual:** Valuing the ideas and opinions of others and collecting their input as part of the decision-making process.
- **Authority:** Showing loyalty to the organisation; respecting the ideas and opinions of people in authority, and using them as resources for information, direction and decisions.
- **Empathy:** Demonstrating an active concern for people and their needs by forming close and supportive relationships with others.

Once the leaders have assessed their own performance in these dimensions, and had their performance assessed by subordinates, peers and superiors they have a wealth of information that can be used to inform their development as leaders. This serves as a basis for them taking action to improve their performance. This does not necessarily mean performing well in all dimensions, rather they take action to address areas that need to be developed if they are to become a rounded leader.

As noted earlier it is unrealistic to expect individuals to be able to function well in all of these 'sets'. However, knowledge concerning performance can be very useful for individuals so that they can become aware of how they are perceived by others and what they may need to do to improve as leaders. It is also clear that different sets will be required at different times. It is difficult to demonstrate excitement and restraint at the same time, however each of these qualities may be needed at different times by an individual if he or she is to be an effective leader. Participants need to have a high degree of self awareness and be committed to this type of programme if they are to benefit from it. The other point to add is that although leaders can influence the environment or the culture of an organisation, there remain other powerful forces that can constrain the efforts of even the most effective leaders.

This illustrates how clinical leadership development is being implemented at a strategic level in the NHS and how it draws in theory development in the wider literature. There is also a series of initiatives being undertaken at other levels. This includes the Leading Empowered Organisations programme.

Leading empowered organisations

The NHS modernisation agenda rests on having people in the range of organisations that make up the NHS who can act as leaders. Leading empowered organisations (LEO) is a three-day programme developed by the Centre for the Development of Nursing Policy and Practice (CDNPP) at the University of Leeds. It is based on work conducted by Creative Health Care Management based in the USA. Central to the LEO programme are the principles of respect, dignity and empowerment. Empowerment is defined as 'creating an environment in which people can behave as responsible adults' (NHSE 2001a). LEO is designed to help sisters, charge nurses and front line team leaders lead change in their organisations. It aims to enable empowerment in the participants by addressing the following areas: responsibility, authority, accountability, articulating expectations, developing autonomy, resolving conflict, risk taking, problem solving and positive discipline (CDNPP 2000). On completion of the programme they should be able to:

- Challenge in a constructive manner the current level of authority they have for finance, personnel and quality. They will be skilled at clarifying and negotiating that authority with the intention of ensuring improvements in patients' experience of healthcare, and the working environment in the clinical setting.

- Accept responsibility for reducing the level of administration and bureaucracy in the service by challenging the status quo.
- Challenge the misuse of resources caused by the lack of cross boundary participation and collaboration, and to build relationships of trust, openness and honesty.
- Influence changes to front line services, which will begin to address the deterioration of the environment as perceived by the public, and to introduce new, innovative practice with confidence and enthusiasm.
- Improve access to services for patients through partnership working and effective problem solving (NHSE 2001a).

It involves a preview day, a three-day programme, and is followed by a review day six months after the main programme. Such programmes are being accessed by a wide range of health professionals. For example, by December 2001 in the Eastern Region of the NHS, 72 LEO programmes had been provided and eleven trainers were working together to deliver further programmes (NHSE 2001b). Here is another example of theory into practice, whereby the principles of leadership have been used to inform a development programme for health professionals within the NHS.

Local leadership

At a more local level an action research project designed to discover more about what leadership means in a modernised NHS was conducted in the London region. Members of a workforce and development leadership working group set out to provide a summary of the attributes, qualities and skills and actions that are central to the exercise of good leadership in the NHS. Drawing on consultation with 'a wide range of leaders and professionals across the NHS in London' a framework was devised that summarises contemporary views of leadership in the NHS (Workforce and Development Leadership Working Group 2000). This report usefully summarises much of the theoretical material covered earlier in the chapter and demonstrates how theory has informed views of good leadership practice in the NHS. The key themes identified in this project are outlined below and in Figure 6.2. They are broken down into sections relating to what good leaders do and what this means for practice. The descriptions of what good leaders do are summarised below and the implications of this for practice are listed in the figure. This illustrates how management theory can be synthesised and be used to guide practice.

Embodying Leadership in the NHS

What do Good Leaders do?

A framework for developing the individual and the organisation

ARTICULATE VISION
Communicate a broad vision for the whole health community.
• Have a clear picture of the world and aspire to create it.
• Communicate vision with passion and conviction.
• Engage people in developing it.
• Make vision reflect diversity of communities served.

EMBODY VALUES
Have a clear sense of personal values and commitment.
• View excellence in public sector leadership in a positive light.
• Demonstrate fairness in all dealings.
• Ensure equity of access to services for all members of the community.
• Persuade others of values – through day-to-day actions – not impose them.

MOTIVATE
Understand the need for a highly motivated organisation.
• Prioritise motivating and supporting people.
• Listen.
• Identify various ways to acknowledge effort and achievement.
• Inspire through action and example.
• Encourage and value high standards of work and loyalty.

RELEASE TALENT
Act on the belief that people have many talents and potential.
• Actively seek out potential at all levels.
• Ensure that individual development needs are identified and met.
• Encourage and support risk taking by individuals and teams.
• Minimise forces that can hold back talent, e.g. bureaucracy.

TAKE DECISIONS
Identify and carry out decisions which need to be taken.
• Anticipate and take difficult decisions.
• Recognise that effective decisions are more achievable than perfect decisions.
• Seek and take account of relevant views.
• Monitor effects of decisions and adjust as necessary.
• Learn from previous decision taking.

Figure 6.2 What do good leaders do? (Workforce and Development Leadership Working Group 2000).

ENCOURAGE CREATIVITY
Show innovation and creativity are highly valued.
- Create a climate which encourages purposeful innovation by anyone.
- Shop openness to new ideas and learning from others.
- Get new ideas into practice and evaluate impact.
- Use success or failure of new ideas as impetus for further learning.

VALUE RESPONSIVENESS
Encourage individuals, teams, organisations, to think and act flexibly.
- Combine clear sense of direction with readiness to adapt and change.
- Manage uncertainty in exemplary ways.
- Find change enlivening rather than stressful.

WORK ACROSS BOUNDARIES
Demonstrate ability to work across professional, team and organisation boundaries.
- Develop capacity for new ways of working across boundaries.
- Recognise and respect perspectives of others.
- Negotiate conflicting priorities with partners.
- Focus on sustaining energy and commitment to common goals.

DEVELOP PERSONAL RESOURCES
Demonstrate resilience and ability to call upon reserves of energy.
- Show self confidence and confidence in team.
- Show insight into personal strengths and weaknesses, knowing when to seek help.
- Develop strategies for avoiding burnout.
- See things through and handle unanticipated difficulties.

Figure 6.2   Continued.

Theme 1: Articulating a vision

Communicating a broad vision for the whole health community
Leaders have a positive sense of how their vision accords with peers and the organisation as a whole. The vision takes a wide perspective and encompasses how the organisation contributes to creating the future. Leaders are able to show why their vision is worth striving for and how it can be brought into reality.

Theme 2: Motivation

Understanding the need to have a highly motivated organisation
Leaders behave in ways which demonstrate that they believe supporting and motivating staff is important. They make time for people and take an interest in them and their problems.

Theme 3: Decision-taking

Being dynamic and proactive in identifying decisions which need to be taken
Leaders are proactive in identifying the decisions that need to be taken in simple and complex situations. They define the decisions that need to be taken and the criteria for evaluating their effectiveness.

Theme 4: Releasing talent

Demonstrating a belief that the people within the organisation are individuals with many talents and potential
Leaders recognise the value of ensuring that people's talents and skills are not lost to the organisation. They ask how the organisation can facilitate people's development and take pride in the achievements of their staff.

Theme 5: Responsiveness and flexibility

Valuing flexibility and responsiveness in the organisation
Leaders recognise that they as individuals and the organisations they lead need to be light on their feet and ready to adapt to changes in the world. They build flexibility into their own working patterns and into the organisation as a whole to ensure that both have the capacity to respond quickly to change.

Theme 6: Embodying values

Having a clear sense of personal values
Leaders demonstrate their personal integrity and command the respect of the people they work with. They show respect for others and behave consistently and acknowledge that values and convictions are best conveyed by personal example.

Theme 7: Innovation and creativity

Demonstrating that innovation and creativity are highly valued in the organisation
Leaders strive for better ways to run their organisations and teams to achieve the goal of delivering high-quality services to users. They create safe havens where people can experiment and innovate. They are adept at challenging, and when necessary, changing their preferred ways of working to become more effective as leaders.

Theme 8: Working across boundaries

Demonstrating ability to work across professional, team and organisational boundaries

Leaders recognise and acknowledge the complexities within which they work and are willing to cross boundaries in pursuit of more effective learning, working, creative solutions and a better service. They are able to identify tensions that cause problems in cross boundary working which prevent innovation. They build the capacity to work more effectively on difficulties that occur and develop actions that change and improve practice within and between organisations.

Theme 9: Personal resources

Demonstrating resilience and the ability to call upon reserves of energy

Leaders demonstrate a profound sense of responsibility and endeavour to make well balanced judgments. They are always ready to think through the longer term and wider implications of their decisions and actions. They have reserves of energy that can be drawn upon to see things through and to handle unanticipated difficulties and problems.

It can be seen from the terminology used to articulate these themes and in the activities described that some familiar trends emerge. The importance of having vision, drive and energy, an understanding of how to motivate people, and how to bring about change are aspects of leadership that appear in a number of accounts. It is also clear that it takes a very special individual to be 'competent' in all of these areas. Leadership is a complex and challenging role. There is no one 'best' style of leadership (Mullins 2002, Crainer 1998) nor is there a definitive guide of how leaders should behave. As Grint (1997) concluded, despite an enormous outpouring of material in the second half of the twentieth century, we appear to be little closer to understanding leadership than either Plato or Sun Tze, who began the written debate several thousand years ago. It may seem strange that despite the amount that has been written about leadership there is no accepted single way of achieving effective leadership, however this only serves to emphasise the need to examine the theory. What has been demonstrated is that it is not possible to arrive at a prescription for leadership that will work for all people in all situations. However, there are some general principles that are evident in the literature and which form the content of the leadership development programmes that have been discussed. Although there is a risk of oversimplifying the situation when drawing out the key points from this work, it has been summarised by Bennis & Nanus (1997).

They suggest leaders who will succeed are those who are best able to:

- set direction during turbulent times
- manage change while still providing service and quality
- attract resources and forge new alliances
- harness diversity
- inspire a sense of optimism, enthusiasm and commitment among people
- be a leader of leaders.

The challenge comes when an attempt is made to apply these principles, and indeed the other recommendations made by writers on leadership, to the reality of health care organisation. The temptation is to seek recourse to a step-by-step guide. However, the lack of agreement as to what leadership is, and the fact that different approaches are required in different settings and at different times render this a redundant approach. A more fruitful approach may be to use the theory that has informed the study of leadership to understand what is going on in health care organisations and ultimately to use this theory to inform leadership in health care.

Embodying leadership in the NHS

It is clear that there is a great deal of work and investment going into the development of leadership in the NHS. The Royal College of Nursing (RCN) Clinical Leadership Programme which started in 1994 has now been attended by almost 2,000 nurses from 140 NHS Trusts in England, Scotland and Wales (Pearce 2002). Evidence concerning the effectiveness of such approaches is beginning to emerge. Cunningham & Kitson (2000), for example, found that the RCN leadership programme improved the leadership capabilities of ward sisters and senior nurses and thereby contributed to improvements in patient care.

However, Edmonstone & Western (2002) found that there is confusion among programme participants and NHS employers surrounding the appropriateness of particular programmes for particular groups of staff. They suggest that wide ranging discussion is needed to explore the assumptions underlying approaches to leadership development in the NHS. In the evaluation studies they examined, no attempt had been made to establish baseline measures of leadership effectiveness; no specific organisational benefits were identified; and there was no consensus over what organisational benefits may be anticipated.

Werrett *et al.* (2002) conducted a regional evaluation of an LEO programme involving 3,870 nurses and 314 allied health professionals in the West Midlands. Although the overall evaluation was positive and the programme was recognised as useful by the participants, it is interesting to note that few participants were able to report a specific example of the impact the LEO programme had had on their delivery of clinical care. They had developed a range of new skills and knowledge, but the extent to which this had 'improved' practice was less clear. This is partly because the evaluation was conducted three months after the completion of the programme, and as Werrett *et al.* (2002) suggest, a more longitudinal evaluation is necessary to evaluate fully the impact of the programme. The work that has been conducted thus far indicates that leadership is only one element in the management and organisation of health care, yet the current emphasis on leadership in health care does not appear to be diminishing. In a recent editorial in the *British Medical Journal* it is stated: 'We need transformational leaders who will redefine purpose, vision, and values and align those values within the organisations they lead' (*BMJ* 2002, p. 1351). However, if large numbers of staff undergo development and are expected to function as leaders, what specific benefits will this bring to patient care? It has been demonstrated that a wealth of theory exists and yet we are still some way from having the 'answers' as regards leadership. It may be that training large numbers of professionals to become leaders is an appropriate strategy that will help improve the management and organisation of health care. Alternatively it has been suggested that the popular (and officially sanctioned) idea that leadership at all levels of the NHS is a more or less politically legitimate and desirable goal could usefully be subjected to critical scrutiny rather than merely assumed (Learmonth 2003). Learmonth goes on to argue:

> Health care institutions are workplaces replete with people who are not formal leaders and who may resist managerial attempts to define them as such, yet surely remain intelligent actors whom it would be an insult to conceptualise as individuals who passively follow leaders. Nevertheless a critical reading of much managerially-oriented leadership research suggests that this is indeed how they are conceived. (Learmonth 2003, p. 112)

The material presented in this chapter can be used as a basis for studying and monitoring this development as it is important to have an understanding of the major theoretical themes informing our understanding of leadership both to apply and to critique them.

Conclusion

Good clinical leadership is central to the delivery of the NHS plan. We need leaders who are willing to embrace and drive though the radical transformation of services that the NHS requires. Leaders are people who make things happen in ways that command the confidence of local staff.

They are people who lead clinical teams, people who lead service networks, people who lead partnerships, and people who lead organisations (Hunt 2000).

This statement made by the Health Minister of the time Lord Hunt, emphasises the importance attached to leadership in current health policy and management. It is an area that all health professionals will have to engage with in the next few years and the theoretical material examined in this chapter can serve as a resource in understanding more about leadership as well as carrying it out.

It is a very challenging role and there is no simple model that applies in all situations. However, there is a wealth of material that can be accessed to further understanding and capability in this area. This may seem an inadequate answer, yet perhaps it is more realistic than issuing another set of guidelines or recommendations indicating 'what good leaders should do'. If such an aphorism were demanded it would be: good leaders recognise the complexity of leadership and combine it with their experience to lead in a way that works for them and their teams.

7. Hybrid Management

Introduction

The traditional view of health professionals' involvement in the management of health care is summarised by Paton (1995) in that professional management concerns the internal management of the responsibilities and workload of a profession governed by professional values. General management, on the other hand, is a different discipline concerned with the operational and strategic issues taking the organisation and its effective functioning as its rationale (Paton 1995).

The purpose of this chapter is to chart the increasing involvement of non-medical professionals in 'generic' management and identify the nature of this new role. Much of the literature discussing this trend raises issues of concern but is generally not supported with empirical evidence. A central theme of the chapter is that the movement of non-medical health care professionals into management represents the development of a new form of management increasingly referred to as 'hybrid' management. This also emphasises the importance of health professionals building their understanding of management theory, which is the central theme throughout this book. The fact that nurses and members of the allied health professions are taking on management roles in increasing numbers suggests there is a need to understand the theoretical and conceptual basis of this development. The intention here is to draw on emerging theoretical accounts of hybrid management as a means of tracing and explaining this development.

This serves as a basis for an examination of the implications of this development and consideration of the training needs for professionals in the future if they are to be equipped to take on these new roles. Finally conclusions will be presented aimed at summarising the current situation in theoretical and empirical terms.

To this end the chapter will:

- establish that management has always been a feature of the work of health professionals
- examine the implications of health professionals taking on management roles

- discuss the notion of hybrid management as a means of making sense of this development
- consider the training needs of nurses and the professions allied to medicine.

Management in the NHS

It has already been established that the 1980s and 1990s witnessed major changes in the organisation of the UK public services, including the NHS (chapters 1 and 2). These included the introduction of market-based approaches to the management and delivery of services, increased emphasis on financial accountability, and a drive to do 'more with less' (Ferlie *et al.* 1996, Flynn *et al.* 1996). The Government did not commission an evaluation of these changes and therefore it is difficult to make any definitive judgment about their success (Allsop 1995). What is clear though is that health services have changed and as Hunter (1996) concludes, what this amounts to is a hybrid model of organising and managing health care that combines both planned and market systems.

This has been reinforced by the introduction of the *NHS Plan* (DOH 2000a) with its emphasis on the 'third way', combining command and control management approaches with public service values. This in turn has wider effects as changes at the level of politics, social life and economics impact upon organisations in terms of structures, people, tasks and processes and have an effect on the way people carry out their roles (Lawton 1998). This is certainly the case with health professionals moving into management.

Professionals into management

If Paton (1995) presents the traditional view of the separation of professionals and managers then Mackay *et al.* (1995) summarise a contrasting view of current and future prospects for health professionals. They argue that professional ideals have been replaced by managerial values and this has 'weakened' professionals, consensus management has been replaced by executive management and health professionals are seldom to be found in general management roles. Yet, writing in the same year, Owens & Petch stated:

> In the years that have followed the implementation of the Griffiths proposals the movement of professionals into management has been dramatic, and nurses have been foremost in taking on general

management roles at all levels in the health service. (Owens & Petch 1995, p. 45)

Øvretveit (1994b) also notes the increasing numbers of health professionals in management roles.

However, there is some information which indicates the extent to which professionals have assumed management roles. The Creative Career Paths, project conducted by the Institute of Health Services Management Consultants on behalf of the NHS Women's Unit, for example, includes some useful figures. It was found that of the 599 top managers throughout the NHS who returned usable questionnaires (from an original target sample of 894), 11 per cent were non-medical health professionals (IHSM Consultants 1995a). Lower down the organisation 33 per cent of middle managers, defined as those in posts directly accountable to a senior manager, were from a non-medical health professional background (IHSM Consultants 1995b).

This suggests that health professionals have not been excluded from management but that their involvement may have been overlooked because it has been assumed that general management is the territory of former administrators, who accounted for the majority of appointments following the *Griffiths Report* (DHSS 1983) (Ham 1992). Indeed, in the wake of the Griffiths proposals and later *Working for Patients* (DOH 1989), there was little examination of professionals as managers. Research tended to focus on the impact of the reforms as a whole (Strong & Robinson 1990, Harrison *et al.* 1992, for example). Where there was an intention to examine the effects on a professional group the movement into management roles did not feature prominently in the work (Owens & Glennerster 1990). Similarly later work on the reforms following *Working for Patients* (DOH 1989) also adopted a 'macro view' (LeGrand *et al.* 1998).

Thus it can be argued that this role has been overlooked, in terms of research, in the past. Owens & Petch have commented:

> Analysts of the management of organisations have tended to ignore the professionals within, and sociologists have similarly paid little attention to the organisation in which they work, or have portrayed them as antithetical to professional values. The separate and different educational backgrounds and socialisation of managers and professional groups has reinforced these problems of co-existence. (Owens & Petch 1995, p. 37)

The way some health professionals work has changed and there is an increasing involvement of professionals in management at all levels in health care organisations. What effects are these new organisational arrangements having on the professionals concerned? How easily have they managed the transition from professional to manager?

Transition

Individual practitioners report that the transition to management can be a difficult process. Zeller (1995), for example, summarises the experience of a delegate at a conference convened to address the question 'Manager or Therapist?' She states: 'One of the major changes in her experience was that of losing professional identity and a sense of loneliness in being separate from a professional group'. Zeller goes on to conclude:

> Making the transition from therapist to manager is a steep learning curve but, although stressful, it provides the opportunity to influence management structure, skill mix and service developments. (Zeller 1995, p. 35)

In a study, employing an initial multidisciplinary workshop and two career transition workshops conducted in 1993, Edmonstone & Harvegal (1993) explored the career transition from functional management roles in the NHS to general management and 'hybrid' roles on the part of health care professionals. The workshops involved 32 participants from a range of trusts in Scotland who held a variety of posts including theatre services manager, clinical nurse manager, business manager and services manager. The participants were asked 'to provide written evidence of the nature of the career transition through which they were moving' and this information was explored further during the workshops. The data were then 'analysed' and 'themed' using the Seven S framework, developed by the McKinsey Management Consultant Company and made famous by Peters & Waterman (1982) in their book *In Search of Excellence*. The picture presented is one in which the participants were appointed to posts in structures that lacked clarity and cohesion, in many cases this move was enforced or involuntary. Often they did not have a job description and there was uncertainty surrounding the role and its content. Lines of responsibility were unclear and the boundaries between professional and managerial accountability were 'blurred'.

Conflict

The participants suggested that from the viewpoint of former colleagues, functional managers who moved into general management posts were seen as 'traitors' to their profession. There were also difficulties in convincing other managers of the reality of the new general management roles because they were still seen as occupying the old professional management roles. There was found to be a powerful contrast between the professional and managerial 'world views' and there was a lack of management training in preparation for their roles. This was also reflected in the language used in the conduct of the role. The old professional/clinical language was increasingly regarded as irrelevant and there was seen to be a need to use a business-oriented management language, on the part of the hybrid managers.

Organisational life was described as fragmented, characterised as being made up of factions and they felt they had little support in making the transition to their new roles. Edmonstone & Harvegal (1993) go on to produce a list of recommendations centred mainly around training and career development which they located under the headings of remedial and developmental action. However, in later reflections on this work (Edmonstone 1997a, b), it is interesting to note a much more pessimistic outlook for 'clinical management', indeed it is seen as a 'fragile flower' which has bloomed, but which 'may whither due to lack of care and attention' (Edmonstone 1997b). The conflict for professional managers occupying these 'dual' or hybrid roles can be overwhelming. However, elsewhere a process of accommodation was adopted which resulted in different outcomes.

Adaptation

In a study of decentralisation of community services Exworthy (1994) found that although the introduction of general management encroached upon professional territory and caused some friction, the dual professional managers were able to exert a considerable degree of power over the policy process. They achieved this by adopting a limited managerial 'framework' whilst retaining an allegiance to their professional group. Using a case study approach, involving participant observation of meetings, analysis of policy documents and interviews, the research timetable coincided with the timescale of the policy change under review. Conducted between 1988 and 1991 it spanned the publication of the White Paper *Working for Patients* (DOH 1989) and was based in 'a small compact area' of inner London which included ten health centres, a 'high number' of single-handed GPs and one district general hospital.

Exworthy's (1994) focus was primarily on how different groups can influence the implementation of the policy process and he ascribes a considerable degree of power, in this respect, to community health nurses who assumed management roles. In terms of their opposition to the process of decentralisation of services he states: 'Whilst they could not be certain that they would succeed in shelving the policy, they wanted to make sure that they achieved the best possible deal in the discussions that took place' (p. 25). This reflects an ambivalence in the role, noted by Exworthy, in that the professional managers opposed the particular course of action yet were instrumental in its implementation. He argues this is consistent with Lipsky's (1980) notion of street level bureaucracy, where professionals working at 'street level' are able to exert influence over the way policy is put into action. This indicates that the effects of managerialism on professionals are variable. Also the influence of managerialism is pervading professional life and central government policies have attempted to 'tie professionals into managerial approaches' (Exworthy 1994). Accommodation and adaptation is one response to this trend; however, there are likely to be others. Forbes & Prime (1999), for example, found that although they experienced some tensions and conflicts, radiographers taking on management roles had 'done so with relative ease' and were effective managers.

A clash of values?

One of the main features of the difficulties experienced by individuals in the transition from a professional role to a hybrid managerial role is the perception that there are conflicting value systems for the two activities. Hunter (1996) has suggested that one explanation for the confusion, instability and low morale among health care staff is a clash of values between the public service ethos and a private sector market-based approach to the organisation of services. This conflict has also been noted by others (see Sutherland & Dawson 1998, Harvey 1994, for example) and is considered in chapter 10 in the context of domain theory.

Cole & Perrides (1995) surveyed three local authority social service departments and focused directly on the ways in which health and social services organisations invest in their workforces. They found conflict in health authorities arising largely from professional-managerial clashes over priorities in decision making. They also suggested how events would unfold:

> Health and social care professionals are moving through role changes. They will need to decide whether they remain in 'practice' for which they were trained and continue to maintain their skills, or whether they wish to embrace the new world in which there is a marriage between clinical practice and business ethics. This remains unresolved for these professionals. (Cole & Perrides 1995, p. 73)

This is also an issue that has not been addressed in the context of the training health professionals receive during their preparation for professional practice (see below). It appears that the challenge is to find a congruence between the values of the professional and the objectives and ethical framework of the organisation (Owens & Petch 1995).

It has been suggested that professional work has always contained a management function (Clarke 1995, Paton 1995, Walby *et al.* 1994), yet it has assumed greater prominence in recent times. This has led to concern in some quarters that the clash between professional values and the new management culture is having a negative effect (Williams 1995, Owens & Petch 1995). Hart (1991), for example, discusses the nature of nursing as an activity, and contends that attempts to reduce it to measurable categories, or describe it using managerial language fail because there is no vocabulary available to express the emotional, intuitive and creative dimensions of the work. The basic theme in Hart's article is that managerial and professional values are incompatible. Traynor (1994) has also reported on the conflict between managerial and professional views. However, these concerns reflect only one aspect of the situation. There is an increasing recognition that some health professionals may become managers while others retain what they consider to be 'professional values' and remain in opposition to management.

Conversely others have suggested that the professions and management are not as different as often claimed (Walby *et al.* 1994) and that the debate needs to move on from simple and superficial characterisations of managers as being primarily concerned with money and balancing the books (Draper 1998). Harrison & Pollitt introduce another dimension to the complex picture that is emerging:

> it is quite conceivable that professionals may acquire management skills without necessarily also embracing a 'managerialist' ideology. To put it in more concrete terms, we may witness the appearance of more and more doctors and nurses who are to some extent management trained but who do not identify themselves with either a management career or the prevailing managerial predilection for economic rationalism. (Harrison & Pollitt 1994, p. 137)

The merging of professional and management approaches in the form of a hybrid manager may be one outcome. Indeed this is advocated as a positive development by some authors. Øvretveit (1994b) contends there is an argument that physiotherapist managers, when appropriately trained, have the expertise to supervise junior staff, decide on the best use of time, determine the parameters of practice, and have the credibility to lead quality assurance. Similarly the Department of Health (DOH 1995b) suggests nurses and midwives as managers, practitioners who pursue careers in general management can bring the special experience of caring for people to the business of provider and strategic health care. Therefore, despite the difficulties, professionals are becoming managers and this can be regarded as a positive outcome in terms of the improved management of health care. However, the term hybrid management requires further consideration if it is to be useful in illuminating the changes that are occurring.

Hybrid management

It has been suggested that the traditional dichotomy between professional and managerial activity is becoming less relevant as the two spheres of work overlap increasingly. The perceived differences are characterised by Flynn

Table 7.1 Ideal type contradictions between managerialism and professionalism (Flynn 1999). Reproduced with permission.

	Managerialism	Professionalism
Source of legitimacy	Hierarchical authority	Expertise
Goals/objectives	Efficiency/profit maximisation	Effectiveness/ technical competence
Mode of control	Rules/compliance	Trust/dependency
Clients	Corporate	Individuals
Reference group	Bureaucratic superiors	Professional peers
Regulation	Hierarchical	Collegial/self-regulation

(1999) as a series of Ideal Type contradictions and are summarised in Table 7.1.

However, this form of analysis does not fully account for the new managerial forms that are emerging. Harrison & Pollitt comment:

> Certainly an analysis based solely on a simple bipolar division between 'managers' and 'professionals' would be too crude to take us very far. A more convincing picture of the future would include various groups *within* management and other groups *within* each major profession manoeuvring for advantage across the new organizational terrain populated by different kinds of purchasers and providers. (Harrison & Pollitt 1994, p. 144) (Emphasis in the original)

This prediction is echoed by Flynn (1999) who suggests that there will be variation within and between professional and managerial groups concerning the right services to provide.

Similarly Causer & Exworthy (1999) contend that in so far as there is a tension between managerial imperatives and professional autonomy, this will be expressed not through the imposition of these imperatives on professionals, but rather through the work of those professionals who work as managers. They conclude that for many people engaged in professional work it may become increasingly inappropriate to ask whether they are a professional or a manager, for the essential nature of their work will lie in a combination of both elements.

A typology of hybrid management

In an attempt to provide a means of increasing understanding of the nature of hybrid management Causer & Exworthy (1999) propose the following typology. They identify three broad roles, each of which may itself be differentiated into two types.

1. *Practising (rank and file) professional*
   Pure practitioner, whose primary function is to engage in the day-to-day exercise of professional activities and who does not have any supervisory or resource allocation responsibilities.
   Quasi managerial practitioner, who does have managerial responsibilities as well as a clinical workload, although not formally designated as a manager.

2. *Managing professional*
   Practising managing professional, who is drawn from the ranks of a profession whose primary responsibility is the management of the day-to-day work of practising professionals and of the resources used in the conduct of that work, whilst maintaining some direct engagement in professional practice.
   Non-practising managing professional, who manages the work and associated resources of a defined professional group but who no longer manages in direct professional practice.

3. *General managers*
   Professionally grounded general manager, who is responsible for the overall management of professional employees but not concerned with the day-to-day practice and is from a professional background.
   Non-professional general manager, who is responsible for the overall management of professional employees but not concerned with the day-to-day practice and is not from a professional background.

However, even in demonstrating the complexity of the new and emerging configurations of management roles, this typology is incomplete. Professionals who take on management roles can also be responsible for the work of groups of staff not regarded as 'professionals', e.g. clerical and ancillary staff. Also large parts of 'professional' activity can be regarded as managerial in nature as care and therapy involve the organisation and mobilisation of people and resources in order to care for/treat patients. Therefore more work will need to be done to increase our knowledge in this area. However, the notion of hybrid management provides us with a useful conceptual device for understanding the changing role and function of health professionals.

Training hybrid managers

The recognition of these changes is evident in the benchmark statements for health care programmes (QAA 2001a). The Quality Assurance Agency for Higher Education is the body responsible for setting and monitoring standards in relation to the undergraduate education of health professionals.

The benchmark statements are a means of describing the nature and characteristics of programmes of study and training in health care. They represent an attempt to make the general academic characteristics and standards of health professional courses explicit. This includes indicating the management content of such programmes. In general terms all such programmes should prepare practitioners to:

- uphold the principles and practice of clinical governance
- participate effectively in inter-professional and multi-agency approaches to health and social care
- demonstrate an ability to deliver quality patient care
- demonstrate an understanding of government policies for the provision of health and social care
- demonstrate an understanding of the relevance to the social and psychological sciences to health and health care.

More detailed requirements are included in the specific statements for each course in relation to management and some examples are listed below.

Nursing (QAA 2001a)
Management of self and others' reflective practice.
- leadership
- principles of management within organisations
- clinical governance and maintaining/monitoring standards.

Physiotherapy (QAA 2001b)
Professional relationships.
- deploy and manage support staff effectively and efficiently.

Personal and professional development.
- managing uncertainty and change
- team working and leadership skills.

Context of service delivery and professional practice.
- an appreciation of the implications of different organisational settings and patterns of working
- quality assurance frameworks encompassing clinical governance, clinical guidelines and professional standards
- the planning of service delivery and its associated workforce.

Occupational therapy (QAA 2001c)
Professional relationships of the occupational therapist.
- participate in the management of staff and students according to organisational policy and accepted standards.

Evaluation of professional practice.
- participate in clinical effectiveness and clinical audit procedures, interpret the outcomes and relate to the practice of occupational therapy as part of the uni- and interprofessional evaluative process.

Subject knowledge understanding and skills.
- Understand the principles of management of people and resources as they apply to the organisation of occupational therapy services within a broader context.

So although Hunter identified a deficit in the training of health professionals some years ago:

> What is offered often fails to prepare students for the world they will eventually enter. In particular there is little grounding in management, health economics, medical sociology and other skills that would prepare professionals for a change management role, which ... is what will be expected. (Hunter 1996, p. 806)

It seems the situation has now changed and student health professionals are receiving education and training that will prepare them for the hybrid management roles they are likely to take on.

Conclusion

The prominence given to management in the reforms of the Health Service in the 1980s and 1990s has resulted in the research and policy focus being directed on managers as a new group within health care. It is evident that many managers are health professionals and the implications of this development have not been examined fully. There is an emerging area of work addressing the notion of hybrid management and it is to be hoped that this will increase our understanding of this role. It is important to consider the theoretical notion of 'hybrid' managers; however, it is equally important that this information helps those who are involved and those who will become involved in managing health care. The transition from professional to manager can be a difficult one, and an awareness of the different dimensions of hybrid roles can help practitioners understand their situation.

8. *Middle Management in the NHS*

Introduction

The level of the organisation where clinical leadership (chapter 6) and hybrid management (chapter 7) often come together is in the role of the middle manager. Torrington & Weightman (1987) have commented that to be a middle manager is the ambition of hardly anyone. It is generally regarded as a time of transition after the escape from the routine of technical specialism and before promotion to the realms of senior or even top management. It is a role, therefore, that is little understood and seldom examined by researchers, whose attention is drawn to the top of the organisational hierarchy. Yet for professionals in health care, middle management roles have become increasingly significant (Thompson 1994). Changes in structures and the flattening of hierarchies have resulted in a large number of professionals occupying middle management roles.

The health care management reforms discussed earlier (see chapters 1 and 2) have resulted in diverse organisational structures being put in place, usually accompanied by a reduction in the number of managerial levels within them. In contrast to some of the more gloomy predictions concerning the fate of middle management as an activity, this process has tended to increase the range of functions and responsibilities associated with these roles in health care. However, before such assertions can be made it is necessary to examine the relevant literature for the following reasons: to arrive at a 'working definition' of the term middle management and to place it in context, and to highlight the fact that little work has been carried out on middle managers in general and even less on middle managers in health care. The discussion will then move on to address the implications this has for health professionals taking on management roles.

Consequently this chapter will:

- define the term middle management
- examine the experience of middle management in general and in the NHS in particular

- discuss the research evidence relating to middle management in health care
- identify the essential features of contemporary middle management.

Defining middle management

> Middle managers integrate the organization as a whole or various parts of it within the organization. They transfer information and materials to different parts of the organization and co-ordinate organizational activities. (Schlesinger & Oshry 1984, p. 8)

This definition arises from Schlesinger & Oshry's (1984) characterisation of organisations as being made up of three layers: an outer layer of top managers which runs the organisation; an inner core of workers, which produces the products or services; and between the two are middle managers whose primary function is to act as organisational integrators. This is consistent with earlier and more recent work. Pugh *et al.* (1968), for example, suggested that middle managers link the activities of vertically related groups and are responsible for at least sub-functional workflow, but not the work of the organisation as a whole. Similarly Floyd & Wooldridge state:

> In general the purpose of middle management is to take responsibility for, and control the managerial problem. As boundary spanners, middle managers mediate between the organization, its customers and its suppliers. As administrators, middle managers direct the organization's overall task. (Floyd & Wooldridge 1997, p. 466)

Again this definition arises from an analysis of organisations which recognises the various levels of activity that are part of the functioning of large and complex organisations. In terms of the public sector the work that has been conducted in this area (Keen 1997, Keen & Vickerstaff 1997, Keen & Scase 1996, see below) uses the definition which was first employed by Dopson & Stewart (1990a,b, see below). However, there is a need to examine the existing literature in an effort to determine the scope of the term.

Being a middle manager

Dopson & Stewart (1990b) observe that, in the past, work on middle management has been characterised by a gloomy view, in that the middle manager is portrayed as a frustrated and disillusioned individual caught in the middle of the hierarchy, impotent and with no real hope of career progression. The work is dreary, frustrating and the introduction of information technology is set to make the role yet more uninteresting and mundane. The elements of this gloomy view are derived from a number of studies. However, most of the more pessimistic writers draw on their experience in consultancy and teaching to chart the decline of middle management. Peters (1992), for example, states categorically that middle management is dead and middle managers are 'cooked geese' (p. 755). However, he does go on to outline how people in these roles should re-create their own function within organisations. This assertion would seem to be borne out by the huge reduction in middle management jobs, totalling one fifth of all job losses in the US since 1988 (*The Economist* 1995). Similarly Pilla *et al.* (1984) found that on average companies are cutting middle management positions by one third. The 'downsizing' and 'de-layering' reflected in a figure of only 33 per cent of British people over the age of 55 years in paid employment (Handy 1994) further illustrates the recent reduction in middle managers, traditionally drawn from this age group. It would seem, on the basis of this evidence, that middle management no longer exists. Yet even in the early 1980s some writers were beginning to recognise that there was a need for middle managers, albeit in a changed form.

The 'plight' of the middle manager can be summarised under four main headings.

1. Being in the middle of a long hierarchy, although this is being negated by the flattening of organisational structures and greater levels of devolved responsibility and self-managed teams, which is leaving the managers isolated.
2. Having to cope with conflicting expectations.
3. Loss of technical expertise.
4. Career disillusionment (Dopson & Stewart 1990b, Schlesinger & Oshry 1984).

The changing role of the middle manager

Jackson & Humble (1995) contend that organisations will always have a role for middle managers but it will change as a result of a number of trends. These are broadly in line with those identified by Dopson & Stewart (1990b). However they are far from pessimistic suggesting that middle managers are needed because they transform the expressed values of the organisation into reality and that they will need to develop new roles as coaches and change agents.

This assertion is in agreement with a study by Scase & Goffee (1989) which involved 374 managers in large organisations in Britain. They found that there are a substantial number of 'reluctant' managers which adversely affects many organisations' performance. Many felt their skills were not being utilised and they reported a lack of management training and education. However, they echo Jackson & Humble (1995) by posing the question: who ensures that the strategies formulated by top executives will actually be implemented if it is not the middle managers? Middle managers are key people in all organisations and greater understanding of their experiences and ways of working is vital if those same organisations are to function effectively.

Middle managers as innovators

Moss Kanter (1982) also feels middle managers are crucial to the success of the organisation. Based on a study of 165 middle managers in five companies she found that middle managers can make a significant contribution to organisational success if they possess the following qualities: comfort with change; clarity of direction; thoroughness; a participative management style; persuasiveness and discretion. All of the managers studied were deemed 'effective' by their companies and 99 of the 165 had made innovations. She explored the types of organisations in which this occurs and the importance of the qualities, listed above, in achieving innovation. She concluded:

> If empowered, innovative middle managers can be one of America's most potent weapons in its battle against foreign competition. (Moss Kanter 1982, p. 105)

This is also the conclusion reached by Pilla *et al.* (1984) who contend that, despite their falling numbers, middle managers will assume greater freedom and authority and will need to find innovative ways of operating. Keys & Bell (1982) suggest that in order to meet these expectations the middle manager requires a number of skills. In a similar tone to Moss Kanter they outline what middle managers need to do. They characterise this package of skills as being able to face and manage four sets of relationships.

> Managers in middle ranks must simultaneously present the proper face upward to superiors, downward to their employees, laterally to their peers, and outward to outside groups. (Keys & Bell 1982, p. 59)

Each 'face' requires particular skills and abilities some examples being:

- Facing upward: the ability to form coalitions.
- Facing downwards: serving as a buffer.
- Facing sideways: developing integrative skills.
- Facing forward: learning to live with ambiguity.

The main themes that emerge from the general literature, then, is that although several writers have predicted the demise of middle management it is still an essential function within organisations. In terms of health care the significance of middle management as an activity has increased as new organisational arrangements have been instituted. Far from being ousted from the organisation, middle managers in health care have taken on an increasing amount of responsibility for managing the service. Also many of the people occupying these roles are drawn from the health professions. This development has been somewhat hidden in the past, but recent work has uncovered the nature and content of this developing role.

Middle management in the public sector

The definition of middle management in the public sector that has been used in previous work, and thus has the potential to provide some points of comparison with other studies, is that of Dopson & Stewart (1990a,b). That is, middle managers are those who have first-line managers/supervisors reporting to them, and who report in turn to more senior managers (Dopson & Stewart 1990b) and middle management is below the very top management and above supervisor level (Dopson & Stewart 1990a). There has been a relatively small amount of research conducted in this area in the public sector generally (Keen 1997, Keen & Vickerstaff 1997, Keen & Scase 1996, for example), and these papers report different aspects of the same research project. This was a case study of a large (40,000 employees) county council. The main body of the research consisted of semi-structured interviews with 48 middle managers.

It was found that many of the managers experienced greater levels of job satisfaction following the introduction of organisational changes which resulted in increased devolution of responsibilities. The authority to take decisions and allocate resources was felt to be an improvement. The associated 'performance culture' did mean that the managers were working longer hours and that job security had been reduced. The precise nature of middle management as an activity varied according to the function the manager was responsible for and it was noted that tensions were experienced by professional staff who derived their identity from a 'public service' ethos, who were then required to exchange this for a managerial role identity (Keen & Scase 1996, p. 179). There was also a recognition that the rhetoric of change was not always reflected in reality and that the tensions between flexibility and control were an issue of concern for the middle managers in the study (Keen & Vickerstaff 1997).

Middle management in the NHS

Middle management in health is similar to management in general in some ways, but there are also some distinguishing features which render private sector models of only limited relevance (Harrow & Willcocks 1990). As far back as 1992 Harrison & Thompson recognised that in the NHS, managers had moved from a largely maintenance function to a challenging one, calling into question their own and others' public service values. However, effective middle managers are vital if stated policy objectives are to be implemented (Harrison & Thompson 1992).

In order to locate this consideration of middle management in health care in its context, and to demonstrate its relevance to health professionals, it is helpful to refer briefly to some findings from the Creative Career Paths project, conducted by IHSM consultants on behalf of the NHS Women's Unit. Based on four postal surveys of: 894 top managers in all sectors of the NHS, 213 managers who have left the NHS, 816 managers spanning first-line, middle and senior management positions and finally 695 senior nurses in the NHS, this study helps to quantify some of the effects of the recent structural changes in health care on managers (IHSM Consultants 1994a,b, 1995a,b).

A clear link is established between management and the professional/ work background of the post holder. The proportion of those with an administrative, management, financial or medical qualification increases with seniority, whereas the reverse is true for nurses and the professions allied to medicine. Taking the figures as a whole (i.e. incorporating medicine and dentistry as well), 41 per cent of managers included in the third survey had a clinical background. This gives some indication of the involvement of people from a range of clinical backgrounds in management. In terms of middle managers, defined in the report as those in posts directly accountable to a senior manager, 22 per cent were from a nursing background and 10 per cent from the allied health professions.

These findings indicate the extent of the involvement of people from a clinical background in middle management roles. They also illustrate the concentration of nurses and the allied health professions in middle management. Therefore understanding this role and its function is of particular relevance to health professionals.

Researching middle management in health care

In one of the earliest studies which specifically investigates the effects of recent structural changes on middle managers in health care, as part of a broader study, Dopson & Stewart (1990a) conducted a comparative investigation using five case studies: three in the public sector (the Inland Revenue, the NHS and a new public agency – Her Majesty's Stationery Office) and two in the private sector (a traditional manufacturing company and a distributor of automobile parts). In general most middle managers saw themselves as playing a more generalist role in their organisations and as a result of this they were required to change their attitudes and become more flexible and adaptable. They were required to acquire new managerial skills including financial knowledge, the ability to manage a wider group of staff, skills in marketing and strategy development and a wider understanding of the organisation (Dopson & Stewart 1990a).

In the NHS the main source of stress for middle mangers was the feeling that their health district could not give as good a service as it should because of limited resources. The public sector managers in the study commented on the paradoxical nature of the demands being placed on them by government in that they felt they were being given the responsibility but not the power to meet specified targets. Dopson & Stewart (1990a) believe this cautious approach by middle managers in the public sector is born out of a tendency, both at the organisational and the individual level, to criticise mistakes rather than to recognise accomplishments. Also in line with previous work conducted by Stewart (1982) they refer to the excessive number of constraints on the actions of middle managers in the public sector. Another factor in this cautious outlook is the primary identity of many of the middle managers in the public sector. Dopson & Stewart (1990a) argue that occupational groups who see themselves as professionals will identify more readily with their professional role than with their managerial function and so resent and oppose reforms which they see as politically motivated and imposed, rather than necessary. They go on to outline a number of issues that need to be addressed, the main one being the fostering of a culture in which accomplishments are recognised and rewarded. This will then progress on to a situation where greater care is taken over the introduction of concepts and terminology from the private sector, managers are given greater control over their own resources and positive leadership is developed. They conclude:

> For the public sector, change is likely to increase as government policies are implemented and the effects of such policies become clearer. Traditionally, public sector managers have not been expected to be leaders but administrators. Now they are expected to be managers. (Dopson & Stewart 1990a, p. 39)

However, as Dopson & Stewart (1990a) concede, one small-scale study cannot permit any firm generalisations and it is necessary to examine more recent work to assess how the situation has developed.

Boundary spanning

In a study investigating the influence of middle managers on the business planning process in the NHS, Currie (1999) employed a qualitative methodology, within a processual approach, which incorporated observation, interviewing and documentary analysis. It was discovered that middle managers modify the implementation of strategy by contesting the performance indicators that form the basis of the business planning framework. It was also found that the managers could have a significant upward influence on decision making and initiate change. Currie (1999) concluded that there is enough evidence of innovation from middle managers, even within the constraints of the business planning process, to challenge pessimistic readings of the role in influencing change. In this way he challenges the limited and negative conceptualisation of middle management which is prevalent in much of the literature.

In a later paper (Currie 2000) the influence of middle managers on the process of strategy formation is reported. Drawing on case study data involving observation, 85 interviews and documentary analysis, Currie (2000) concludes middle managers can have an enhanced role and 'add value' to the NHS. However, this will require that they have the necessary skills to 'boundary span', as identified by Floyd & Wooldridge (1997), to link the network organisations that are likely to be the shape of health and social care in the future.

In a paper reporting dimensions of a related study Procter *et al.* (1999) examined how an organisational attempt to empower middle managers had been received. Using a case study methodology involving 47 interviews with middle and other managers in an NHS community trust, they discovered that there was variation in the degree of power middle managers experienced as part of this initiative. In many cases the areas where the managers were empowered were fairly mundane and their decision-making powers were constrained by other departments in the trust that had not been reformed along similar lines. Also the policy environment meant that the nature of the middle management role was subject to constant change and it was difficult to maintain a focus on key activities. The fact that there are no firm conclusions forthcoming from this work indicates that more work is needed to build an understanding of how middle management operates in health care. However, it does suggest that middle managers were regarded as an important resource and that the attempt to 'empower' them, although not successful, represents a recognition of the influence middle management can have in an organisation.

McConville & Holden (1999) also employed case study methodology involving interviews and a survey in two acute NHS Trusts to discover more about the role of the middle manager in human resource management. They found that managers want to be active in managing and developing their staff but are constrained in this because decisions with implications for financing these activities are taken at a higher level in the organisation. The managers were found to be isolated from others in the management hierarchy and experienced 'role dissonance' because they occupied a contradictory position in the organisation, situated between senior management and the work teams. Indeed McConville & Holden (1999) found that the middle managers were acting as a source of mediation between the various conflicts at work in the organisation:

> The incumbents of the role are far from being power-hungry, self serving individuals, seeking a means to justify their existence. Rather they are fulfilling a vital role in balancing tensions and mediating potential conflict, often at personal, emotional costs. (McConville & Holden 1999, p. 422)

The boundary spanning role identified by Floyd & Wooldridge (1997) finds its expression here in the actions of middle managers and this imposes a particular strain on the individual managers. In striving to ensure the organisation continues to function they have to span a range of boundaries and work hard to offset conflict and dysfunction which is inherent in such complex organisations (see chapter 10). The feelings of isolation and distress this engenders can be exacerbated by other factors.

Constraints in the role

For example, Preston & Loan-Clarke (2000) report work from another case study of an NHS community trust, in which they focused on the third stage of a project based on 39 interviews, 27 of these being with middle managers. They found that the managers were aware of the negative view the public and some colleagues had of their role; they knew that other staff believed they (the managers) were withholding information from them; and they expressed their view that they had an unpopular, difficult but essential job to do. This stage of the study explored the perceptions the managers had of themselves and their beliefs concerning how others saw them. This is confirmed by Learmonth (1997) who found that in a survey of 124 members of the public that there was a distinct lack of sympathy for NHS managers. More than 65 per cent of Learmonth's respondents were unsympathetic to managers. Whilst not surprising this indicates that managers are operating in an environment where they are often seen as part of the problem, rather than as a team member who is working hard in the pursuit of good quality care.

More recently Hewison (2002) confirmed some of these findings in concluding that middle management is a difficult and diffuse role, although currently it is an unrealised resource in health care. It emerged from a study of middle managers at work that there was a lack of clarity surrounding the role and that they were often in competition with each other for scarce resources. The scope of the role was potentially open ended and there was a lack of effective training. These factors militated against middle managers being instrumental in the achievement of inclusive, evidence guided services, developed in partnership with key stakeholders.

One way of conceptualising the work of middle mangers in health care is to characterise it partly as being a means of resolving conflict; conflict between professional and managerial concerns and priorities in the way the work is conducted, and internal conflict as the individual attempts to integrate the values and aims of management into the professional value set. Health professionals may take on managerial roles for a whole range of reasons but ultimately they will have to come to some conclusions as to how they will cope with the transition.

Conclusion

This chapter has demonstrated that although research has been carried out to investigate the nature of management, very little work has focused specifically on middle management. Similarly there is relatively little research which examines middle management in health care. For example, recent research evaluating the health management reforms of the 1990s did not address this area (LeGrand *et al.* 1998). The related literature, which can be used to shed more light on the activity of middle management, has been reviewed and it is possible to draw out some general trends, usefully summarised by Wall (1999):

- Middle managers are essential to organisations but they are often unsupported by those above them and reviled by those they supervise.
- Effective middle managers keep top managers in touch with reality and reinterpret policy and strategy so operational staff understand it.

Wall (1999) concludes by suggesting that middle managers should receive recognition for the vital work they do. The concentration of health professionals in middle management posts suggests that an understanding of the issues affecting middle managers and their experience within health care will be useful to all professionals because it is a role they may undertake at some point. For those who do not, knowledge of the middle management function is still necessary in order to understand how the organisation operates. One of the areas of responsibility that can fall within the broad remit of the middle manager is the co-ordination and monitoring of multidisciplinary teams and this is the focus of the next chapter.

9. *Interprofessional Working*

Introduction

There has been a surge of interest in interprofessional working in recent years. This interest has been spurred in part by concerns with quality, both inside and outside the health care system (Mackay *et al.* 1995, Scholes & Vaughan 2002). There are several other developments that have contributed to the increased attention currently being focused on the work of the professions and interprofessional working: these include the demand for greater flexibility from professional workers to respond to changing health care needs (Beattie 1995), a general challenge to the notion of exclusivity of knowledge, the increasingly complex nature of patient care needs, and the influence of the commercial sector in terms of teamworking. Furthermore, this concern with effective interprofessional working as a means of delivering improved patient services has been given added impetus because the current cost containment culture in health care has put all professional roles under new scrutiny (Owens & Petch 1995).

The importance of interprofessional working has been emphasised in a series of government White Papers addressing primary care (DOH 1996a,b,c) which call for more teamworking, extended roles for professionals and the removal of obstacles to collaboration. Most recently this has been taken forward in the *NHS Plan* (DOH 2000a) and in the paper reporting on progress made with increasing the number of staff in the NHS (DOH 2001). To ensure this demand for greater teamwork is met the new workforce development confederations, which have replaced the 39 educational consortia and local medical advisory groups (the bodies responsible for commissioning professional education and training), have been given a specific remit to promote multiprofessional training. The confederations will be central to driving change both in the way in which staff are trained and educated, ensuring that education and training is sensitive to the needs of employers and increasingly undertaken on a multidisciplinary basis (DOH 2001).

So there are clearly several factors that have combined to render interprofessional working a central concern in the organisation and management of health care. Yet the precise meaning of the terms employed in this area is not clear. Prefixes such as inter-, multi- and trans- are used randomly and in different contexts, and the descriptions in the professional literature are so diverse that their meaning is 'murky' (McCallin 2001).

The purpose of this chapter, then, is to examine the nature of multiprofessional and interprofessional working and to determine what the theory that has been developed in this area has to offer. As with many other aspects of health care organisation it is a complex area which is not amenable to straightforward explanation and solution. It needs to be addressed in the context of the theoretical accounts that have been presented to increase our understanding of this vital element of contemporary health care.

In outline this chapter will:

- explore the definitions that have been developed to describe interprofessional working
- examine the models of interprofessional working that have emerged from research in this area
- identify the barriers to effective interprofessional working
- consider the role of professional codes of conduct in promoting and preventing interprofessional working.

Defining the terms

There are many problems associated with defining the terms interprofessional, multiprofessional and transprofessional. They are used to refer to a wide range of different sorts of teams and activities. However these terms are used widely and there have been many calls for more effective multidisciplinary teamwork and interdisciplinary working, despite the fact that there is little evidence of the cost effectiveness of these approaches when compared with separate profession services (Øvretveit 1997). Similarly there is little evidence to substantiate the view that collaboration leads to an increase in the quality of care which has furthered the well-being of patients (Leathard 1994a). This has led to calls for more research because more evidence is needed to evaluate whether interprofessional work affects patient outcomes (McCallin 2001). If it is also considered that both interprofessional education and practice lack a theoretical basis (Leathard 1994a) then the need to engage with the terminology and the concepts that have been developed to explain this area of practice becomes clear.

Øvretveit suggests:

A general definition of a multidisciplinary team is: a group of practitioners with different professional training (multidisciplinary), employed by more than one agency (multiagency), who meet regularly to co-ordinate their work providing services to one of more clients in a defined area. (Øvretveit 1993, p. 9)

On the other hand, Leathard (1994a) argues interdisciplinary practice refers to people with distinct disciplinary training working together for a common purpose, as they make different yet complementary contributions to patient focused care. These definitions are fairly similar although they are ostensibly referring to two different terms. This problem is evident in other applications of the term.

Gill & Ling (1995), for example, found that the term interprofessional shared learning appears in a range of situations and contexts and that its precise meaning, and the expectations that accompany its use, are seldom made explicit. However, as they go on to comment: 'This lack of precision does not appear to daunt the large number of individuals and authorities who recommend its adoption'. It seems then that even though there is no agreement as to what interprofessional working is, it is regarded as a 'good thing' and an objective that is worth pursuing. In the remainder of this chapter some of the different dimensions of interprofessional working will be examined as a basis for suggesting how this objective can be achieved. Although there is no universal agreement around the terminology, there has been a lot of work conducted to clarify the issues and this will serve as the focus for what follows.

The nature of interprofessional working

The nature of interprofessional working remains an issue of concern and has been the focus of much analysis and debate (see, for example, Owens *et al.* 1995, Soothill *et al.* 1995). Davis (1988) suggests that learning to work with others can be seen as taking place on a continuum of growth. This continuum is made up of the following levels of interprofessional work:

- **Unidisciplinarity**: Feeling confident and competent in one's own discipline.
- **Intradisciplinarity**: Believing that you and fellow professionals in your own discipline can make an important contribution to care.
- **Multidisciplinarity**: Recognising that other disciplines also have important contributions to make.
- **Interdisciplinarity**: Willing and able to work with others in the joint evaluation, planning and care of the patient.
- **Transdisciplinarity**: Making the commitment to teach and practice with other disciplines across traditional boundaries for the benefit of the patient's immediate needs.

Different groups of professionals and teams will be at different points on this continuum and this will affect the way they operate. In a similar way

Øvretveit (1997) suggests that a more fruitful approach in developing understanding of the nature of interprofessional working is to consider the different types of interprofessional working that exist and use this to design and improve interprofessional working arrangements. This has a dual purpose in that those working in and/or responsible for such teams can identify which type of team he/she is in or wishes to build, while those wishing to study and understand the nature of interprofessional working have ways of describing and evaluating the different sorts of teams. The four ways of describing and defining teams advocated by Øvretveit centre around the following key terms: integration; team membership; team process; team management. These will now be considered in turn.

Integration

This refers to the degree of integration that exists within a multidisciplinary team. Øvretveit (1997) maintains that the best way to think of this is by means of a continuum of 'degree of integration'. At one end of the continuum is a loose-knit team called a 'network', which some would not actually regard as a team because its membership changes frequently and it is voluntary. At the other end of the continuum is a closely integrated team where members' workload and clinical decisions are governed by a team policy and decisions made at team meetings. This continuum accounts for much of the experience of 'closeness' of interprofessional working. The location of the team, in terms of this continuum, will affect the experience of those working in the team and the type of service it provides. This is influenced by whether or not the team is formally constituted to serve a defined population or whether it is a 'looser' group that comes together as the need arises. Also the degree of collective responsibility felt by the team will determine its location on the continuum. Clearly structural matters are also important here in that the way the team is established in the first place is a crucial factor in terms of where it sits on the continuum.

Team membership

Membership defines a group's boundaries and often becomes an issue as teams develop. Clarifying membership tends to mark the transition from an informal loose-knit group to a more formal and organised team and this generally happens as a result of building a clearer agreement as to the purpose of the group. This involves the assignment of different categories of membership often differentiating 'core' and 'associate' members, dependent on their function and contribution. This process can also entail taking decisions on the skill-mix needed within the team to meet the demands made by client needs. Often though, team membership is the result of historic staffing decisions. The other element that Øvretveit (1997) believes it is important to consider in this area is the specific skill levels of each individual member and the contribution made to the team's work. The extent to which the team is comfortable with and able to discuss differences between team members, in terms of status and function, will also affect the way the team operates.

Team process

This aspect of interprofessional working is concerned with how the work teams make decisions about the patient's 'journey' through the health care system. Øvretveit (1997) has identified six common types of team process which can be used to identify differences in the way teams work.

Type 1. Parallel pathway team
Each profession has its own pathway and team meetings are for the purpose of referring patients across onto other pathways.

Type 2. Allocation or 'post box' teams
The team meeting serves as a starting point where professional teams pick up referrals and take them back to the separate professional pathway. The initial referral may be brought to the meeting either by a team secretary or team leader, alternatively an individual professional may receive the initial request and bring it to the meeting for discussion.

Type 3. Reception and allocation team
In these teams there is a short-term response at the reception stage. Team members take turns on duty to receive referrals, and this is formally organised.

Type 4. Reception-assessment-allocation teams
As the name suggests, in this type of team there is an initial detailed assessment of the client's needs before decisions are made about who in the team becomes involved in the care package.

Type 5. Reception-assessment-allocation-review teams
The inclusion of a review stage represents a means of self monitoring. It helps the team monitor client care and to exert more control over resources. To operate effectively it requires closer team integration which in turn depends on the existence of a clear structure. This can reduce team members' autonomy.

Type 6. Hybrid-parallel-pathway teams
Øvretveit (1997) found that in reality many teams are characterised by a mixture of these 'types' which he labels hybrids. He contends that mapping

client pathways in this way helps to describe and differentiate teams and this information can then be used to improve decision making and resource use within teams.

Team management

Within this dimension Øvretveit (1997) has identified five main categories of team management which are: profession-management; single manager; joint-management; contracted-profession-managed; hybrid managed teams. There are two main challenges in managing multidisciplinary teams. The first is the establishment of a structure which allows for appropriate autonomy for practitioners from different backgrounds who are at different levels of seniority. The second is establishing clear lines of responsibility for the management of the team's resources. These central concerns are dealt with differently depending on the team structure.

Type 1. Profession-managed structure
As the name suggests, practitioners are managed by their profession-managers who all manage in different ways because of their professional background. This structure is generally associated with loosely coupled network teams.

Type 2. Single management structure
In this model all the practitioners within the team are managed by one manager. This arrangement is common in the USA and Australia but less common in the UK.

Type 3. Joint-management structure
Within this structure a team co-ordinator and a professional in the team agree how to divide the managerial responsibilities associated with running the team.

Type 4. Team manager-contracted structure
This model gives the manager control over team members through contract arrangements. Team members are part of profession-managed services and are 'contracted in' for particular service provision over a specified period of time. It allows the managers flexibility to contract in the skills that are needed.

Type 5. Hybrid management structure
A mixed management structure with the team manager managing core staff, coordinating some under a joint management agreement and contracting others in.

The range of team structures together with the team process, membership and degree of integration indicate the complex nature of interprofessional working. There are other ways to consider teams and teamworking (see below), however Øvretveit (1997) maintains that considering where a team lies on the four dimensions he has devised can help us to understand more about multiprofessional teams. More recent work on the nature of interprofessional working (Miller *et al.* 2001) reached similar conclusions to those of Øvretveit (1993, 1997) concerning the complexity of this area, and offers another way of explaining the way different interprofessional teams operate.

Three types of multiprofessional working

As part of a three year research study into multiprofessional working and shared learning Miller *et al.* (2001) conducted in-depth case studies of six multiprofessional teams in a range of specialisms. Arising from this work they identified three main types of interprofessional working: integrated, fragmented, and core and periphery. This provides further evidence for the variety of team structures and ways of working. This means that the term interprofessional is only of limited use as it can only describe a broad area of study. The specific type of interprofessional working needs to be identified if it is to be managed appropriately.

Integrated

This type of working existed in an organisational context of stability and predictability. This enabled the team to plan its work and to develop in-depth knowledge of colleagues and patients. It tended to occur where professionals were designated to a particular specialism and did not have extensive demands on their time from other teams. This allowed for the development of team allegiance and group identity.

Such teams served the same population of patients, so there was only one focus for practice. This led to a joint approach to the organisation of the team involving joint meetings, joint care planning and evaluation of care. This way of working was based on openness in communication, with team members being encouraged to raise issues about patients and professional concerns. In order to ensure that team practice remained dynamic, challenge to the status quo was encouraged by means of facilitative leadership within a strong, safe learning environment. Integral to this way of working was the development of professional skills and knowledge. It was found that teams operating in this way brought several benefits to patients.

Continuity

Professionals learned skills and gained knowledge from each other and so were able to continue with patients' treatments when their colleagues were not there. Care plans were adhered to because different practitioners could 'slot into' the care process as necessary.

Consistency

Knowledge of how colleagues interpreted patients' needs served as a basis for acting in a similar way and thus providing a consistent service.

Reduction of ambiguity

Because of joint practice there was a high level of 'team knowledge' and so there was no conflict in the messages given to patients about their diagnosis and care.

Appropriate and timely referral

The team members had a detailed and accurate knowledge of each others' roles and boundaries. They were therefore able to judge when it was appropriate to refer patients to other team members for assessment and treatment.

Actions and decision based on an holistic perspective

Through the use of in-depth discussion the team was able to develop a complete picture of the patients and their needs. These multiple perspectives enabled decisions to be made using a wider knowledge base and facilitated effective collaboration in care planning.

Actions and decisions based on problem solving

This wider knowledge base provided by the team also led to more creativity in solving patients' problems.

Interestingly in the research only one example of this type of team was found. It was a neuro-rehabilitation team which was based in a purpose-built twenty bed unit and cared for patients who were medically stable. In many ways this represents the ideal conditions for interprofessional working, yet even within this setting there were still some rifts and problems. However, it does indicate that interprofessional working can occur and benefits can accrue when the setting and focus are 'right'. However, in many instances such ideal conditions are not present.

Fragmented working

The second type of working discovered by Miller *et al.* (2001) was what they termed fragmented working. As the name suggests these teams worked in a more fragmented fashion. Aspects of patient management such as problem solving, decision making and responsibilities for actions taken related to single profession groups. Partly as a result of this, communication between members was brief and related more to the giving of information rather than to the sharing of professional perspectives. Consequently, role understanding was superficial and role boundaries were actively protected, thus reinforcing the monoprofessional nature of practice.

Leadership was problematic in this type of working because those in power were either autocratic and took decisions without consulting staff, or they steered decision making without consensus. This created an environment that was not conducive to communication and learning.

Unlike the integrated team, there was a lack of awareness of the benefits to patients that could be achieved through collaboration. The teams did not come together to discuss how effective teamwork could be achieved and so agreement on how to operate as a team was not reached. Thus the potential benefits of working in this way were not being realised.

Core and periphery working

This form of interprofessional working incorporated both integrated and fragmented working within the team. These tended to have a core group, which displayed features of integrated working, with the remainder of the team being peripheral to the core and functioning in a fragmented way. The dislocation of the peripheral group from the core meant that communication between the two groups was poor. This also contributed to a lack of understanding of others' roles.

The development of this type of working can have a historical component in that the original members know each other well and have established effective ways of working. This arrangement continues to operate as new members join the team leading to exclusion of the new members from the core group. It was also found that sometimes roles which require practitioners to be part of other teams led to them not being regarded as 'core members' of the multiprofessional team.

Miller *et al.* (2001) conclude that although integrated working seems to be the most effective way of providing benefits for patients, setting this up as a 'yardstick' for multiprofessional working may ultimately be self-defeating. They recognise that the circumstances necessary to achieve this in its 'pure form' are seldom in place and if working in this way is presented as the way to operate it could lead to demoralisation. Rather they argue along similar lines to Øvretveit (1997) that their work be used as a basis for discussion and reflection on the nature of interprofessional teamwork in order to assist team members in developing appropriate approaches for their own teams. These approaches to conceptualising interprofessional working can aid practitioners in a number of ways:

- to plan and design the best type of team for a particular population or service
- to enable teams to clarify how they are organised and the choices open to them in the future
- to enable managers to understand and review the teams they are responsible for.

Barriers to interprofessional working

Nonetheless, there are many barriers which impede successful inter-professional working. Also as Rawson (1994) has observed:

> Even if it is agreed that inter-professional working is the most appropriate and worthy means of establishing positive ways of working together, it is important to remain open to the possibility that it can also generate counter productive practice. (Rawson 1994, p. 57)

Some of these barriers, described by Mackay *et al.* (1995) include: ascribed and perceived occupational status; occupational knowledge and the perceived importance of that knowledge for health care; and fear, even distrust, of the perspectives of other occupational groups. The term commonly used to describe this situation is 'tribalism'. It was coined by Strong & Robinson (1990) in their research on the effects of the *Griffiths Report* (DHSS 1983) and has now become part of the language of the NHS. It has been claimed that, whether motivated by the service ideal or professional self-interest, there is a lack of collaboration between health and social care professionals (Carrier & Kendall 1995). Clearly if interprofessional working is to be achieved, as well as recognising the different types of teams and settings involved, it is also important to have an appreciation of the potential barriers to this way of working.

In general terms there are many factors that can impede interprofessional working:

- A large number of organisations may be involved in providing a variety of different caring and accommodation services.
- These organisations have different structures, which makes communication at various levels difficult.
- Different organisations have different budgets and financial arrangements.
- Some of the organisations have different geographical boundaries.
- There has been weak legislative and policy guidance on interprofessional working.

- Workers within organisations have different backgrounds, remuneration, training, culture and language, which can contribute to professional barriers, mistrust, misunderstanding and disagreements.

Organisational barriers

It is not possible to examine all of these factors in detail, however, because service provision for individuals and communities takes place in the context of an organisation. The work of Miller *et al.* (2001) will be used again as it addresses some of the important areas listed above, and then attention will be directed as to how the nature of the professions can militate against collaboration.

Miller *et al.* (2001) identified four main organisational issues which influence teamwork and these are: recent government policies; the diversity of patient populations the teams have to work with; the extent of team-oriented structures and processes; and opportunities for working closely. While these factors are all interrelated, it is useful to look at them in turn to build an appreciation of the challenges involved in developing genuine interprofessional working.

The effects of recent government policy on teamworking

Bed management policy

Waiting list targets, throughput requirements, and the high bed occupancy rates that this has led to has resulted in patients being moved frequently and dispersed around a large number of wards within acute trusts. This results in fragmented working simply because there is no base for the team. The professionals in Miller *et al.*'s (2001) study had to visit a large number (8–10) of wards and departments, and this made it difficult to develop the relationships necessary to foster effective teamwork.

This was compounded by the fact that medical staff had become more specialised, necessitating the input of a greater number of team members to each ward. Ultimately this leads to a situation where there are a lot of patients dotted around the hospital and there are lots of professionals visiting wards at different times. One or two major medical ward rounds are replaced with several smaller ones leading to disruptions in the patterns of working. Often this is compounded by high levels of staff turnover and staff shortages.

This resulted in breakdowns in communication, because the large numbers of people visiting to make decisions about patients' care and treatment may or may not find someone to pass the information on to. In many instances it was found that messages were not passed on because nursing staff were conducting direct care and could not be found. The visiting professional wrote in the patients' records but did not inform anyone. This had implications for the care of the patients, for example missed appointments, and incorrect preparation for investigations.

This all contributes to an unstable and uncertain working environment which is not conducive to interprofessional working. Also opportunities for patient-focused discussion are missed and opportunities for the team to build up understanding of each others' roles is lost.

Interestingly in many trusts this situation has led to the introduction of a new team member or members. For example, bed managers, discharge planning coordinators, and delayed discharge managers are employed in many trusts to deal with the problems arising from this particular policy. The irony is that there are now more team members who need to visit the wards and communicate with different staff thus exacerbating the difficulties.

Care programme approach

Another example of policy directly affecting teamwork identified by Miller *et al.* (2001) is CPA (care programme approach). This is a particular approach to the care of people with mental health problems. The intention was that clients with greatest need, or those who were most severely ill, should receive the fullest range of services and be closely monitored. Three different levels of need are identified in this approach. In practice the needs of clients were assessed using different forms by community psychiatric nurses and social workers. This separate approach to the same programme reinforced the differences between the agencies and their ways of operating. Confusion over the key worker role, identified in the policy as a central component of the CPA, also led to difficulties. It was interpreted differently by health and social care personnel and exacerbated disputes over social and nursing needs such as housing.

In this situation the way the new policy was implemented had an effect on teamworking. If a joint approach had been taken based on a meeting of minds between the managers of the respective services, there might have been a different outcome. However, two distinct organisations came into conflict and an opportunity to foster teamworking was lost because of the inconsistencies in the policy and its implementation at organisational level.

Diversity of patient populations

The specific client group served by the team can enhance team identity and focus. The more diverse the population the greater the calls on the time of team members. This diversity also demands that decisions to prioritise and target effort need to be made. Different team members may have different demands on their time, depending on their role. The example given in the study is of a diabetes care team. Some team members focused solely on patients with diabetes, whereas others, such as the dietitians, had other patients as well. This was interpreted by the 'focused' members of the team as a lack of commitment to the central mission of team.

In essence the greater the diversity of needs of the patient group served by the team the more difficult it becomes to develop shared approaches to care and service delivery. The team members are also less able to develop specific expertise in the area, because of its diversity, and this can weaken the team ethos. Again there is a link here to the organisational structure in that if professionals are grouped together without a single focus for their work, in terms of the patient population, they are unlikely to develop into a cohesive and integrated team. Øvretveit (1993) has observed that organisation affects our lives in profound ways and that people working in groups need suitable organisation if their constructive and creative potential is to be allowed expression. This is examined below.

The team orientation of organisational structures and processes

If teamworking is an organisational priority, the way in which an organisation develops its structures and processes needs to reflect an emphasis on teams rather than on individual professional groups. If interprofessional working is to be achieved it can be enhanced if structures and procedures are in place to support it. For example, simply holding meetings where different members of the team come together on a regular basis and have the opportunity to discuss care and treatment of clients supports teamwork. This needs to be built into people's working day and not regarded as an 'add on' or optional extra. If this is underpinned by communication between the managers of the different professional groups, then success is more likely.

Miller *et al.* (2001) also suggest there is a need to recognise that it is more difficult to manage than a uniprofessional team. For example, if the issue of accountability is considered, in uniprofessional teams the lines of accountability are relatively straightforward, whereas in interprofessional teams different professionals may be accountable to different people for different aspects of their role, for example professional and managerial accountability.

Another challenging issue is the existence of separate communication systems in different professional groups. Each professional group maintains patient records/notes in different ways. If single patient records are developed by the organisation as a whole and used by all practitioners, then such problems can be overcome, and communication enhanced as team members will have access to all relevant patient information in one place. However, if it is left to individual teams to solve it may result in a range of record keeping systems developing within an organisation and so complicate the situation and impede interprofessional work.

Opportunities for working closely

If integrated interprofessional working is to become a reality it is vital that people have opportunities to work closely together in order to build up personal relationships and to understand the roles of others. One of the main factors in creating opportunities for people to work closely is the location and the base for the team. It is important that the team has a 'place' that is its focus. This does not necessarily mean a permanent base, rather an area where the team is able to meet, or which is recognised as the centre of the team's activities. This can also bring benefits if it provides opportunities for team members to observe the practice of colleagues. It can help build an appreciation and understanding of what they do.

Yet in some ways the NHS as an organisation is not geared up for fluid arrangements such as multidisciplinary teams. It is a large and traditional organisation which in many instances works against effective interprofessional working. An awareness of this can be useful in appreciating some of the difficulties that exist in trying to achieve this goal. However, as the work of Øvretveit (1993, 1997) and Miller *et al.* (2001) demonstrates, it is not impossible. Even when the circumstances are problematic, interprofessional working can occur. The more we know about the processes involved and the circumstances necessary for interprofessional working to occur, the greater the likelihood that realistic progress can be made. Another potential barrier is the existence of professional boundaries.

Professional codes and interprofessional working

With regard to health professionals, a key part of their professional identity is the adherence to professional codes of conduct, and this can be a factor in making interprofessional working difficult. When specific codes of ethics in health care are examined, it is interesting to note that this issue is addressed fairly explicitly. Within the codes promulgated by the COT, CSP and the NMC, the following statements would seem to lay a firm foundation for effective interprofessional working:

Occupational therapists respect the needs, traditions, practices, special competencies and responsibilities of other professions, institutions and statutory and voluntary agencies that constitute their working environment. (COT 1995, p. 13 [section 5.3])

You are expected to work collaboratively within teams and to respect the skills, expertise and contribution of your colleagues. (NMC 2002, clause 4.2)

Chartered physiotherapists shall communicate and co-operate with professional staff and other carers in the interests, and with the consent of, their patient; and shall avoid criticism of any of them. (CSP 1996, p. 19 [rule 4])

Indeed, codes of ethics in other health professional areas echo this concern:

Speech therapists should recognise the limits of their professional competence and, as appropriate, refer patients to other professionals where these limits are exceeded. (CST 1988)

Radiographers should work in a collaborative and co-operative manner with other members of the health care team. (COR 1994)

Also, the code of conduct for NHS managers requires that as a manager you must:

demonstrate your commitment to team working by cooperating with all your colleagues in the NHS and in the wider community. (DOH 2002)

Yet despite these professed sentiments of co-operation and collaboration, one of the main barriers to interprofessional working is what Hugman (1991) has termed 'professionalism as demarcation'. This is characterised by a focus on the uniqueness of the profession and a concern for the public image of the individual occupational group concerned. These considerations are not necessarily inappropriate or unjustifiable, but imply a greater concern with notions of professional self-interest than with those of interdisciplinarity or client welfare. Carrier & Kendall (1995) contend:

It should come as no surprise that calls for interprofessional collaboration have proved to be more an aspiration than an easily achieved reality. Such collaboration implies the sharing of knowledge; respect for individual autonomy of different professional groups and administrators; the surrender of professional territory where necessary; and a shared set of values concerning appropriate responses to shared definitions of need. (Carrier & Kendall 1995, p. 18)

Specific codes of ethics also reflect this concern with demarcation:

Chartered physiotherapists shall adhere at all times to personal and professional standards which reflect credit on the profession. (CSP 1996, p. 31 [rule 8])

The profession has a right to expect that its good name shall not be brought into disrepute by public argument. (APA 1990, p. 118)

Any reference to the quality of service rendered by, or the integrity of, a professional colleague will be expressed with due care to protect the reputation of that person. (COT 1995, p. 11 [section 4.7])

A similar process can be seen at work when claims to competence in dealing with particular problems are examined. These tend to emphasise differences rather than similarities between occupations, and this can lead to the separation of occupational groups which may in fact share much in common (Hugman 1991). There is a danger that with the current emphasis on 'outcomes' and the need to 'measure' the effectiveness of practitioners' interventions, the professions may become inward looking, attempting to describe and justify their unique contribution in a spirit of competition, rather than looking outwards to work collaboratively with other groups.

Interprofessional learning

Interprofessional learning has been widely advocated as the means of overcoming some of the barriers to interprofessional working. As Funnell (1995) observes, there is a common-sense attractiveness to the view that enhanced service delivery will result if those who must work together learn together. However, as he goes on to conclude, despite this there is little empirical evidence to support this view or to demonstrate that anything other than short-term benefit will accrue from shared learning interactions.

In a recent review Cooper *et al.* (2001) found that although there are a range of initiatives underway to promote interprofessional learning, there is little evidence that the perceived benefits of this educational approach are transferred into the students' practice. It was noted earlier that despite the lack of evidence for its effectiveness interprofessional learning has been identified as a priority by the government, and programmes of study for health professionals are increasingly required to include an inter-professional approach to learning and teaching. It seems therefore that an understanding of this area is likely to become more important. The absence of extensive evidence does not devalue the underlying principle of interprofessional working. Indeed its value is widely recognised (McCallin 2001, Soothill *et al.* 1995, Øvretveit 1997, Øvretveit *et al.* 1997), and Leathard (1994b) argues that the case for interprofessional education and practice is 'strong', but it needs support. Developments over the next few years will determine the extent to which the various varieties of interprofessional working examined in this chapter are adopted.

Conclusion

Multiprofessional teamwork has become a major issue for heath and social care over the past ten years and some of the reasons for this have been examined in this chapter. The main focus, however, has been on examination of different accounts of interprofessional working that have been produced in order that the complex nature of this area is not overlooked as a result of applying terminology in a simplistic way.

In the final part of the chapter, the current efforts to increase the levels of interprofessional education have been referred to as this is likely to be a feature of educational provision and practice over the next few years. It is clear that interprofessional working is a major policy objective and that its achievement is expected. To summarise, a list of key requirements is included below as it usefully draws together some of the main themes explored in the chapter. If interprofessional work is to become an effective contribution to health and social care the following recommendations will have to be met:

- an emphasis on increased interprofessional education and training which is focused on the needs of practice
- further research and studies to clarify the strengths and weaknesses of the present educational and training input and practice outcomes
- forums to establish consensus on interprofessional criteria, values, methods of communication, goals and accreditation
- the political will and management resource support to enable professionals, users and carers to work together in times of change which require an approach of flexibility, cohesion and mutual understanding. (Leathard 1994b)

Such lists of recommendations need to be considered in the context of the pressures at work, and if this is done, managers and policy makers can create an appropriate environment for interprofessional work. Realistic progress towards integrated interprofessional teamwork is then more likely.

10. Domain theory

Introduction

In the earlier chapters specific elements of management and management theory have been examined and the relevance and usefulness of the theory assessed. The range of material covered indicates that there is no right answer to the 'problem' of management in health care. Similarly there is no single theory that provides a universal framework for managing health care. The specific dynamics of a given situation influence the applicability and usefulness of any theory, also the wider social and political environment are particularly significant in terms of the effect they can exert on an organisation. Rather than advocating a single theory the intention has been to present different theoretical accounts all of which can help nurses and allied health professionals both understand the organisation they work in and play a part in its management.

In this chapter a theoretical account of public service organisations is introduced to make a further contribution to the achievement of this aim. Health care organisations are extremely complex and the forces that impinge on them vary between organisations depending on a whole range of factors such as location, staffing, political and social environment, and governing values. This suggests that constant development and refinement of theoretical explanations will be needed to help us make sense of health care organisations that are themselves in a constant process of development. One theory which may prove particularly useful in this respect is domain theory (Kouzes & Mico 1979), and it is included here because it draws together a number of themes that have been developed earlier.

First the theory will be explained and then summaries of studies that have applied it in a health care setting will be presented to illustrate how its use has contributed to our understanding of health care delivery. The intention is to demonstrate how theory can operate on two levels in studying management and its relevance for nurses and allied health care professionals. It can function at a 'macro' level of theoretical explanation of health care systems and organisations, and it can function at the 'micro' level of serving as a framework for research. This will confirm the underlying argument presented throughout the book that management theory is useful to health professionals in a number of ways.

Consequently this chapter will:

- examine the development of domain theory
- evaluate its utility as a means of explaining the complex dimensions of health care organisation
- discuss research findings arsing from the application of the theory
- identify topical issues in health care organisation and management that can be illuminated using domain theory.

Domain theory

First propounded by Kouzes & Mico (1979), domain theory suggests that the different domains in public service organisations promote separate identities and inhibit the development of a common vision for the organisation. This contributes to a loss of a sense of coherence and results in an 'identity crisis' for professionals who become managers. Human service organisations (HSOs) are defined as those concentrated in the fields of health, education and social welfare and are distinctive in that they have contrasting attributes to business organisations. Their primary motive is service to clients (not customers); they are primarily resourced from public taxation (not private capital); their goals are ambiguous; the outputs are relatively unclear and often indeterminate; and they exist in a political environment.

Drawing on their own work in organisation development and extending the work of Bell (1976), Jacques (1976) and Weick (1976), they propose domain theory as a means of explaining behaviour in human service organisations. In many ways the basis for this theoretical approach arises from analyses which conclude that the differences between private and public sector organisations are significant and that this needs to be accounted for in any explanation of how health care organisations function. The nature of these contrasts is summarised in Table 10.1. It should be noted that not all of these contrasts apply to all HSOs and private sector/commercial organisations. For example, many private sector commercial organisations are in the 'service sector' and so would be primarily involved in 'staff-client interaction'. Similarly health care organisations are not judged solely on 'qualitative' measures of performance. Waiting list figures, patient throughput and waiting times in A&E departments are all quantitative measures. Also the increasing emphasis in government policy on public/private partnerships and the Private Finance Initiative suggest that such divisions are becoming less and less useful as a basis for analysis.

However, significant differences do still exist and it is important to consider elements that have contributed to the development of Kouzes & Mico's theory. The conclusion they reached that 'human service organisations are different' prompted Kouzes & Mico (1979) to weave together their own experiences and

Table 10.1 Contrasting attributes of human service organisations and business industry. Reproduced with permission from Kouzes J.M. & Mico P.R. (1979) Domain Theory: an introduction to organizational behaviour in human service organizations. *Journal of Appled Behavioural Science*, 15(4), 169–174.

Dimension	Human service organisations	Business/industrial organisations
Primary motive	Service	Profit
Primary beneficiaries	Clients	Owners
Primary resource base	Public taxes	Private capital
Goals	Relatively ambiguous and problematic	Relatively clear and explicit
Psychosocial orientation of the workforce	Professional	Instrumental
Transformation processes	Staff client interactions	Employee-product interactions
Connectedness of events and units	Loosely coupled	Tightly coupled
Means-ends relation	Relatively indeterminate	Relatively determinant
Outputs	Intangible	Tangible
Measures of performance	Qualitative	Quantitative
Primary environmental influences	The political and professional communities	The industry and suppliers

observations with those of other theorists, researchers and practitioners to develop their theory. This work has been taken forward and applied by others, such as Edmonstone (1986) and Mark & Scott (1992), and a diagrammatic representation of domain theory that has been developed as part of this process is presented in Figure 10.1.

The domains

Kouzes & Mico (1979) define the different domains in the following way.

Policy domain
The level of the organisation at which governing policies are formulated. This often involves the interaction of the executive board and national

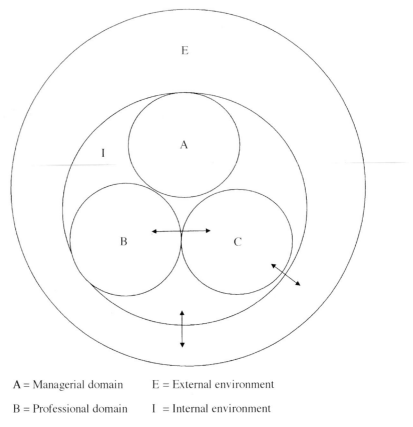

A = Managerial domain   E = External environment

B = Professional domain   I = Internal environment

C = Political domain

Figure 10.1 Domain theory. Reproduced with permission from Mark & Scott (1992) Management in the National Health Service, in Willcocks & Harrow (eds), *Rediscovering Public Services Management*, McGraw-Hill Book Company, London, pp. 197–234.

Notes: Arrows indicate the movement of issues, groups and individuals between internal and external environments and any of the domains. Each domain also has reference points for its value system or parts of it within the external environment.

politicians. The success of the policy domain is measured in terms of equity. It operates on the axial principle of legitimacy by the consent of the governed.

Management domain
The management domain mirrors the model of business and industrial management, and because of the dominance of the 'technocratic

bureaucracy', it operates on the governing principles of hierarchical control and co-ordination. It attempts to rationalise the organisation and accepts cost efficiency and effectiveness as its measures of success.

Service domain/professional

Those who provide the services to the clients of the HSOs see themselves as having rights to control what they define as their professional domain. They regard themselves as capable of self-governance and believe they have the necessary expertise to respond to the needs of their clients. The principles of self-governance and autonomy govern the service domain. Success is measured in terms of quality of care and professional standards.

Kouzes & Mico (1979) suggest that for each domain there is a set of governing principles, success measures, structural arrangements and work modes which is incongruent with those that apply in the others. Similarly each domain gives rise to its own legitimating norms which are in conflict with the norms of the others. They go on to conclude that the result of the interactions of these domains is an organisation that is internally disjunctive and discordant. This situation contributes to the destruction of a sense of coherence and connectedness and is felt particularly acutely by professionals who take on management roles. They pass through the 'zone' from professional service to management which leads to a loss of identity whilst former colleagues wonder if they can be trusted (Kouzes & Mico 1979). The existence of the domains, as distinct spheres of influence, is a useful theoretical model for exploring such conflict.

The Rashamon effect

Kouzes & Mico (1979) draw on the work of Schön (1971) to illustrate how the different domains in human service organisations affect the people who work within them. People who occupy roles in the different domains view the organisation from different vantage points and construct different versions of the reality of the situation based on this perception. Schön (1971) refers to this phenomenon as the 'Rashamon effect' in which the same story told from the point of view of several participants is presented differently by each person and often the accounts conflict. This is a feature of human service organisations and can be helpful in explaining internal conflicts and problems.

The term is derived from a classic Japanese film in which the observers of an incident all give different accounts of an event that has occurred. In health care organisations the actors in each domain collect the information they need to perform their own roles and in the process of doing this often ignore or discount information available from other sources, thus arriving at conclusions or plans that are incompatible with those in other domains. The actors in each domain define problems only in terms of how things affect their own measures of success, and often one domain's solution is another domain's problem. While this selective perception causes overall organisational problems, it serves to preserve each domain's integrity (Kouzes & Mico 1979). Some examples of this dynamic in action are included below to illustrate how domain theory can be applied to help account for the way health care organisations function.

In such organisations where disjunctive domains and discordant relationships prevail, where different perceptions of the purpose of the organisation exist, uncertainty and confusion abound. The existence of multiple domains creates a situation in which tasks are unpredictable, highly variable and extremely difficult (Kouzes & Mico 1979). Domain theory does have some explanatory utility in terms of conceptualising contemporary health care organisation. The different guiding principles and contrasting measures of success that pertain in the different domains can help to uncover inherent conflicts with health care. Also the refinements added by Mark & Scott (1992), which locate the domains more clearly in the external environment, facilitate the consideration of a wider collection of forces that can impinge on the organisation and management of HSOs. For example, government targets to increase the numbers of patients treated and reduce the length of hospital stay (policy domain) is often in conflict with the desire of health professionals to deliver individualised care and maintain continuity of care through the 'patient journey' (service domain). Similarly, management actions (management domain) to ensure spending does not exceed the allocated budget (policy domain) is often manifested in limitations placed on staff employed and impairs standards of care that can be delivered (service domain). This illustrates how the domains interact and result in conflict. Therefore domain theory can be useful in explaining the conflict and difficulties that are inherent in working in health care at an 'abstract' or macro level.

A useful framework?

This raises a number of implications. The discordance, disjunction and conflicts between the three domains engenders struggles for power, control and stability that in themselves have to be managed. Thus additional managerial tasks result from the uncertainty the domains produce (Willcocks & Harrow 1992). This renders management in health care distinctive in that it is about balancing and managing competing interest groups in an intensely political environment. Willcocks & Harrow (1992) go on to conclude:

> Domain theory provides a major basis for assessing the degree and importance of the plurality of managerial activity within and between

public services, so diminishing the appropriateness of reference to a unified public sector. One inherent danger with utilizing domain theory is that it can become a managerial alibi for things never going right, for accepting domain walls and the presence of conflict as reasons for non-achievement, and for refusing to learn from possibly applicable management practices originating outside a specific domain. (Willcocks & Harrow 1992, p. xxvii)

Edmonstone (1986) was also of the view that domain theory is an appropriate framework for understanding health care. Indeed he suggests that it is 'the most useful approach to understanding the unusual nature of management in health care' (p. 9). Whilst recognising its usefulness, Smith (1984) suggested how some of the difficulties might be overcome, outlining how the theory can be used and prevent it becoming an alibi for failure as feared by Willcocks & Harrow (1992).

Towards Conciliation (Smith 1984)
1. Members of all three domains need to understand the others.
2. The pressures one domain exerts on the others needs to be appreciated.
3. Change needs to be planned, taking into account the needs of the different domains.
4. Personnel should be encouraged to work across the domains.

Whilst this prescription is unlikely to provide a solution for all the management ills of health care organisations, it does indicate how the theory can be used in a constructive way. It can also serve as a framework for specific research projects aimed at discovering more about the way health care operates.

Research using domain theory

There is a collection of work in which domain theory has been applied to the UK public sector. Willcocks & Harrow (1992) maintain that domain theory can be operationalised comfortably in British public service organisations. One example of this is Kakabadse's (1982) study in which he investigated social services departments and produced a threefold classification of power, role and task cultures functioning largely in the way described by Kouzes & Mico (1979). Similarly Harrow & Willcocks (1992) used domain theory to categorise and explain the range of organisational learning that occurred in public sector organisations in the early 1990s. This approach has also been applied to the use of information technology in health care (Willcocks & Mark 1989) and to investigate the work of doctors

(Brazell 1987, Mark 1995). These two studies are examined in more detail here to further demonstrate the utility of this particular theoretical approach.

Doctors' views of management

Brazell (1987) conducted a small study based on fifteen interviews with doctors at various levels in the organisation and a survey of a larger group, concerning their views on management. The findings of the research are summarised in Figure 10.2.

Brazell used domain theory as a framework for the analysis of her data. She found the views expressed by the doctors to be consistent with the characterisation of the service domain. They felt they had the 'right' to act as independent practitioners and make the decisions which they felt were in the best interest of their patients. Activity in the management domain was regarded as bureaucratic and a waste of their time. The application of domain theory provided a mechanism for Brazell to locate the doctors' reluctance to become involved in management in the broader context of the way the organisation operates. At the time of her research the *Griffiths Report* was taking effect and there were expectations that doctors would take on management roles.

However this study, utilising the framework of domain theory, is useful in explaining why this did not happen. Doctors did not come forward in large numbers to be managers following the *Griffiths Report* and between 1985 and 1991 the number of doctors heading the management of districts and hospitals halved from 120 to 58 (Salter 1998). Domain theory, as applied by Brazell (1987), offers an explanation of why this was the case. The management domain in the NHS was bureaucratic and involved strong conformity to rules and procedures and team decision making; consequently doctors viewed involvement in this process with distaste (Brazell 1987). Based on these findings Brazell (1987) was able to make some

---

- The doctors studied accepted they had a management role to play.
- They did not regard management as an essential part of their work.
- Doctors are used to making decisions on their own and do not function well in team decision making.
- They identified poor communication throughout the service as a problem.
- They did not want to become managers.

Figure 10.2 Research into the role of doctors as managers (Brazell 1987).

recommendations relating to the training of doctors for management roles that addressed the particular concerns of doctors as a group. This indicates how the application of theory in research can result in the analysis of findings that renders them useful in informing the formulation of future training programmes.

Management development

Domain theory was also employed in research conducted by Mark (1995). However, in this case it was used as a point of reference to indicate that it does not adequately explain some elements of managing in health care. Reflecting on the findings of a study which evaluated the outcomes of a management development programme for consultant medical staff conducted within 14 regional heath authorities, and a case study carried out in a London hospital, Mark (1995) identified the personal consequences for those involved. She argues that the role overload, role ambiguity, and professional isolation experienced by the doctor managers can all be explained in terms of domain theory. The movement between the different domains of management and service (or professional) is difficult for the individuals concerned because no frame of reference exists for the environment and cultures through which these transitions are being experienced at the front-line of change (Mark 1995). The doctor managers were undertaking the roles for the first time and use of domain theory could help identify why they were fraught with difficulty. The movement between the competing and conflicting domains resulted in the tension this caused being experienced at an individual level.

However, Mark (1995) also called into question the enduring utility of domain theory as an explanatory framework. She states:

> This interpretation of the organisation and the individuals changing role in it may clarify the personal costs and benefits to individuals but still leaves a number of areas unaddressed which, research has revealed, are causing concern. (Mark 1995, p. 255)

She then goes on to list what these concerns are, which include the relatively low numbers of women in management; the lack of team development; and the lack of succession planning. Unfortunately, though, she does not examine any further why domain theory was not useful in revealing these aspects of the experience of the participants. Indeed it could be argued that the difficulties experienced by women in becoming managers could be explained in terms of the management domain reflecting a version of management which is associated with 'male' qualities, which leads to the exclusion of women from management roles. Collins (1998), for example, contends that organisations in highly masculine societies tend to be structured around the expectation that people live to work, and as a result qualities such as strength and assertiveness are rewarded. However, it provides further evidence concerning the utility of domain theory as a device for understanding more about management in health care.

Willcocks & Harrow (1992) concluded that domain theory provides a good basis for assessing the degree and importance of the plurality of managerial activity within and between the public services (see p. 156). In this chapter it has been employed to illustrate how theory can be used to help explain the way health care is organised and managed and some more examples of this are explored below.

Further applications of domain theory

The modern matron

Three recent developments in health care include the introduction of the modern matron role (DOH 2000a); and increasing emphasis on the importance of continuing professional development (CPD) (DOH 1998); and the refinement of the performance assessment framework (NHSE 1999). These are all areas where the difficulties and challenges involved can be clarified if they are considered in the context of domain theory. For example, the modern matron role was introduced as part of the *NHS Plan* (DOH 2000a) and was intended to be a solution to a particular set of problems such as poor standards of cleanliness, poor quality hospital food, high rates of hospital acquired infection, and lack of progress with clinical governance. It was stated in the plan that:

> The public consultation provoked a strong call for a 'modern matron' figure – a strong clinical leader with clear authority at ward level – and we will do it. The ward sister or charge nurse will be given authority to resolve clinical issues, such as discharge delays and environmental problems such as poor cleanliness ... They will be in control of the necessary resources to sort out the fundamentals of care, backed up by appropriate administrative support. (DOH 2000a, p. 86)

There are three main strands to the matron role (DOH 2001):

- Securing and assuring the highest standards of clinical care by providing leadership to the professional and direct care staff within the group of wards for which they are accountable.
- Ensuring that administrative support services are designed and delivered to achieve the highest standards of care within the group of wards for which they are accountable.

- Providing a visible, accessible and authoritative presence in ward settings to whom patients and their families can turn for assistance, advice and support.

The response to this policy proposal within nursing has been mixed. There was relatively little discussion of this initiative and most of the comment was in the form of editorials and letters. It was welcomed by some as a positive development for nursing (Castledine 2000, Thomas 2000, Young 2001), including the Royal College of Nursing (Carvel 2001, Snell 2001). Whereas others condemned it as a retrograde step (Buswell *et al.* 2000, Metherall 2000, Peterson 2000), and 'sexist' (Brown 2000). This indicates that even within one domain (professional) there can be disagreement as to the appropriate course of action in the face of the challenges posed by organising care.

If the policy domain is considered it can provide an insight into why the success or otherwise of this initiative can be difficult to evaluate. For example, improvements in cleanliness in one hospital, attributed to the advent of the modern matron by the Secretary of State for Health, had actually occurred before a matron had been appointed (Lipley 2001). The need to present the policy in a positive light resulted in inaccurate claims for its effectiveness.

Insufficient attention to the management domain may result in problems with the introduction of this new role over time. Introduction of modern matrons at a local level was left to the particular trusts concerned. The guidance was that no single model would be universally applicable and that it was inappropriate to proscribe any particular approach, provided that the model adopted locally delivered the policy objectives (DOH 2001). However, without some indication of how the new role could be integrated into existing management structures, and without clear guidance on issues of professional and managerial accountability, there are likely to be areas of conflict as the role develops (Hewison 2001). This illustrates how domain theory can be used as a framework for directing attention to particular components of an aspect of health care and thereby increase our understanding of it. Another example where such an approach may be helpful is in examining continuing professional development.

Continuing professional development (CPD)

It was demonstrated in chapter 3 that CPD is a major component of the current approach to improving quality in health care as part of the clinical governance framework (DOH 1998). However, there are different interpretations that can be made of the term which can be explained, in part, by locating them in the relevant domain. It is stated in *A First Class Service* (DOH 1998) that:

Health professionals, professional bodies and local employers need to discuss a locally based approach to CPD, centred on the service development needs of the local community and learning needs of the individual. It is for local health service employers to decide on the level of investment needed to support CPD programmes for professional, managerial and other staff. (DOH 1998, p. 45)

In terms of the policy domain it can be regarded as a national approach to the minimisation of risk and the improvement of standards. The requirement that all professional staff engage in continuing professional development is central to clinical governance (chapter 3) and targets have been set (DOH 1998). However, at a management level the needs of the organisation as a whole may be interpreted in such a way that individual professional aspirations are overlooked.

For example, the need within a particular trust may be to direct investment towards basic hygiene training for all staff in preference to specialised courses for particular groups of professionals. This may be necessary to comply with other targets arising from the 'policy domain' relating to Health and Safety and adherence to budgets. Complying with a health and safety requirement to have all trust staff trained in basic hygiene procedures may mean that most of the training budget is spent on achieving this objective. Therefore, in order to stay within overall spending limits set at a policy level, the trust is unable to fund other training needs identified by individual professionals or professional groups as essential to their development. In this way the pressures from inputs in the different domains can lead to conflict. The constant drive for improvement and effectiveness in health care has led to the development of a range of policies aimed at bringing this about. Another example is the performance assessment framework.

Performance assessment

The NHS performance assessment framework has two main stated purposes: to assist the NHS in improving the health of the population and to provide a framework for assessing how well the NHS is performing (NHSE 1999). The framework addresses six areas.

Health improvement
To reflect the over-arching aims of improving the general health of the population and reducing health inequalities, which are influenced by many factors reaching well beyond the NHS.

Fair access
To recognise that the NHS's contribution must begin by offering fair access to health services in relation to people's needs, irrespective of geography, socioeconomic group, ethnicity, age or sex.

Effective delivery of appropriate health care
To recognise that fair access to care is effective, appropriate and timely and complies with agreed standards.

Efficiency
To ensure that effective care is delivered with the minimum waste, and that the NHS uses its resources to achieve value for money.

Patient/carer experience
To assess the way in which patients and their carers experience and view the quality of the care they receive, to ensure that the NHS is sensitive to individual needs.

Health outcomes of NHS care
To assess the direct contribution of NHS care to improvements in overall health.

Once again there are several issues associated with the assessment of performance that can be illuminated if considered from the perspective of domain theory. The requirements at a policy level are that overall perform-ance can be demonstrated to be continually improving; however, achievement of success in all areas identified in the performance assessment framework is very difficult. Just as it was noted in chapter 3 that there are differing perceptions of quality, similarly different interpretations of the elements within the performance assessment framework are possible.

For example, at a policy level 'fair access' may mean access to a hospital that is able to treat you anywhere in the UK or mainland Europe. At a management level it may mean the extent to which this can be done within cost limits, ultimately resulting in fair access being regarded as affordable access. Finally, when located in the service domain, fair access incorporates models of care and treatment that are seen to be desirable by health professionals and easily accessible, in terms of distance, for clients. Stewart & Walsh (1994) concluded that no set of indicators can ever be assumed to be complete, since in the public sector no relevant issues can be excluded. This is not to suggest that attempts to measure performance are inherently flawed, rather it is to illustrate some of the complexities involved. As Sheldon observes:

The NHS, its aims, its role in society, and its activities are complex and multidimensional. Not all of the outputs that are valued by society can be measured easily and some of these unfold over several years and cannot be measured accurately at any one time. (Sheldon 1998, p. 47)

There are no simple explanations to account for the way health care is managed and delivered and a range of theoretical approaches can be employed to contribute to our understanding of this aspect of health care. Domain theory can be used as a conceptual tool to shed some light on the problems and challenges involved in monitoring performance.

Conclusion

The discussion of domain theory indicates that nurses and health professionals can access a wide range of theoretical explanations for the management 'problems' in health care. As has been argued throughout, theory, in the context of the management of health care, does not provide all the answers, rather it provides a different way of looking at the problem. One of the most useful functions it can fulfil is to encourage us to look at aspects of the 'problem' that were previously hidden, or we were unaware of. Domain theory is particularly useful in this respect as it directs attention towards three key levels of activity within health care organisations.

When applied as a framework for research or an analytical framework for the consideration of particular issues, it can help us to develop fresh insights on familiar and seemingly intractable problems. In practice-based disciplines such as nursing and the allied health professions to medicine, 'useful' theory is needed if it is to impact on practice. Domain theory is one such theory as it is directly relevant and can be applied to help us understand and manage health care.

11. *Evidence-based Management*

Introduction

West (2001) has suggested that few would now question that management matters in delivering quality health care. However, she goes on to concede that knowledge about the nature of the relationship between management and quality care is incomplete. This recognition of the importance of management has been carried forward into recent policy developments in the UK, such as clinical governance (DOH 1998) (chapter 3) and the *NHS Plan* (DOH 2000a), where emphasis is given to the central role of leadership (chapter 6) and management at all levels of the UK National Health Service in improving quality and carrying out the modernisation agenda. This reliance on management as a means of improving health care delivery could be regarded as surprising given West's observation. Not only that, there is no agreed set of guidelines which indicate the best way to manage. Some of the reasons for this are summarised by Loughlin:

> It is possible to talk and to think sensibly about management; it is just that most management theorists fail to do so and the last thing you need if you are to 'manage well' is to learn what is called 'management theory'. The health service and the public services in general need critical thinkers, able to reflect on the problems of their own practice with acuity and intellectual honesty, not decision makers whose specialist areas are in jargon and the creation of paperwork. (Loughlin 2002, p. 66)

The assumption underlying Loughlin's view is that management and 'critical thinking' are mutually exclusive. However, the overall purpose of this book has been to demonstrate how management theory can be useful in helping us to understand management in health care. One area where clearer links between theory and practice may be established is evidence-based management. The aims of this chapter are to:

- outline the development of evidence-based practice
- define the term evidence-based management
- discuss the role of theory in informing management activity.

Evidence-based practice

Evidence-based practice (EBP) has been defined as 'doing the right things right' (Muir Gray 1997). This summarises the key elements of EBP, which has developed from the approach adopted in medicine to generate and use better evidence in the pursuit of effective patient care. It is the conscientious and judicious use of best evidence in making decisions about the care of individual patients (Sackett *et al.* 1996). Although the emphasis in much of the work addressing EBP is on generating and using research as the primary form of evidence, there is also a growing recognition of the importance of 'best practice' and 'expert consensus' as other forms of evidence (Kovner *et al.* 2000). As Kitson (2002) argues, definitions of evidence need to be understood in the context of establishing effective therapeutic relationships with clients and by balancing evidence from patients, clinical experience and research in order to make 'best' decisions about clinical care. An extensive literature has developed around the purpose and introduction of EBP (see for example Sackett & Rosenberg 1995, Muir Gray 1997, Nutley & Davies 2000, Craig & Smyth 2002) and it will not be rehearsed here, rather the aim is to establish a context for the subsequent development of evidence-based management. Part of this context though is the acknowledgement that EBP is far from being an uncontested concept. Indeed Traynor (2002) refers to it as being comprised of 'movements' and examines some of the controversies and conflicts that characterise this area. These include disagreements as to the nature and relative weight of different types of evidence (chapter 5) (Forbes & Griffiths 2002, Traynor 2002); the difficulties associated with changing practice in the light of evidence (Davies *et al.* 1999, Kitson *et al.* 1998, Wood *et al.* 1998); and concerns about the impact of EBP on professional groups (Wiles & Barnard 2001, McInnes *et al.* 2001), yet these factors have not reduced the impetus of EBP. It is beginning to have an impact at the policy level (Black 2001, Niessen *et al.* 2000) and more latterly management.

As Spurgeon has observed: 'One of the repercussions of evidence-based medicine may be a challenge to management in terms both of the evidence available and of the nature and processes of research used to collect the evidence' (Spurgeon 1999, p. 29). On one level this should be a straightforward process because as Reedy & Learmonth (2000) suggest:

> the dominant view of what management is . . . sees it as a rational, scientific and professional activity. From this view of management, it follows that it should be possible to identify a common core of generic knowledge, techniques and competencies, which are always applicable no matter what type of organisation is being managed. (Reedy & Learmonth 2000, p. 155)

However, the reality is more complex than this and in the NHS no real 'axiomatic' management principle has been officially endorsed at either an implicit or explicit level (Harrison *et al.* 1992, p. 78). Reedy & Learmonth (2000) also go on to conclude that no consensus regarding the nature and content of management exists, nor that there is any sense of a developing body of knowledge in health care management, which stems from early research that is recognised as the foundation of later work, and from which major new developments can be traced (Stewart 1999, p. ix). Yet this has not exempted health care management from the 'repercussions' that Spurgeon identified.

The impact of managerialism

The impact of managerialism on health care and the public sector more generally is a relatively recent phenomenon (Pollitt 1993a) and was examined in chapter 2. It can be defined as a set of beliefs, at the core of which burns the seldom tested assumption that better management will prove an effective solvent for a wide range of economic and social ills (Pollitt 1993a). The policies that were introduced arising from this belief led to the application of management techniques and major structural changes in health care, in particular the 'internal market' in the NHS (Cutler & Waine 2000). This ultimately led to demands for evidence to support clinical interventions and practices in order to inform 'purchasing' decisions thus conferring EBP with the status of 'an idea whose time has come' (Harrison 1998).

Evidence-based management

The key factor in the drive for evidence-based management is summarised by Walshe & Rundall:

> There is certainly considerable scope for making better use of research evidence when deciding how to organize, structure, deliver or finance health services. Managers and policy makers are on shaky ground if they argue that the principles of evidence-based health care – which they have advocated so enthusiastically for clinical practice – do not apply to them. (Walshe & Rundall 2001, p. 451)

Evidence-based management means that managers should be encouraged to examine critically the scientific basis for their practice. They should learn to search and critically appraise empirical evidence from management research as a basis for their decisions (Axelsson 1998). In a review of the literature which included the term evidence-based management as applied to health care, Young (2002) found there were two main categories of interpretation of the term. It was used to indicate the management of clinical practice based on agreed evidence, and to advocate the application of the principles of EBP to the practice of management itself. However, as Walshe & Rundall (2001) note, evidence-based management seems to have made little or no progress in health care when compared with its clinical cousin and they go on to conclude that we are still a long way from seeing managers make proper use of evidence in their decision making. The nature of management as an activity means that adoption of the principles of EBP in the same way that they have been applied to clinical care is unlikely and more importantly inappropriate. As noted above, the process of evidence-based practice is itself problematic and it is questionable whether strict application of the principles of EBP to management is possible or desirable. An application of the evidence-based approach from medicine to management cannot be done without some modifications (Axelsson 1998).

Stewart (2002) argues that the scientific standards required for evidence-based medicine are rarely feasible in management let alone necessary. She goes on to contend that what is needed is information which is useful in reaching management decisions and which is as reliable as possible within the constraints of the situation. Thus, in management, a broad view must be taken of what is meant by current best evidence (Stewart 2002). Evidence-based management is primarily a questioning attitude of mind. The same approach is also part of good management, but one that is too often neglected. The practice of evidence-based management can provide the impetus to overcome this neglect (Stewart 2002, p. 23).

However, rather than looking to the central tenets of EBP for answers, it may be more fruitful for management to look to its own history. Indeed it has been noted that a number of techniques that characterise EBP were originally developed in university business schools. Examples include decision analysis, cost benefit analysis, decision modelling and statistical process control (Neuhaser 2000). Axelsson (1998) also points to 'scientific management' (Taylor 1947) as an early application of research evidence to the practice of management. A more appropriate and useful tradition associated with management, which could be developed to support the 'questioning attitude' of mind advocated by Stewart is that of craft.

Craft

The concept of craft is a familiar one in managerial practice and can serve as a means of resolving the tensions inherent in balancing the demands for evidence-based management and dealing with the reality of health care. The way the term has been used will be examined briefly as a basis for suggesting that management in health care may progress if founded on a reformulation of a 'craft-based' approach.

The craft of management

The term 'craft' evokes notions of traditional skill, dedication, and perfection through the mastery of detail (Mintzberg 1987). Wright Mills (1953) argued that craftsmanship (sic) as a fully idealised model of work gratification involves six major features:

- There is no ulterior motive in work other than the product being made and the processes of its creation.
- The details of daily work are meaningful because they are not detached in the workers' mind from the product of the work.
- The worker is free to control his (sic) own working action.
- The craftsman is thus able to learn from his work and to use and develop his capabilities and skills in its prosecution.
- There is no split of work and leisure or work and culture.
- The craftsman's livelihood determines and influences his entire mode of living.

However, he concluded that its realisation is impossible for the modern white collar worker. This set of features is an 'ideal type', ideal in the sense that it represents a set of characteristics itemising elements of a fully formed notion of craft. An ideal type is a model of a phenomenon or situation which conveys its essential constituents. It represents what, in this case craft, would look like in its 'pure' form (Watson 1995b). This can then be used to study the phenomenon or situation and serve as a basis for developing different ways of using it (see also chapter 2). It can also serve as a basis for suggesting that a 'reformulation' of the notion of craft can be applied to current developments in evidence-based management.

For example, Mintzberg (1987) discusses the craft involved in moulding clay as a metaphor to explain how management strategy making should be approached. Central to this is the combination of thought and action, as he observes: no craftsman thinks some days and works others. The utility of the concept of 'craft' as a means of conveying the complexity of management is also evident in more recent work. Watson (1994) suggests that in carrying out their craft, managers are rhetoricians or wordsmiths, using words to make sense of what they are doing and to persuade others. He goes on to conclude: 'Management and management research can both be usefully labelled as crafts. Shaping and crafting are very similar notions. Managers craft and shape things to get the level and quality of work tasks done which will enable their organization to continue its business' (Watson 1994).

This represents a particular strand in management thought summarised by Schön (1991) and it is this view which can be used to help managers in health care incorporate the principles of EBP into their work. He argues that the manager is a craftsman (sic), a practitioner of an art of managing that cannot be reduced to explicit rules and theories (Schön 1991, p. 236). Rather than applying a series of techniques and seeking evidence for all aspects of their practice, managers need to blend their tacit knowledge, their experience of the organisation and the evidence that is available as appropriate as a basis for management action and decisions. The notion of management as an 'intellectual craft' (Wright Mills 1959, Watson 1994) appears to be consistent with the 'questioning attitude of mind' which is seen by Stewart (2002) and Axelsson (1998) as essential for the advancement of evidence-based management. The rediscovery or surfacing of this tradition in the context of EBP indicates how management may best proceed.

Notions of craft also have some resonance with professional practice. The importance of combining the different elements of professional knowledge in the pursuit of EBP is beginning to be recognised. Pearson & Craig (2002), for example, discuss the integration of systematically derived research-based knowledge with the practitioner's tacit knowledge drawn from experience and their interpretation of the needs and perspectives of each person with whom they interact in individual clinical encounters. This is similar to definitions of the craft of management and both approaches can be summarised as forms of 'knowing-in-practice' (Schön 1991) where intuitive judgment, skill, a feeling for phenomena and action are brought together as a basis for understanding and action. However, the generation of knowledge through rational processes and the development of knowledge through experience are regarded as incompatible activities by some. For example, White argues that knowledge and judgment which are intuitive and gained through experience are not reducible to formal scientific knowledge (White 2001, p. 142). Yet adhering rigidly to such a division may serve to impose a limit on practice. New ways of thinking about management which combine elements of both indicate a way forward.

The craft of health care management

The focus in the final part of this chapter is on the work of Mintzberg, a noted management theorist and researcher, who has coined the term 'blended care' to illustrate the congruence between nursing and management. He characterises blended care as the insightful or craft manager model which involves informed and involved management with respect for the professional competence of people (Mintzberg 1994a). He also contends that if a natural balance of analysis and intuition is considered desirable, then women might be more predisposed to the practice of management (p. 35). Nurses in general seem to step into the managerial role most comfortably and perhaps more readily than doctors (p. 36). These conclusions are based on his earlier work in developing a comprehensive model of management (Mintzberg 1994b), carried forward into an observational study of managers at work (Mintzberg 1994a). This is a theme he returns to later: organizations need continuous care, not interventionist cures. That is why nursing is a better model for management than medicine and why women may ultimately make better managers than men (Mintzberg 1996, p. 66). The same parallels could also be drawn between some of the other allied health professions and management. In reality things are not quite so straightforward and many health professionals experience considerable difficulties in taking on management roles (Edmonstone 1997a,b), and in some instances fundamental differences between managerial and professional values can lead to conflict (Traynor 1994, 1999). However Mintzberg's conclusions do suggest that there is potential in pursuing this reformulated craft-based view as a basis for the advancement of health care management. The Chief Nursing Officer for England has argued that there is no single management approach that can be applied and that the most effective managers are able to apply a range of approaches in dealing with different situations (Mullally 2003). This degree of flexibility is inherent in the notion of craft.

The need to develop such new models to generate fresh thinking about managing health care could also be regarded as an appropriate response to the effects of the managerialism that have affected UK public services in recent years. The forces of managerialism have created 'hybrid' formations through which professionals become managers and managerial consciousness is more widely dispersed (Clarke & Newman 1997) (chapter 7). The emergence of hybrid managers, whereby professionals take on management roles, is a new development which challenges traditional ways of thinking about managerial and professional work (Causer & Exworthy 1999, Flynn 1999). Combining elements from nursing and the allied health professions (AHP) and management to further the 'craft' of management represents a useful model for the future for health professionals who take on management roles.

This craft style of managing is about inspiring and involves leadership based on common experience and deep understanding. The experience and focus of nurses and AHPs predisposes them to this type of management. Also it is regarded as the most appropriate approach to further the development of evidence-based management. Stewart (2002) comments that a craftsperson should understand the nature of the material with which he or she works and be skilful in his or her use of it (p. 43), and this is central to evidence-based management.

This is necessary because as Thompson and Learmonth (2002) conclude, 'Evidence-based culture is one which is totally committed to balanced decisions that give due weight to research evidence, patient preference, available resources and clinical expertise' (p. 235). The effective combination of these different elements in order to adapt the principles of EBP to management will require focused 'critical thinking', such as that advocated by Loughlin (2002) at the start of this chapter. Drawing together the work of Schön and Mintzberg demonstrates that a firm foundation for this approach exists. The reflection in action of managers is distinctive in that they operate in an organisational context and deal with organisational phenomena. They draw on cumulatively developed organisational knowledge which they transform in the context of some unique situation (Schön 1991, p. 265). If this is combined with Mintzberg's (1994a) notion of blended care, the prospect of managers taking the informed decisions referred to by Thompson & Learmonth (2002) becomes more likely. Managerial culture is pragmatic and value is placed on the application of ideas, rather than the generation of evidence, and so either substantial changes in managerial practice are required or adaptation of the ideas of EBP so that they are more congruent with the existing values and beliefs of managers (Walshe & Rundall 2001).

This can also be compatible with nursing because despite the value conflicts referred to earlier, there is much common ground between nursing and management (Hewison & Stanton 2002, 2003) which has been confirmed by some recent work. Based on her research into the changing shape of nursing practice, Allen (2001) has characterised the nature of nursing as being essentially about boundary management. Nurses work at the boundary of life and death, the boundary of individual patient need and organisational constraint, interagency and interorganisational boundaries, and at the boundaries of families, carers and professionals (Allen 2001). This involves the combination of high levels of technical, management and interpersonal skills, and a flexible approach to their work. Yet she concludes that nursing has yet to find an adequate language with which to articulate its function and thus elements of it remain invisible to those outside the occupation (Allen 2001, p. 178). Recourse to the concept of the craft of management represents a means of developing a creative approach to the organisation and management of health care.

Conclusion

Mullally (2003) suggests that just as we draw on and contribute to the evidence base for clinical practice in nursing we must use the models and tools available in the management literature, including management psychology and organisational development, to build the body of evidence on which to base effective nursing management (p. 3). Yet these models and tools need to be combined and applied in a way that differs from the prescription for evidence-based medicine. If evidence-based management is to be more than the latest fashion it needs to be integrated into the craft of

172

management (Stewart 2002). The history and traditions of nursing and the allied health professions and management point to their integration in the form of blended care as a model for an adapted form of evidence-based healthcare management. As Mintzberg concludes: 'Organizations need to be nurtured – looked after and cared for, steadily and consistently. They don't need to be violated by some dramatic new strategic plan or some gross new reorganization every time a new chief executive happens to parachute in' (Mintzberg 1996, p. 66).

Health professionals as managers are in an ideal position to undertake this nurturing and to advance the adapted form of evidence-based management. There is also the possibility that a more comprehensive management science could be built by extending and elaborating on what they, as skilful managers, actually do. Practitioners might then become not only the users but the developers of management science (Schön 1991, p. 266)

Nursing and the allied health professions are dynamic and developing disciplines. Health professionals as managers have an opportunity to lead the way in providing the sort of management needed to deliver the quality that West (2001) has attributed to effective management. In taking this new form forward it may also be possible to demonstrate more clearly the links between management as blended care and quality.

Conclusion

The focus of this book has been on examining how theory related to management can be useful to nurses and other health professionals in managing and understanding the organisations they work in. This is necessary because the organisation and management of health care are very complex activities and health professionals are increasingly expected to play an active part in them. However despite its importance there is no one right or agreed way to manage (Ranade 1997). Also there is no body of evidence that has been accumulated that can serve as the basis for developing guidelines for best practice, as is the case in evidence-based practice. In terms of health policy Smith *et al.* (2001) have noted that the NHS reorganisation, arising from the recommendations made in the *NHS Plan* (DOH 2000a), is an 'evidence free zone'. Although not 'evidence free' Stewart concludes:

> In management, it is harder than in medicine to assess what evidence is necessary and how to find it, and it is often more difficult to know how to interpret it. Also there is no equivalently rigorous research information to inform decision making. (Stewart 2002, p. 12)

In the absence of definitive evidence which indicates the best way to manage there is a need to seek recourse to theory in order to develop a workable framework for management. However, knowledge of theory alone is not sufficient, it is also important to reflect on experience, seek the views of others, particularly colleagues and patients, and to remain open to new ideas. The hope is that the material addressed in the earlier chapters has indicated some of the key areas that need to be thought about if this is to occur.

The intention has been to present a range of resources and approaches that can provide fresh insights on familiar management problems. Indeed the sub-title of the book 'theory into practice' reflects this intention. Theory can be perceived as being somewhat distant from the reality of practice (Hewison & Wildman 1996) yet it can be a valuable tool for nurses and other health professionals. Loughlin has argued:

> Theory can only affect the world insofar as it affects the minds and attitudes of human beings searching for just and humane solutions to the problems

174

they encounter. A good theory is distinguished by the way in which it affects people: it should enable them to understand the causes of their problems and to think creatively about them. It should not encourage them to delude themselves with simplistic or bogus solutions. Instead, it should teach them to identify and examine fundamental assumptions critically and with intellectual honesty and to pursue a line of argument to its logical conclusion, however incompatible that may turn out to be with the accepted dogma of the day. (Loughlin 2002, p. 21)

Although he has little time for management theory Loughlin explains clearly the role it can play in assisting health professionals understand and manage the organisations they work in. He goes on to contend that every organisation needs to be organised and some are better organised than others, this begs the questions 'what is good organisation and how can it be achieved?' He believes if answers to these questions can be found then good management can be applied to all organisations (Loughlin 2002). However Stewart (2002) observes that the attempt to find universal principles was abandoned with the discovery of how organisations vary thus discrediting the classical school of management which produced just such a set of fundamental principles.

What seems to be in little doubt though is that exploration, under-standing and, where appropriate, application of management theory is important. Loughlin (2002) despite his reservations goes so far as to suggest that management is not only a sort of science, it is surely the most important science of all since it tells us how to do just about anything as efficiently and effectively as possible. Although he proceeds to question this assertion the underlying premise emphasises the role of management in contemporary health care. It is regarded as central to the organisation and delivery of health services.

A critical practical perspective

Nursing and management have embraced a succession of ideas and ideologies in order to try and make sense of, and exert some control over a complex practice environment (Hewison & Stanton 2003). This has led to the repackaging of old ideas as new solutions to current problems, and the sometimes unquestioning acceptance of the latest 'panacea' to improve and explain practice before it has been thoroughly evaluated (McKenna 1997). There is a need to employ what Collins (2002) has described as a 'critical-practical perspective' to management theory and ideology. That is, an approach which locates theory in its context and facilitates its critique. If this approach is adopted the applicability of the theory or ideology can be assessed and its practicability, in terms of its use in practice, can be determined. A similar approach for nursing theory has been advocated by McKenna (1997) who calls for 'credibility determination' to be conducted before the widespread adoption of new approaches. In this way theory and new prescriptions for the practice environment can be analysed and their applicability assessed before they are adopted.

This is not to suggest that the advancement of clinical and management practice should be halted, rather it is to recommend that such advancement needs to be informed by a careful consideration of the basis on which any claims for improvement and change are made. An understanding of the origins and development of management theory is central to such assessment and evaluation.

The future?

Mintzberg (1994a) concludes, we have a long way to go in understanding this most important of jobs. He then goes on to suggest a 'new' model for understanding management which consists largely of very familiar concepts, these include: Communicating, controlling, leading, linking, and doing. This emphasises the point made in the introduction that in many ways there is nothing 'new' in management and organisation theory, rather it is the way it is put together and applied to new situations which changes.

In terms of testing his model Mintzberg (1994a) spent time with managers to see how closely it reflected the reality of their work (chapter 11). Based on his observation of the work of a head nurse (Mintzberg 1994b) he concludes that nurses step into managerial roles comfortably because they have a lot of the skills necessary for managing in health care. He characterises this as a 'third style', an insightful approach that facilitates empowerment. It is informed and involved management based on respect for colleagues' professional competence. He describes how the head nurse he observed 'works mostly on her feet, with nurses, doctors and others flowing around her so that linking, leading, and other roles seem to happen spontaneously and interactively.' Also 'everything flowed together in a natural rhythm'.

This suggests that some nurses and health professionals may have a propensity for management because of their interpersonal and organisational skills. If this is underpinned by a thorough understanding of the nature of organisations and an openness to new approaches then the 'managing as blended care' described by Mintzberg (1994b) may become more widespread throughout the service.

The need for health professionals at all levels of the NHS to become more involved in management is unlikely to diminish and because management is by no means an 'exact science' this presents particular challenges to those

Conclusion

involved. Some recommendations are outlined below which suggest how health professionals can develop as managers. This is followed by some suggestions for further reading which will inform this process. Cowley has suggested:

> the aspirations represented in managerialism and professionalism are changing; new visions are being set out for both spheres that, increasingly, follow a shared agenda and similar values. There is an enormously exciting potential for nursing and the population this group serves, if it is only possible to harness and capitalise on that momentum. (Cowley 1999, p. 17)

These recommendations indicate how nurses and other health professionals can be part of this 'momentum'.

Recommendations

- Read widely about management issues and management theory (see list that follows).
- Seek involvement in organisational management through committee membership, participation in working groups, and commenting on local policy proposals.
- Observe managers in 'action' and try to understand why some are effective and why others are not.
- Reflect on your own activities as a manager and record these in your professional portfolio to be used as a source of learning.
- Actively seek out secondment opportunities to develop and test your abilities as a manager.
- Look beyond purely professional perspectives on health care issues and seek to understand the 'management view'.
- Ask managers about their work and what they see as the key components of the role.
- Endeavour to find evidence for the management action you take and those taken by others.

Further Reading

The material listed here is restricted to books. There is also a wealth of information available in journals which provides a useful resource for studying and learning about health care management. A list of journals where research and analyses of health care management issues are published is included below.

The history of the NHS

Allsop J. (1995) *Health Policy and the NHS Towards 2000* (Second Edition). Longman, London.

Butler J. (1992) *Patients, Policies and Politics*. Open University Press, Buckingham.

Ham C. (1992) *Health Policy in Britain* (Third Edition). Macmillan, Houndmills.

Harrison S. (1988) *Managing the NHS – Shifting the Frontier*. Chapman and Hall, London.

Klein R. (2001) *The New Politics of the NHS* (Fourth Edition). Prentice Hall, Harlow.

Powell M.A. (1997) *Evaluating the National Health Service*. Open University Press, Buckingham.

Ranade W. (1997) *A Future for the NHS? Health Care for the Millennium*. Longman, London.

Rivett G. (1998) *From Cradle to Grave: Fifty Years of the NHS*. King's Fund, London.

Salter B. (1998) *The Politics of Change in the Health Service*. Macmillan, Houndmills.

Webster C. (1988) *The Health Services since the War: Volume 1 Problems of Health Care in the National Health Service before 1957*. HMSO, London.

Webster C. (1998) *The National Health Service: A Political History*. Oxford University Press, Oxford.

These books provide useful insights on the historical development of organised healthcare in the UK. Some understanding of the history and politics of healthcare is helpful as a basis for making sense of more recent developments in management and organisation.

Management theory

Handy C. (1993) *Understanding Organizations* (Fourth Edition). Penguin Books, London.

Huczynski A. & Buchanan (2001) *Organizational Behaviour: An Introductory Text* (Fourth Edition). Financial Times/Prentice Hall, Harlow.

Mullins L.J. (1999) *Management and Organisational Behaviour* (Sixth Edition). Prentice Hall, Harlow.

Pugh D. (ed) (1990) *Organization Theory*. Penguin, London.

Pugh D. & Hickson D.J. (1996) *Writers on Organizations*. Penguin, London.

Shafritz J.M. & Ott J.S. (eds) (2001) *Classics of Organization Theory* (Fifth Edition). Harcourt College Publishers, Fort Worth.

Watson T.J. (1995) *Sociology Work and Industry* (Third Edition). Routledge, London.

The best way to examine particular theories and ideas about management is to access the original sources. There are too many to list here so the texts suggested above are intended to serve as a 'halfway house'. They are discussions and summaries of organisational and management theory which provide guidance and commentary on the original theories. They can be a useful starting point for finding out more about organisation and management theory.

Management and health care

Blundell B. & Murdoch A. (1997) *Managing in the Public Sector*. Butterworth Heninemann, Oxford.

Dowding L. & Barr J. (2002) *Managing in Health Care: A Guide for Nurses, Midwives and Health Visitors*. Prentice Hall, London.

Green J. & Thorogood N. (1998) *Analysing Health Policy: A Sociological Approach*. Longman, London.

Martin V. & Henderson E. (2001) *Managing in Health and Social Care*. Routledge, London.

In recent years more books have appeared that relate wider management principles and theory to health care.

Journals

British Journal of Health Care Management

Journal of Health Organisation and Management (formerly *Journal of Management in Medicine*)

Health Services Management Research

Journal of Nursing Management

These are journals which have a specific focus on management issues in health care.

Other journals

British Journal of Management
Journal of Advanced Nursing
Journal of Management Studies
Policy & Politics
Public Administration
Public Money & Management
Social Science & Medicine
Sociology of Health and Illness

The primary focus of these journals is not necessarily management, however they often contain useful research reports and discussion papers relating to health care management.

References

Abercrombie N., Hill S. & Turner B.S. (1988) *Dictionary of Sociology*. Penguin Books, London.

Abrahamson E. (2000) Change without Pain. *Harvard Business Review* July–August, 75–79.

Ackroyd S., Hughes J.A. & Soothill K. (1989) Public services and their management. *Journal of Management Studies* **26** (6), 603–619.

Adair J. (1988) *Effective Leadership*. Pan Books, London.

Albrow M. (1997) *Do Organizations have feelings?* Routledge, London.

Allaire Y. & Firsirotu M. (1984) Theories of organizational culture. *Organization Studies* **5** (3), 193–226.

Allen D. (2001) *The Changing Shape of Nursing Practice: The Role of Nurses in the Hospital Division of Labour*. Routledge, London.

Allsop J. (1984) *Health Policy & the National Health Service*. Longman, London.

Allsop J. (1995) *Health Policy and the NHS Towards 2000* (Second Edition). Longman, London.

Alvesson M. (1993) *Cultural Perspectives on Organizations*. Cambridge University Press, Cambridge.

Ansoff H.I. (1987) *Corporate Strategy*. Penguin, London.

Anthony P. (1994) *Managing Culture*. Open University Press, Buckingham.

APA (1990) Australian Physiotherapy Association: Ethical principles. *Australian Journal of Physiotherapy* **36**, 117–121.

Appleby J. (1994) The reformed national health service: a commentary. *Social Policy & Administration* **28** (4), 345–358.

Ashford J., Eccles M., Bond S., Hall J. & Bond J. (1999) Improving health care through professional behaviour change: introducing a framework for identifying behaviour change strategies. *British Journal of Clinical Governance* **4** (10), 1–13.

Audit Commission (1995) *A Price on their Heads: Measuring management costs in the NHS*. HMSO, London.

Axelsson R. (1998) Towards and evidence-based health care management. *International Journal of Health Planning and Management* **13**, 307–317.

Baggott R. (1997) Evaluating health care reform: the case of the NHS internal market. *Public Administration* **75**, 283–306.

Baggott R. (1998) *Health and Health Care in Britain* (Second Edition). Macmillan Press, Basingstoke.

Banyard R. (1988a) How do UGMs perform? *Health Service Journal* **98** (5110) 21 July, 824–825.

Banyard R. (1988b) Management Mirrored. *Health Service Journal* **98** (5111) 28 July, 858–859.

Banyard R. (1988c) More power to the units. *Health Service Journal* **98** (5112) 4 August, 882–883.

Banyard R. (1988d) Watching the revolution. *Health Service Journal* **98** (5113) 11 August, 916–917.

Barley S. R. & Kunda G. (1992) Design and devotion: surges of rational and normative ideologies of control in managerial discourse. *Administrative Science Quarterly* **37**, 363–399.

Barrett S. & McMahon L. (1990) Public management in uncertainty: a micro-political perspective of the health service in the United Kingdom. *Policy and Politics* **18** (4), 257–268.

Beattie A. (1995) War and peace among the health tribes. In Soothill K., Mackay L. & Webb C. (eds), *Interprofessional Relations in Health Care*. London: Edward Arnold, 11–26.

Beckhard R. & Harris R. (1987) *Organisational Transitions: Managing Complex Change*. Addison-Welsley, Wokingham.

Bell D. (1976) *The Cultural Contradictions of Capitalism*. Basic Books, New York.

Bennis W. (1996) Comments from an interview during the Radio 4 Programme *Attacking the Organisation*. 22 May.

Bennis W. & Nanus B. (1997) *Leaders – Strategies for Taking Charge* (Second Edition). Harper Business, New York.

Bero L.A., Grilli R., Grimshaw J.M., Harvey E., Oxman A.D. & Thomson A. (1998) Closing the gap between research and practice: an overview of systematic reviews of interventions to promote the implementation of research findings. *British Medical Journal* **317**, 465–468.

Berwick D.M. (2001) Not again! Preventing error lies in redesign-not exhortation. *British Medical Journal* **322**, 247–248.

Black N. (2001) Evidence-based policy: proceed with care. *British Medical Journal* **323**, 275–279.

Bond J. & Bond S. (1986) *Sociology and Health Care*. Churchill Livingstone, Edinburgh.

Bouckaert G. (1995) Measuring quality. In Pollitt C. & Bouckaert G. (eds), *Quality Improvement in European Public Services*, Sage Publications, London, pp. 20–28.

Bourne M. & Ezzamel M. (1986) Organisational culture in hospitals in the National Health Service. *Financial Accountability and Management* **2** (3), 203–225.

Boyett I. & Currie G. (2001) The failure of competence-based management education in the public sector. *Personnel Review* **30** (1), 42–60.

Bradshaw P.L. (1999) A service in crisis? Reflections on the shortage of nurses in the British National Health Service. *Journal of Nursing Management* **7** (3), 129–132.

Brazell H. (1987) Doctors as managers. *Management Education and Development* **18** (2), 95–102.

British Medical Journal (2002) Editorial: Needed: Transformational leaders. *British Medical Journal* **325**, 1351.

Broussine M. (1990) Across the sectoral divide: how managers see each other. *Public Money & Management* **10** (1), 51–55.

Brown C. (2000) Battle of sexes still raging on the ward (letter). *British Journal of Nursing* **9** (18), 2004.

Brown H. & Goss S. (1993) Can you hear the sound of breaking glass? *Health Service Journal* 23 September, 26–27.

References

Buswell K., Hehir B. & McMahon B. (2000) Manager by another name (letter). *Nursing Standard* **14** (50), 23.

Butler J. (1992) *Patients, Policies and Politics*. Open University Press, Buckingham.

Caldwell K., Francome C. & Lister J. (1998) *The Envy of the World: The past and future of the National Health Service*. NHS Support Federation, London.

CAIPE (1996) *Principles of Interprofessional Education*. Centre for the Advancement of Interprofessional Education, London.

Carpenter M. (1977) The new managerialism and professionalism in nursing. In Stacey M., Reid M., Heath C. & Dingwall R. (eds), *Health and the Division of Labour*, Croom Helm, London, 165–193.

Carrier J. & Kendall I. (1995) Professionalism and interprofessionalism in health and community care: some theoretical issues. In Owens P., Carrier J. & Horder J. (eds), *Interprofessional Issues in Community and Primary Care*, Houndmills, Macmillan.

Carroll S.J. & Gillen D.J. (1987) Are the classical management functions useful in describing managerial work? *Academy of Management Review* **12** (1), 38–51.

Carvel J. (2001) Matron's rule returns in NHS quality drive. *The Guardian* April 5, 7.

Castledine G. (2000) A new matron: a positive initiative for nursing? *British Journal of Nursing* **9** (16), 1110.

Causer G. & Exworthy M. (1999) Professionals as managers across the public sector. In Exworthy M. & Halford S. (eds), *Professionals and the New Managerialism in the Public Sector*, Open University Press, Buckingham, 88–101.

Cavanaugh S.J. (1996) Mergers and acquisitions: some implications of cultural change. *Journal of Nursing Management* **4**, 45–50.

Centre for the Development of Nursing Policy & Practice (2000) *Leading an Empowered Organisation*. http://www.leeds.ac.uk/healthcare/centre/progs/leo.html

Centre for the Development of Nursing Policy & Practice/The Royal Marsden (2000) *National Cancer Nursing Leadership Programme*. Centre for the Development of Nursing Policy & Practice/The Royal Marsden, London.

Chamings A. & Keady P. (1995) Safety first. *Health Service Journal* **105** (5443), 30–31.

Chandler J.A. (1991) Public administration and private management. Is there a difference? *Public Administration* **69** (3), 385–392.

Chartered Society of Physiotherapy (1996) *Rules of Professional Conduct*. Chartered Society of Physiotherapy, London.

Cheater F.M. & Keane M. (1998) Nurses' participation in audit: a regional study. *Quality in Health Care* **7**, 27–36.

Child J. (1981) *The Challenge to Management Control*. Kogan Page, London.

Clarke J. (1995) Nurses as Managers. In Baly M.E. (ed.), *Nursing and Social Change* (Third Edition), Routledge, London, 277–294.

Clarke J. & Newman J. (1997) *The Managerial State*. Sage Publications, London.

Clarke J., Cochrane A. & McLaughlin E. (1994) Mission accomplished or unfinished business? The impact of managerialization. In Clarke C., Cochrane A. & McLaughlin E. (eds), *Managing Social Policy*, Sage Publications, London, 226–242.

Cole R.E. (1998) Learning from the quality movement: What did and didn't happen and why? *California Management Review* **41** (1), 43–73.

Cole R. & Perrides M. (1995) Managing values and organisational climate in a multi-professional setting. In Soothill K., Mackay L. & Webb C. (eds), *Interprofessional Relations in Health Care*, Edward Arnold, London, 62–74.

College of Occupational Therapy (1995) *Code of Ethics and Professional Conduct for Occupational Therapists*. College of Occupational Therapists, London.

College of Radiography (1994) *Code of Professional Conduct*. College of Radiographers, London.

College of Speech Therapists (1988) *Code of Ethics and Professional Conduct, with Ethical Guidelines for Research*. College of Speech Therapists, London.

Collins D. (1998) *Organizational Change: Sociological Perspectives*. Routledge, London.

Collins D. (2000) *Management Fads and Buzzwords: Critical Practical Perspectives*. Routledge, London.

Connelly J. (2000) A realistic theory of health sector management the case for critical realism. *Journal of Management in Medicine* **14** (5/6), 262–271.

Connolly M. (1995) Editorial: Managers and professionals. *Public Money & Management* **15** (2), 3.

Cooper H., Carlisle C., Gibbs T. & Watkins C. (2001) Developing an evidence base for interdisciplinary learning: a systematic review. *Journal of Advanced Nursing* **35** (2), 228–237.

Coulter A. (2002) After Bristol: putting patients at the centre. *British Medical Journal* **324**, 648–651.

Cowley S. (1999) Nursing in a managerial age. In Norman I. & Cowley S. (eds), *The Changing Nature of Nursing in a Managerial Age*, Blackwell Science, Oxford, 3–17.

Cox D. (1991) Health service management- a sociological view: Griffiths and the non-negotiated order of the hospital. In Gabe J., Calnan M. & Bury M. (eds), *The Sociology of the Health Service*, Routledge, London, 89–114.

Cox D. (1992) Crisis and opportunity in health service management. In Loveridge R. & Starkey K. (eds), *Continuity and Crisis in the NHS The politics of design and innovation in health care*, Open University Press, Buckingham, 23–42.

Craig J. V. & Smyth R. L. (eds) (2002) *The Evidence-Based Practice Manual for Nurses*. Churchill Livingstone, Edinburgh.

Crainer S. (1998) *Key Management Ideas* (Third Edition). *Financial Times*/Pitman Publishing, London.

Crosby P. (1979) *Quality Without Tears*. Mentor, New York.

Crosby P. (1985) *Quality is Free*. Mentor, New York.

Cunningham G. & Kitson A. (2000) An evaluation of the RCN clinical leadership development programme: part 2. *Nursing Standard* **13** (15), 34–40.

Currie C. (1999) The influence of middle managers in the business planning process: a case study in the UK NHS. *British Journal of Management* **10**, 141–155.

Currie G (2000) The role of middle managers in strategic change in the public sector – the case of marketing in the NHS. *Public Money & Management* **20** (1), 17–22.

Cutler T. & Waine B. (2000) Managerialism reformed? New labour and public sector management. *Social Policy & Administration* **34** (3), 318–332.

Davies H.T.O., Nutley S.M. & Mannion R. (2000) Organisational culture and quality of health care. *Quality in Health Care* **9**, 111–119.

References

Davies H.T.O., Nutley S.M. & Smith P.C. (1999) What works? The role of evidence in public sector policy and practice. *Public Money & Management* 3–5.

Davis C (1988) Philosophical foundations of interdisciplinarity in caring for the elderly, or the willingness to change your mind. *Physiotherapy Practice* **4**, 23–25.

Dawson P. (1994) *Organizational Change: A Processual Approach*. Paul Chapman Publishing Limited, London.

Dawson S., Winstanley P., Mole V. & Sherval J. (1995) *Managing in the NHS: A Case Study of Senior Executives*. HMSO, London.

Deal T. & Kennedy A. (1982) *Corporate Cultures: The Rites and Rituals of Corporate Life*. Addison-Wesley, New York.

Decker D. (1995) Market testing – does it bring home the bacon? *Health Service Journal* **105** (5436), 26–28.

Deming W.E. (1988) *Out of the Crisis*. University Press, Cambridge Mass.

Denison D. (1984) Bringing corporate culture to the bottom line. *Organization Dynamics* Autumn, 5–22.

Denzin N.K. (1989) *Interpretive Interactionism*. Newbury Park, Age Publications.

Department of Health (1989) *Working for Patients* (Cm 555), HMSO, London.

Department of Health (1993) *Changing Childbirth (Part 1): Report of the Expert Maternity Group*. HMSO, London.

Department of Health (1995a) *NHS and Community Health Services – non medical staff 1989–1994*. HMSO, London.

Department of Health (1995b) *Career Pathways*, DOH, Wetherby.

Department of Health (1996a) *Primary Care: Delivering the Future* (96/395). HMSO, London.

Department of Health (1996b) *The NHS: A Service with Ambitions* (cm 3425). HMSO, London.

Department of Health (1996c) *Primary Care: Choice and Opportunity*. HMSO, London.

Department of Health (1997) *The New NHS Modern Dependable* (Cm3807). HMSO, London.

Department of Health (1998) *A First Class Service: Quality in the New NHS*. DOH, Leeds.

Department of Health (1999) *Working Together – Securing a Quality Workforce for the NHS*. DOH, London.

Department of Health (2000a) *The NHS Plan: A Plan for Investment, a Plan for Reform* Cm 4818–1. DOH, London.

Department of Health (2000b) *A Health Service of all the Talents: Developing the NHS Workforce*. DOH, London.

Department of Health (2000c) *Meeting the Challenge: A Strategy for the Allied health Professions*. DOH, London.

Department of Health (2001) *Implementing the NHS Plan – Modern Matrons*. HSC 2001/010. DOH, London.

Department of Health (2002) *Code of Conduct for NHS Managers*. DOH, London.

Department of Health and Social Security (1972) *National Health Service Reorganisation: England (Foreword)* Cmnd 5055. HMSO, London.

Department of Health and Social Security (1983) *The NHS Management Enquiry (The Griffiths Report)*, DA(83)38. DHSS, London.

Department of Trade and Industry (1995) *The Quality Gurus* (Managing in the '90s). DTI, London.

Dickson A. (1998) Women on top – a study of senior women managers in local authorities. *Social Services Research* **2**, 11–22.

Dixon J. (1998) The context. In Le Grand J., Mays N. & Mulligan J. (eds), *Learning from the Internal Market*, King's Fund, London, 1–14.

Dobson R. (2000) Review condemns poor leadership of Oxford cardiac services. *British Medical Journal* **321**, 1307.

Dopson S. & Stewart R. (1990a) Public and private sector management: The case for a wider debate. *Public Money and Management* **10** (1), 37–40

Dopson S. & Stewart R. (1990b) What is happening to middle management? *British Journal of Management* **1**, 3–16.

Dopson S. & Waddington I. (1996) Managing social change: a process sociological approach to understanding change in the NHS. *Sociology of Health and Illness* **18** (4), 525–550.

Draper H. (1998) Should managers adopt the medical ethic? Reflections on health care management. In Dracopoulous S. (ed), *Ethics and Values in Health Care Management*, Routledge, London, 38–55.

Dunleavy P. & Hood C. (1994) From old public administration to new public management. *Public Money & Management* **14** (3), 9–16.

The Economist (1995) The salaryman rides again. *The Economist* 334 (7900), February 4, 82.

Edmonstone J.D. (1986) If you're not the woodcutter, what are you doing with that axe? *Health Services Manpower Review* **12** (3), 8–12.

Edmonstone J. (1997a) The continuing development of clinical management. *British Journal of Health Care Management* **3** (5), 265–267.

Edmonstone J. (1997b) The continuing development of clinical management II. *British Journal of Health Care Management* **3** (7), 363–365.

Edmonstone J. & Harvegal M. (1993) *Career Transitions from Functional to General Management within the NHS in Scotland.* Management Development Group, Scottish Health Service Centre, Edinburgh.

Edmonstone J. & Harvegal M. (1996) *New Roles for Old: The Roles and Development Needs of Business Managers, Locality Managers and Practice Managers within the NHS in Scotland.* Management Development Group, Scottish Health Service Centre, Edinburgh.

Edmonstone J. & Western J. (2002) Leadership development in health care: what do we know? *Journal of Management in Medicine* **16** (1), 34–47.

Effective Health Care Bulletin (1999) Getting evidence into practice. *NHS Centre for Reviews and Dissemination* **5** (1), 1–16.

Ellis R. & Whittington D. (1993) *Quality Assurance in Health Care: A Handbook.* Edward Arnold, London.

Exworthy M. (1994) The contest for control in community health services: General managers and professionals dispute decentralisation. *Policy & Politics* **22** (1), 17–29.

Exworthy M. (1996) Managers and clinical audit: past, present and future. *British Journal of Health Care Management* **2** (11), 605–608.

Farnham D. & Horton S. (1993) The political economy of public sector change. In Farnham D. & Horton S. (eds), *Managing the New Public Services*, Macmillan, Houndmills, 3–26.

Fayol H. (1949) *General and Industrial Management.* Pitman, London.

Ferlie E., Fitzgerald L. & Wood M. (2000) Getting evidence into clinical practice:

an organisational behaviour perspective. *Journal of Health Services Research & Policy* **5** (2), 96–102.

Ferlie E., Ashburner L., Fitzgerald L. & Pettigrew A. (1996) *The New Public Management in Action*. Oxford University Press, Oxford.

Fiedler F.E. (1967) *A Theory of Leadership Effectiveness*. McGraw-Hill, New York.

Finlayson B., Dixon J., Meadows S. & Blair G. (2002) Mind the gap: the policy response to the NHS nursing shortage. *British Medical Journal* **325**, 541–544.

Fitzgerald L. (2001) Changing clinical practice in primary care: Do we really understand what influences behaviour? *What Matters* (R & D News WM Region) **13**, 12–13.

Fitzgerald L., Ferlie E., Wood M. & Hawkins M. (1999) Evidence into practice? An exploratory analysis of the interpretation of evidence. In Mark A.L. & Dopson S. (eds), *Organisational Behaviour in Health Care – The Research Agenda*, Macmillan Business, Houndmills, 189–206.

Floyd S W & Woolridge B (1997) Middle management's strategic influence and organizational performance. *Journal of Management Studies* **34** (3), 465–485.

Flynn N. (1993) *Public Sector Management* (Second Edition). Harvester Wheatsheaf, New York.

Flynn R. (1999) Managerialism, professionalism and quasi markets. In Exworthy M. & Halford S. (eds), *Professionals and the New Managerialism in the Public Sector*, Open University Press, Buckingham, 18–36.

Flynn R., Williams G. & Pickard S. (1996) *Markets and Networks: Contracting in community health services*. Open University Press, Buckingham.

Forbes A. & Griffiths P. (2002). Methodological strategies for the identification and synthesis of 'evidence' to support decision-making in relation to complex healthcare systems and practices. *Nursing Inquiry* **9** (3), 141–155.

Forbes T. & Prime N. (1999) Changing domains in the management process. Radiographers as managers in the NHS. *Journal of Management in Medicine* **13** (2).

Fox N. (1992) *The Social Meaning of Surgery*. Open University Press, Milton Keynes.

Franks A. (2001) How goes the nightwatchman? An overview of the first annual clinical governance reports 1999/2000 from acute trusts in an English NHS region. *Journal of Management in Medicine* **15** (3), 220–226.

Funnell P. (1995) Exploring the value of interprofessional shared learning. In *Interprofessional Relations in Health Care*, Soothill K., Mackay L. & Webb C. (eds), Edward Arnold, London, 63–171.

Gagliardi P. (1986) The creation and change of organizational culture: a conceptual framework. *Organization Studies* **7** (2) 117–134.

Garside P. (1998) Organisational context for quality: lessons from the fields of organisational development and change management. *Quality in Health Care* **7** (4), S8–S15.

Geertz C. (1973) *The Interpretation of Cultures*. Basic Books, New York.

Gerth H. & Mills C. (1948) *From Max Weber: Essays in Sociology*. Oxford University Press, Oxford.

Gill J. & Johnson P. (1991) *Research Methods for Managers*. Paul Chapman Publishing Limited, London.

Gill J. & Ling J. (1995) Interprofessional shared learning: a curriculum for collaboration. In Soothill K., Mackay L. & Webb C. (eds), *Interprofessional Relations in Health Care*, Edward Arnold, London, 172–193.

Glennerster H., Matsanganis M., Owens P. & Hancock S. (1994) *Implementing GP Fundholding: Wild Card or Winning Hand?* Open University Press, Buckingham.

Gray A. & Jenkins B. (1995) From public administration to public management: reassessing a revolution? *Public Administration* **73**, 75–99.

Green J. & Thorogood N. (1998) *Analysing Health Policy: A Sociological Approach.* Longman, London.

Gregory K. (1983) Native view paradigms: multiple cultures and culture conflicts in organizations. *Administrative Science Quarterly* **28**, 359–376.

Griffiths R. (1992) Seven years of progress – general management in the NHS. *Health Economics* **1**, 61–70.

Grint K. (1995) *Management: A Sociological Introduction.* Polity Press, Cambridge.

Grint K. (1997) *Fuzzy Management.* Oxford University Press, Oxford.

Guest D. (1992) Right enough to be dangerously wrong: an analysis of the In Search of Excellence Phenomenon. In Salaman G. (ed), *Human Resource Strategies*, Sage, London.

Gullick L. & Urwick L. (1937) *Papers on the Science of Administration.* Columbia University Press, New York.

Gunn L. (1988) Public management: a third approach? *Public Money & Management* **8** (3), 21–25.

Hackman R.J. & Wageman R. (1995) Total quality management: Empirical, conceptual, and practical issues. *Administrative Science Quarterly* **40**, 309–342.

Hales C. (1986) What do managers do? A critical review of the evidence. *Journal of Management Studies* **23** (1), 88–115.

Hales C. (1993) *Managing Through Organisation.* Routledge, London.

Halladay M. & Bero L. (2000) Implementing evidence-based practice in health care. *Public Money & Management* **20** (4), 43–50.

Ham C. (1992) *Health Policy in Britain* (Third Edition). Macmillan, Houndmills.

Ham C. (1994) Reforming health services: learning from the UK experience. *Social Policy & Administration* **28** (4), 293–298.

Ham C. (1997) *Management and Organisation in the NHS* (Second Edition). Radcliffe Medical Press, Abingdon.

Hammer M. & Stanton S.A. (1995) *The Reengineering Revolution Handbook.* Harper Collins, London.

Hammersley M. (1985) From ethnography to theory: A programme and paradigm in the sociology of education. *Sociology* **19** (2), 244–259.

Hammersley M. (1990) What's wrong with ethnography? The myth of theoretical description. *Sociology* **24** (4), 597–615.

Hammersley M. (1992) *What's Wrong with Ethnography?* Routledge, London.

Hammersley M. (1995) Theory and evidence in qualitative research. *Quantity & Quality* **29**, 55–66.

Handy C. (1993) *Understanding Organizations* (Fourth Edition). Penguin Books.

Handy C. (1994) *The Empty Raincoat, Making Sense of the Future.* Hutchinson, London.

Handy C. (1997) *The Hungry Spirit.* Hutchinson, London.

Harrison J.H.J. (1999) The rhythm of quality management. *British Journal of Health Care Management* **5** (6), 241–246.

Harrison J. & Thompson D. (1992) A flat earth syndrome. *Health Service Journal* **102** (5320) 17 September, 29.

References

Harrison S. (1988) *Managing the National Health Service: Shifting the Frontier?* Chapman and Hall, London.

Harrison S. (1998) The politics of evidence-based medicine in the United Kingdom. *Policy & Politics* **26** (1), 15–29.

Harrison S. & Pollitt C. (1994) *Controlling Health Professionals.* Open University Press, Buckingham.

Harrison S., Hunter D., Marnoch G. & Pollitt C. (1992) *Just Managing: Power and Culture in the National Health Service.* Macmillan, Houndmills.

Harrow J. & Willcocks L. (1990) Public services management: activities, initiatives and limits to learning. *Journal of Management Studies* **27** (3), 281–304.

Harrow J. & Willcocks L. (1992) Management, innovation and organizational learning. In Willcocks L. & Harrow J. (eds), *Rediscovering Public Services Management,* McGraw-Hill Book Company, London, 50–83.

Hart E. (1991) Ghost in the machine. *Health Service Journal* **101** (5281) 5 December, 20–22.

Harvey S (1994) Trustworthy nurses. *Nursing Management* **1** (2), 16–17.

Haslock I. (2000) Clinical governance: an acute trust's approach. *British Journal of Health Care Management* **6** (1), 21–23.

Hearnshaw H., Reddish S., Carlyle D., Baker R. & Roberston N. (1998) Introducing a quality improvement programme to primary health care teams. *Quality in Health Care* **7** (4), 200–208.

Henry C. (1995) Mismatch of Policy and Practice. In Henry C. (ed), *Professional Ethics and Organisational Change in Education and Health,* Edward Arnold, London, 102–108.

Hersey P. & Blanchard K.H. (1993) *Management of Organizational Behavior: Utilizing Human Resources* (Sixth Edition). Prentice-Hall, New York.

Hewison A. (2001) The modern matron: reborn or recycled? *Journal of Nursing Management* **9** (4), 187–189.

Hewison A. (2002) Exploring middle management in the NHS. *British Journal of Health Care Management* **8** (1), 16–21.

Hewison A. & Stanton A. (2002) From conflict to collaboration? Contrasts and convergence in the development of nursing and management theory (1). *Journal of Nursing Management* **10** (6), 349–355.

Hewison A. & Stanton A. (2003) From conflict to collaboration? Contrasts and convergence in the development of nursing and management theory (2). *Journal of Nursing Management* **11** (1), 15–24.

Hewison A. & Wildman S. (1996) The theory-practice gap in nursing: a new dimension. *Journal of Advanced Nursing* **24**, 754–761.

Holt P.R. (1999) Making incisions into clinical governance decisions. *British Journal of Health Care Management* **5** (7), 290–293.

Honigsbaum F. (1979) *The Division in British Medicine.* Kogan Page, London.

Hood C. (1991) A public management for all seasons. *Public Administration* **69**, 3–19.

Hope V. & Hendry J. (1995) Corporate cultural change is it relevant for the organisations of the 1990s? *Human Resource Management Journal* **5** (4), 61–73.

House R.J. (1971) A path-goal theory of leadership effectiveness. *Administrative Science Quarterly* **16**, 321–338.

Huczynski A.A. (1993) *Management Gurus: What Makes Them and How to Become One.* Routledge, London.

189

Hughes D. & Griffiths L. (1999) On penalties and the Patients Charter: centralism vs decentralised governance in the NHS. *Sociology of Health & Illness* **21**, 79–94.

Hugman R. (1991) *Power in Caring Professions*. Macmillan, London.

Hunt P. (2000) Speech made at the Nursing, Midwifery & Health Visiting Conference, London. http://www.doh.gov.uk/stheast/press128.htm

Hunter D.J. (1992) Doctors as managers: Poachers turned gamekeepers? *Social Science & Medicine* **35** (4), 557–566.

Hunter D.J. (1996) The changing roles of health care personnel in health and health care management. *Social Science & Medicine* **43** (5), 799–808.

Hurley R.E. & Kaluzny A.D. (1987) Organizational ecology and health services research: new answers for old and new questions. *Medical Care Review* **44** (2), 235–255.

Huxham C. & Bothams J. (1995) Bridging the divide: the duality of roles for medical directors and clinicians in the new NHS. *Public Money & Management* **15** (2), 27–34.

Iles V. (1997) *Really Managing Health Care*. Open University Press, Buckingham.

Iles V. & Sutherland K. (2001) *Organisational Change: A Review for Health Care Managers, Professionals and Researchers*. National Coordinating Centre for NHS Service Delivery and Organisation R & D, London.

IHSM (1994a) *Creative Career Paths Report No 1: Top Managers*. Department of Health, London

IHSM (1994b) *Creative Career Paths in the NHS Report No 2: Managers who have left the NHS*. Department of Health, London.

IHSM (1995a) *Creative Career Paths in the NHS Report No 3: Managers in Fifteen NHS Organisations*. Department of Health, London.

IHSM (1995b) *Creative Career Paths Report No 4: Senior Nurses*. Department of Health, London

Jackson D. & Humble J. (1995) Middle managers: new purpose, new directions. *Journal of Management Development* **13** (3), 15–21.

Jackson S. & Hinchliffe S. (1999) Improving organisational culture through innovative development programmes. *International Journal of Health Care Quality Assurance* **12** (4), 143–148.

Jaques E. (1976) *A General Theory of Bureaucracy*. Halsted Press, New York.

Jelinek M., Smirich L. & Hirsh P. (1983) Introduction: a code of many colours. *Administrative Science Quarterly* **28**, 331–338.

Johnston G., Crombie I.K., Davies H.T.O., Alder E.M. & Millard A. (2000) Reviewing audit: barriers and facilitating factors for effective clinical audit. *Quality in Health Care* **9**, 23–36.

Joseph K. (1974) Foreword from *National Health Service Reorganisation:* England. Cmnd 5055, HMSO, London.

Joss R. & Kogan M. (1995) *Advancing Quality: Total Quality Management in the National Health Service*. Open University Press, Buckingham.

Juran J.M. (1992) *Juran on Quality by Design: The New Steps for Planning Quality into Goods and Services*. Free Press, New York.

Kakabadse A. (1982) *The Culture of the Social Services*. Gower, Aldershot.

Keen L. (1997) Markets, quasi markets and middle managers in local government. *Public Policy and Administration* **12** (3), 42–58.

Keen L. & Scase R. (1996) Middle managers and the new managerialism. *Local*

Government Studies **22** (4), 167–186.

Keen L. & Vickerstaff S. (1997) 'We're all human resource managers now': local government middle managers. *Public Money & Management* **17** (3), 41–45.

Kennedy C. (1998) *Guide to the Management Gurus.* Century Business, London.

Keys R. & Bell R. (1982) Four faces of the fully functioning middle manager. *California Management Review* **XXIV** (4), 59–67.

Kilmann R.H., Saxton M.J., Serpa R. & Associates (1985) *Gaining Control of the Corporate Culture.* Jossey-Bass, San Francisco.

Kimberly J.R. & Miles R.H. (1980) *The Organizational Life Cycle.* Jossey-Bass, San Francisco.

Kimberly J.R. & Rottman D. B. (1987) Environment, organization and effectiveness: a biographical approach. *Journal of Management Studies* **24**(6), 595–622.

Kitson A. (2002) Recognising relationships: reflections on evidence-based practice. *Nursing Inquiry* **9** (3), 179–186.

Kitson A, Harvey G and McCormack B. (1998) Enabling the implementation of evidence-based practice: a conceptual framework. *Quality in Health Care* **7**, 149–158.

Klein R. (1995) *The New Politics of the NHS* (Third Edition). Longman, London.

Kmietowicz Z. (2000) NHS Trust 'condoned' abuse of elderly patients. *British Medical Journal* **321**, 1244.

Kouzes J.M. and Mico P.R. (1979) Domain theory: an introduction to organizational behaviour in human service organizations. *Journal of Applied Behavioural Science* **15** (4), 169–174.

Kovner A.R., Elton J.J and Billings J.D. (2000) Evidence-based management. *Frontiers of Health Services Management* **16** (4), 3–24.

Kroeber A. & Kluckholm C. (1952) *Culture: A Critical Review of Concepts and Definitions.* Vintage Books, New York.

Langridge C. (1993) Women on the edge. *Health Service Journal* 7 October 28–30.

Lawton A. (1998) *Ethical Management for the Public Services.* Open University Press, Buckingham.

Le Grand J. (1993) Evaluating the NHS Reforms. In Robinson R. & LeGrand J. (eds), *Evaluating the NHS Reforms*, King's Fund Institute, Hermitage, 243–260.

Le Grand J., Mays N. & Mulligan J. (eds) (1998) *Learning from the NHS Internal Market: A Review of the Evidence.* King's Fund, London.

Learmonth M. (1997) Managerialism and public attitudes towards UK NHS managers. *Journal of Management in Medicine* **11** (4), 1–6.

Learmonth M. (1998) Kindly technicians: hospital administrators immediately before the NHS. *Journal of Management in Medicine* **12** (6).

Learmonth M. (2003) Making health services management research critical: a review and a suggestion. *Sociology of Health & Illness* **25** (1), 93–119.

Leathard A. (1994a) Inter-professional developments in Britain: an overview. In Leathard A. (ed), *Going Inter-Professional: Working together for health and welfare*, Routledge, London, 3–37.

Leathard A. (1994b) Conclusion and future agendas for interprofessional work. In Leathard A. (ed), *Going Inter-Professional: Working together for health and welfare*, Routledge, London, 206–230.

Leatherman S. & Sutherland K. (1998) Evolving quality in the new NHS: Policy, process, and pragmatic considerations. *Quality in Health Care* **7**, S54–S61.

Lewin K. (1951) *Field Theory in Social Science*. Harper Row, New York.

Linstead S. & Grafton-Small R. (1992) On reading organizational culture. *Organization Studies* **13** (3), 331–355.

Lipley N. (2001) Milburn's matrons can't take credit for cleanliness. *Nursing Standard* **16** (8), 8.

Lipsky, M. (1980) *Street-Level Bureaucracy*. Russell Sage Foundation, New York.

Lorbiecki, A. (1995), 'Clinicians as managers: Convergence or collision?'. In Soothill K., Mackay L. and Webb C. (eds), *Interprofessional Relations in Health Care*, Edward Arnold, London, 88–106.

Lord J. & Littlejohns P. (1994) Secret garden. *Health Service Journal* **104** (5417), 18–20.

Loughlin M. (2002) *Ethics, Management and Mythology*. Radcliffe Medical Press, Abingdon.

Lukes S. (1974) *Power – A Radical View*. Macmillan, London.

Lupton C. & Taylor P. (1995) Coming in from the cold. *Health Service Journal* **105**(5444), 22–24.

Macara S. (1995) Culture of consensus. *IHSM Network* **2** (3), 2.

McCallin A. (2001) Interdisciplinary practice – a matter of teamwork: an integrated literature review. *Journal of Clinical Nursing* **10**, 419–428.

McConville T. & Holden L. (1999) The filling in the sandwich: HRM and middle managers in the health sector. *Personnel Review* **28** (5/6), 406–424.

McGregor D. (1960) *The Human Side of Enterprise*. McGraw-Hill, New York.

McInnes E., Harvey G., Duff L., Fennessy G., Seers K. & Clark E. (2001) Implementing evidence-based practice in clinical situations. *Nursing Standard* **15** (41), 40–44.

Macintyre S., Chalmers I., Horton R. & Smith R. (2001) Using evidence to inform health policy: a case study. *British Medical Journal* **322**, 222–225.

Mackay L., Soothill K. & Webb C. (1995) Troubled times: the context for interprofessional collaboration?' In Soothill K., Mackay L. & Webb C. (eds), *Interprofessional Relations in Health Care*, Edward Arnold, London, 1–10.

McKee L., Marnoch G. & Dinnie N. (1997) Medical Managers: Puppet masters or puppets? Sources of power and influence in clinical directorates. Conference Paper, British Sociological Association, Medical Sociology Group Conference, York, September.

McKenna H. (1997) *Nursing Theories and Models*. Routledge, London.

Mackenzie S. (1995) Surveying the organizational culture in an NHS trust. *Journal of Management in Medicine* **9** (6), 69–77.

Malek M., Vacani P., Rasquinha J. & Davey P. (eds) (1993) *Managerial Issues in the Reformed NHS*. John Wiley and Sons, Chichester.

Management Research Group (1998) *Leadership Effectiveness Analysis*. Management Research Group Inc, Portland.

Manson T. (1977) Management, the professions and the unions: a social analysis of change in the National Health Service. In Stacey M., Reid M., Heath C. & Dingwall R. (eds), *Health and the Division of Labour*, Croom Helm, London, London, 196–214.

Mark A. (1995) Developing the doctor manager: Reflecting on the personal costs. *Health Services Management Research* **8** (4), 252–258.

Mark A. & Scott H. (1992) Management in the National Health Service. In Willcocks L. & Harrow J. (eds), *Rediscovering Public Services Management*, McGraw-Hill Book Company, London, 197–234.

References

Marshall G. (1994) *The Concise Oxford Dictionary of Sociology*. Oxford University Press, Oxford.

Maslow A.H. (1970) *Motivation and Personality*. Harper and Row, New York.

Maxwell R.J. (1984) Quality assessment in health. *British Medical Journal* **288**, 1470–1472

Maxwell R.J. (1992) Dimensions of quality revisited: from thought to action. *Quality in Heath Care* **1**, 171–177.

Maynard A. (1994) Can competition enhance efficiency in health care? Lessons from the reforms of the UK National Health Service. *Social Science & Medicine* **39** (10), 1433–1445.

Meek V. (1988) Organizational culture: origins and weaknesses. *Organization Studies* **9** (4), 453–473.

Metcalfe L. & Richards S. (1990) *Improving Public Management*. Sage Publications, London.

Metherall A. (2000) Matron belongs to another age (letter). *Nursing Times* **96** (33), 24.

Meyerson D. & Martin J. (1987) Cultural change: an integration of three different views. *Journal of Management Studies* **24** (6), 623–647.

Miller C., Freeman M. & Ross N. (2001) *Interprofessional Practice in Health and Social Care*. Arnold, London.

Ministry of Health (1946) *The National Health Service Bill*. HMSO, London.

Ministry of Health (1966) *Report of the Committee on Senior Nursing Staff (Salmon Report)*. HMSO, London.

Mintzberg H. (1987) Crafting strategy. *Harvard Business Review* July–August, 66–75.

Mintzberg H. (1994a) Managing as blended care. *Journal of Nursing Administration* **24** (9), 29–36.

Mintzberg H. (1994b) Rounding out the manager's job. *Sloan Management Review* **36** (1), 11–26.

Mintzberg H. 1996. Musings on management. *Harvard Business Review*, July–August: 61–67.

Mohan J. (1996) Accounts of the NHS reforms: macro-, meso- and micro-level perspectives. *Sociology of Health & Illness* **18** (5), 675–698.

Morgan G. (1986) *Images of Organization*. Sage Publications, London.

Morgan G. (1997) *Images of Organization* (Second Edition). Sage Publications, Thousand Oaks.

Moss Kanter R. (1982) The middle manager as innovator. *Harvard Business Review* June/July, 95–105.

Muir Gray J.A. (1997) *Evidence-Based Health Care: How to Make Health Policy and Management Decisions*. Churchill Livingstone, New York.

Mullally S. (2003) Visions from the Chief Nursing Officer. *Journal of Nursing Management* **11** (1), 1–4.

Mullins L.J. (2002) *Management and Organisational Behaviour (Sixth Edition)*. Prentice Hall, Harlow.

Neuhauser D. (2000) The challenge of evidence-based management. *Frontiers of Health Services Management* **16** (4), 39–44.

New B. (1999) A *Good Enough Service: Values, Trade-offs and the NHS*. Institute for Policy Research/King's Fund, London.

Newman J. (1994a) The limits of management: gender and the politics of change. In Clarke A., Cochrane A. & McLoughlin E. (eds), *Managing Social Policy*, Sage Publications, London, 182–209.

Newman J. (1994b) Beyond the vision: cultural change in the public sector. *Public Money & Management* **14** (2), 59–64.

Newman J. & Clarke J. (1994) Going about our business? The managerialization of public services. In Clarke J., Cochrane A. & McLaughlin (eds), *Managing Social Policy*, Sage Publications, 13–31.

NHSE (1999) The *NHS Performance Assessment Framework*. National Health Service Executive, Wetherby.

NHSE (2001) *Leading an Empowered Organisation*. NHSE (http://www.gov.uk/ero/leo.htm

NHSE (2001a) *NHS National Nursing Leadership Project*. http://www.nursing leadership.co.uk/rcn_leo/leo_info.htm

NHSE (2001b) *LEO (Leading an Empowered Organisation)*. http://www.doh.gov.uk/ero/leo.ht.

NHSE/King's Fund (2000) *The Nursing, Midwifery and PAM Leadership Programme 2000 (West Midlands Leadership Programme)*. NHSE/King's Fund, Birmingham.

Niessen L W, Grijseels E W M and Rutten F F H. (2000) The evidence-based approach in health policy and health care delivery. *Social Science & Medicine* **51** (6), 859–869.

Nursing & Midwifery Council (2002) *Code of Professional Conduct*. NMC, London.

Nutley S. & Davies H.T.O. (2000) Making a reality of evidence based practice: some lessons from the diffusion of innovations. *Public Money & Management* **20** (4), 35–42.

Nutley S., Davies H.T.O. & Tilley N. (2000) Getting research into practice. *Public Money & Management* **20** (4), 3–6.

Oakland J.S. (1993) *Total Quality Management* (Second Edition). Butterworth-Heinemann, Oxford.

Office for Public Management/NHS Women's Unit (1994) *Managing Beyond Gender*. OPM, London.

Osborne D. & Gaebler T. (1992) *Reinventing Government: How the entrepreneurial spirit is transforming the public sector*. Addison-Wesley, Reading Mass.

Ouchi W. (1981) *Theory Z: How American business can meet the Japanese challenge*. Addison-Wesley, New York.

Øvretveit J. (1992) *Health Service Quality*. Blackwell Scientific Publications, Oxford.

Øvretveit J. (1993) *Coordinating Community Care – Multidisciplinary Teams and Care Management*. Open University Press, Buckingham.

Øvretveit J. (1994a) All together now. *Health Service Journal* **104** (5437), 24–26.

Øvretveit J. (1994b) Changes in profession management, autonomy and accountability in physiotherapy. *Physiotherapy* **80** (9), 605–609.

Øvretveit J. (1997) How to describe interprofessional working. In Øvretveit J., Mathias P. & Thompson T. (eds), *Interprofessional Working for Health and Social Care*. Macmillan, Houndmills, 9–33.

Øvretveit J., Mathias P. & Thompson T. (eds) (1997) *Interprofessional Working for Health and Social Care*. Macmillan, Houndmills.

Owens P. & Glennerster H. (1990) *Nursing in Conflict*. Macmillan Education Limited, Basingstoke.

Owens P. & Petch H. (1995) Professionals and management. In Owens P., Carrier I. & Horder J. (eds), *Interprofessional Issues in Community and Primary Care*, Macmillan, Houndmills, 37–55.

References

Owens P., Carrier J. & Horder J. (eds) (1995) *Interprofessional Issues in Community and Primary Care*. Macmillan, Houndmills.

Packwood T. (1991) The three faces of medical audit. *Health Service Journal* September **26**, 24–26.

Packwood T., Pollitt C. & Roberts S. (1998) Good medicine? A case study of business process re-engineering in a hospital. *Policy & Politics* **26**(4), 401–415.

Pascale R.T. & Athos A.G. (1986) *The Art of Japanese Management*. Sidgewick and Jackson, London.

Pascale R., Milleman M. & Gioja L. (1997) Changing the way we change. *Harvard Business Review* November–December, 127–139.

Paton C. (1995) *Health Policy and Management*. Chapman and Hall, London.

Pearce L. (2002) Nursing leaders. *RCN Magazine* Autumn, 25–27.

Pearson M. & Craig J. V. 2002. Evidence-based practice in nursing. In Craig J.V. & Smith R.L. (eds), *The Evidence-Based Practice Manual for Nurses*, Churchill Livingstone, Edinburgh, 3–20.

Peters T. (1988) *Thriving on Chaos*. Macmillan, London.

Peters T. (1992) *Liberation Management*. Macmillan, London.

Peters T. & Waterman R. W. (1982) *In Search of Excellence: Lessons from America's best run companies*. Harper and Row, New York.

Peterson D. (2000) Matron must remain an historical figure (letter). *British Journal of Nursing* **9**(17), 1122.

Pettigrew A., Ferlie E. & McKee L. (1992) *Shaping Strategic Change*. Sage, London.

Pilla L., McKendrick J. & Mason J. (1984) The challenge to middle managers. *Management World* **13**(33), 8–33.

Pollitt C. (1993a) *Managerialism and the Public Services* (Second Edition). Blackwell Business, Oxford.

Pollitt C. (1993b) The struggle for quality: the case of the National Health Service. *Policy & Politics* **21**(3), 161–170.

Pollitt C. (2000) Is the emperor in his underwear? An analysis of the impacts of public management reform. *Public Management* **2**(2), 181–199.

Pollitt C. & Summa H. (1997) Trajectories of reform: Public management change in four countries. *Public Money & Management* **17**(1), 7–18.

Pollitt C., Harrison S., Hunter D.J. & Marnoch G. (1988) The reluctant managers: clinicians and budgets in the NHS. *Financial Accountability & Management* **4**(3), 213–233.

Poole L. (2000) Health care: new labour's NHS. In Clarke J. & Gerwitz S. (eds), *New Managerialism New Welfare?* Sage Publications, London, 102–121.

Powell M. A. (1997) *Evaluating the National Health Service*. Open University Press, Buckingham.

Preston D. & Loan-Clarke J. (2000) The NHS manager a view from the bridge. *Journal of Management in Medicine* **14**(2), 100–108.

Procter S., Currie G. & Orme H. (1999) The empowerment of middle managers in a community health trust: structure, responsibility and culture. *Personnel Review* **28**(3), 242–257.

Pugh D.S. (ed) (1997) *Organization Theory: Selected Readings*. Penguin, London.

Pugh D.S., Hickson D.J., Hinnings C.R. & Turner C. (1968) Dimensions of organization structure. *Administrative Science Quarterly* **13**, 65–105.

Quality Assurance Agency for Higher Education (2001a) *Subject Benchmark Statement: Nursing*. QAA, Gloucester.

Quality Assurance Agency for Higher Education (2001b) *Subject Benchmark Statement: Physiotherapy.* QAA, Gloucester.

Quality Assurance Agency for Higher Education (2001c) *Subject Benchmark Statement: Occupational Therapy.* QAA, Gloucester.

Ranade W. (1997) *A Future for the NHS? Health Care for the Millennium* (Second Edition). Longman, London.

Ranson S. & Stewart J. (1989) Citizenship and government: the challenge for management in the public domain. *Political Studies* **XXXVII**, 5–24.

Ranson S. & Stewart J. (1994) *Management for the Public Domain: Enabling the Learning Society.* Macmillan, Basingstoke.

Rawson D. (1994) Models of interprofessional work: likely theories and possibilities. In Leathard A. (ed), *Going Inter-Professional: Working Together for Health and Welfare*, Routledge, London, 38–63.

Reedy P. & Learmonth M. (2000) Nursing managers, transformed or deformed? A case study in the ideology of competency. *Journal of Management in Medicine* **14** (3/4), 153–156.

Repper D. (1996) *Clinical Directors: The Emergence of Clinician Managers and their Meaning for Health Care Policy.* Department of Nursing and Midwifery Studies, University of Nottingham, Nottingham.

Roberts C., Crosby D., Dunn R., Evans K., Grundy P., Hopkins R., Jones P., Lewis P., Vetter N. & Walker P. (1995) Rationing is a desperate measure. *Health Service Journal* **105** (5435), 15,

Robertson D. (1985) *Dictionary of Politics.* Penguin Books, Harmondsworth.

Rogers E.M. (1983) *The Diffusion of Innovations* (Third Edition). Free Press, New York.

Rogers E.M. (1995) *The Diffusion of Innovations* (Fourth Edition). Free Press, New York.

Roland M., Campbell S. & Wilkin D. (2001) Clinical governance: a convincing strategy for quality improvement? *Journal of Management in Medicine* **15** (3), 188–201.

Sackett D.L. & Rosenberg W.C. (1995) The need for evidence-based medicine. *Journal of the Royal Society of Medicine* **88** (11), 620–624.

Sackett D., Rosenberg W., Gray J., Haynes R. & Ricardson W. (1996) Evidence-based medicine: what it is and what it isn't. *British Medical Journal* **312**, 71–72.

Sackman S. (1991) *Cultural Knowledge in Organizations – Exploring the Collective Mind.* Sage Publications, London.

Salter B. (1998) *The Politics of Change in the National Health Service.* Macmillan, Houndmills.

Scase R. & Goffee R. (1989) *Reluctant Managers.* Unwin Hyman, London.

Schein E. (1984) Coming to a new awareness of organizational culture. *Sloan Management Review* Winter, 3–6.

Schein E. (1996) Culture: the missing concept in organization studies. *Administrative Science Quarterly* **41** (2), 229–240.

Schlesinger L.A. & Oshry B. (1984) Quality of working life and the middle manager: muddle in the middle. *Organization Dynamics* Summer, 5–19.

Scholes J. & Vaughan B. (2002) Cross-boundary working: implications for the multiprofessional team. *Journal of Clinical Nursing* **11**, 399–408.

Schön D.A. (1971) *Beyond the Stable State.* Norton, New York.

Schön D.A. (1991) *The Reflective Practitioner: How Professionals Think in Action.* Arena/Ashgate, Aldershot.

References

Senge P. (1992) *The Fifth Discipline: the art and practice of the learning organisation*. Century Business, London.

Shafritz J.M. & Ott J.S. (eds) (2001) *Classics of Organization Theory* (Fifth Edition). Harcourt College Publishers, Orlando.

Sheldon T. (1998) Promoting health care quality: what role performance indicators? *Quality in Health Care* **7** (4), s45–s50.

Short J.H. (2000) A counter proposal on evidence-based management. *Frontiers of Health Services Management* **16** (4), 27–34.

Singh J.V., House R.J. & Tucker D.J. (1986) Organizational change and organizational mortality. *Administrative Science Quarterly* **31** (4), 587–611.

Smircich L. (1983) Concepts of culture and organizational analysis. *Administrative Science Quarterly* **28**, 339–358.

Smith G.W. (1984) Towards an organisation theory for the NHS? *Health Services Manpower Review* **19** (3), 3–7.

Smith J., Walshe K. & Hunter D.J. (2001) The 'redisorganisation' of the NHS. *British Medical Journal* **323**, 1262–3.

Snell J. (2001) Thoroughly modern matron. *Health Service Journal* March 1, 28–31.

Soothill K., Mackay L. & Webb C. (eds) (1995) *Interprofessional Relations in Health Care*. Edward Arnold, London.

Spiers J. (1995) Is Brighton set to rock the NHS? *Health Service Journal* **105** (5439), 21.

Spurgeon P. (1995) *Background to GP Fundholding*. Paper presented at GP Practitioner Fundholding Conference, University of Oxford Department for Continuing Education. 27 June.

Spurgeon P. (1999) Organisational development: from a reactive to a proactive process. In Mark A.L. & Dopson S. (eds), *Organisational Behaviour in Healthcare: The Research Agenda*, Macmillan Business, Houndmills, 25–34.

Spurgeon P. & Barwell F. (1991) *Implementing Change in the NHS*. Chapman & Hall, London.

Stewart R. (1982) *Choices for the Manager: A Guide to Managerial Work and Behaviour*. McGraw Hill Book Company (UK), Maidenhead.

Stewart R. (1989) *Leading in the NHS: A Practical Guide*. Macmillan, Houndmills.

Stewart R. (1999) Foreword. In Mark A.L. & Dopson S. (eds), *Organisational Behaviour in Healthcare: The Research Agenda*, Macmillan Business, Houndmills, ix–xi.

Stewart R. (2002) *Evidence-based Management: A Practical Guide for Health Professionals*. Radcliffe Medical Press, Abingdon.

Stewart J. & Walsh K. (1994) Performance measurement: when performance can never be finally defined. *Public Money & Management* **14** (2), 45–49.

Strong P. & Robinson J. (1990) *The NHS Under New Management*. Open University Press, Milton Keynes.

Sutherland K. & Dawson S. (1998) Power and quality improvement in the new NHS: the roles of doctors and managers. *Quality in Health Care* **7**, S16–S23.

Tannen D. (1995) The power of talk: who gets heard and why. *Harvard Business Review* Sept–Oct, 138–148.

Tannenbaum R. & Schmidt W.H. (1973) How to choose a leadership pattern. *Harvard Business Review*, May–June, 162–180.

Taylor F.W. (1947) *Scientific Management*. Harper and Row, London.

Teasdale K. (1992) *Managing the Changes in Health Care*. Wolfe Publishing Limited, London.

The Inquiry into the Management of Care of Children receiving complex Heart Surgery at the Bristol Royal Infirmary 1984–1995 (2001) HMSO, London. www.bristol-inquiry.org.uk

Thomas L. (2000) Matron makes a comeback. *Nursing Standard* **14** (49), 3.

Thomas P., Griffiths F., Kai J. & O'Dwyer A. (2001) Networks for research in primary health care. *British Medical Journal* **322**, 588–590.

Thomson P. (1992) Public sector management in a period of radical change: 1979–1992. *Public Money & Management* **12** (3), 33–41.

Thomson R.G. & Barton A.G. (1994) Is audit running out of steam? *Quality in Health Care* **3**, 225–229.

Thompson C. & Learmonth M. (2002) How can we develop an evidence-based culture? In Craig J.V. & Smith R.L. (eds), *The Evidence-Based Practice Manual for Nurses*, Churchill Livingstone, Edinburgh, 211–239.

Thompson D. (1994) *Developing Managers for the New NHS*. Longman, London.

Thompson N. (1995) *Theory and Practice in Health and Social Welfare*. Open University Press, Buckingham.

Torrington D. & Weightman J. (1987) Middle management work. *Journal of General Management* **13** (7), 74–89.

Traynor M. (1994) The views and values of community nurses and their managers: research in progress – one person's pain, another person's vision. *Journal of Advanced Nursing* **20**, 101–109.

Traynor M. (1999) *Managerialism and Nursing: Beyond Profession and Oppression*. Routledge, London.

Traynor M. (2002) The oil crisis, risk and evidence-based practice. *Nursing Inquiry* **9** (3), 162–169.

Trisolini M.G. (2002) Applying business management models in health care. *International Journal of Health Planning and Management* **17**, 295–314.

Turner B. (1987) *Medical Power and Social Knowledge*. Sage Publications, London.

Vroom V.H. & Yetton P.W. (1973) *Leadership and Decision Making*. University of Pittsburgh Press, Pittsburgh.

Walby S. & Greenwall J. (1994) Managing the National Health Service. In Clarke J., Cochrane A. & McLaughlin E. (eds), *Managing Social Policy*, Sage Publications, London, 57–72.

Walby S., Greenwall J., Mackay L. & Soothill K. (1994) *Medicine and Nursing: Professions in a Changing Health Service*. Sage, London.

Wall, A. (1996) Travelling without arriving – management training in the NHS. *British Journal of Health Care Management* **2** (4), 217–220.

Wall A. (1999) Courtin' the middle. *Health Service Journal* February 4, 22–25.

Walsh M. & Ford P. (1989) *Nursing Rituals – Research and Rational Actions*. Heinemann Nursing, Oxford.

Walshe K. (2002) The rise of regulation in the NHS. *British Medical Journal* **324**, 967–970.

Walshe K. & Rundall T. G. (2001) Evidence-based management: from theory to practice in health care. *The Millbank Quarterly* **79** (3), 429–457.

Walt G. (1994) *Health Policy: An Introduction to Process and Power*. Zed Books, London.

References

Watson T.J. (1994) Managing, crafting and researching: words skill and imagination in shaping management research. *British Journal of Management* **5** (2), S77–S87.

Watson T.J. (1995a) Rhetoric, discourse and argument in organizational sense making: a reflexive tale. *Organizational Studies* **16** (5), 805–821.

Watson T.J. (1995b) *Sociology of Work and Industry* (Third Edition). Routledge, London.

Weber M. (1948) Bureaucracy. In Gerth H. & Mills C. (eds), *From Max Weber: Essays in Sociology*. Oxford University Press, Oxford, 196–245.

Webster C. (1988) *The Health Services Since the War: Volume I Problems of Health Care in the National Health Service before 1957*. HMSO, London.

Webster C. (1998) *The National Health Service: A Political History*. Oxford University Press, Oxford.

Weick K.E. (1976) Educational organizations as loosely coupled systems. *Administrative Science Quarterly* **21** (1), 1–19.

Werrett J., Griffiths M. & Clifford C. (2002) A regional evaluation of the Leading Empowered Organisation leadership programme. *NTResearch* **7** (6), 459–470.

West E. (2001) Management matters: the link between hospital organisation and quality of patient care. *Quality in Health Care* **10**, 40–48.

West E., Barron D.N., Dowsett J. & Newton J.N. (1999) Hierarchies and cliques in the social networks of health care professionals: implications for the design of dissemination strategies. *Social Science & Medicine* **48**, 633–646.

White K. (2001) Professional craft knowledge and ethical decision-making. In Higgs J. & Titchen A. (eds), *Practice Knowledge and Expertise*, Butterworth Heinemann, Oxford, 142–148.

Whitley R. (1989) On the nature of managerial tasks and skills: their distinguishing characteristics and organization. *Journal of Management Studies* **26** (3), 210–224.

Wiles R. & Barnard S. (2001) Physiotherapy and evidence based practice: an opportunity or a threat to the profession. *Sociological Research Online* **6** (1), 1–18.

Willcocks L. & Harrow J. (1992) Introduction. In Willcocks L. & Harrow J. (eds), *Rediscovering Public Services Management*, McGraw-Hill Book Company, London, xiii–xxxi.

Willcocks L. & Mark A. (1989) IT systems implementation: research findings from the public sector. *Journal of Information Technology* **4** (2), 92–103.

Williams A., Dobson P. & Walters M. (1993) *Changing Culture – New Organizational Approaches* (Second Edition). IPM, London.

Williams J. (1995) Revival of the fittest. *Health Service Journal* **105** (5476), 24 August, 24–25.

Willmott H. (1984) Images and ideals of managerial work: a critical examination of conceptual and empirical accounts. *Journal of Management Studies* **21** (3), 349–368.

Willmott H. (1987) Studying managerial work: a critique and a proposal. *Journal of Management Studies* **24** (3), 250–270.

Willmott H. (1993) Strength is ignorance; slavery is freedom: Managing culture in modern organisations. *Journal of Management Studies* **30** (4), 515–552.

Wilson E. & Doig A. (1996) The shape of ideology: structure, culture and policy delivery in the new public sector. *Public Money & Management* **16** (2), 53–61.

Wood M., Ferlie E. and Fitzgerald L. (1998) Achieving clinical behaviour change: a case of becoming indeterminate. *Social Science & Medicine* **47** (11), 1792–1738.

Workforce and Development Leadership Working Group (2000) *Workforce and Development – Embodying Leadership in the NHS*. NHS Executive, London.

Wright S. (1994) Culture in Anthropology and Organizational Studies. In Wright S. (ed), *Anthropology in Organizations*, Routledge, London, 1–31.

Wright Mills C. (1953) *White Collar*. Oxford University Press, New York.

Wright Mills C. (1959) *The Sociological Imagination*. Penguin Books, Harmondsworth.

Young A.P. (2000) 'I'm just me' A study of managerial resistance. *Journal of Organizational Change* **13** (4), 375–378.

Young A. (1994) Unravelling the tightrope tensions. *Nursing Management* **1** (3), 16–17.

Young L. (2001) Bringing back matron. *Primary Care Network*, **32**, 4.

Young S. K. (2002) Evidence-based management: a literature review. *Journal of Nursing Management* **10** (3), 145–151.

Zeller M. (1995) Manager or therapist? *British Journal of Occupational Therapy* **58** (1), 34–36.

Index